CONTENTS

ABOUT THE AUTHOR

Jerry Lee Ford, Jr., is an author, instructor, and a security analyst with over 13 years experience in the information technology field. He holds a Masters in Business Administration from Virginia Commonwealth University in Richmond, Virginia and has over five years of teaching experience in information technology. Jerry has authored seven other books including *Practical Microsoft Windows Peer Networking* and *Absolute Beginner's Guide to Personal Firewalls*. He lives in Richmond, Virginia with his wife, Mary, and their children, Alexander, William, and Molly.

DEDICATION

To Mary, Alexander, William, and Molly.

ACKNOWLEDGMENTS

This book is the result of the combined efforts of a number of people. First, I want to thank Sharry Lee Gregory for her work as the book's Acquisitions Editor and for working so hard to make this book a reality. I want to thank Mark Reddin for his work as the book's Development Editor, David Eytchison for providing his services as Technical Editor, and Jill Hayden, and Greg Wiegand, the Associate Publishers who helped shepherd me and this book through to completion. I should also thank Andrew Guest from TechTV who provided valuable assistance during the development of the book.

TELL US WHAT YOU THINK!

As the reader of this book, *you* are our most important critic and commentator. We value your opinion and want to know what we're doing right, what we could do better, what areas you'd like to see us publish in, and any other words of wisdom you're willing to pass our way.

As an Associate Publisher for Que, I welcome your comments. You can fax, e-mail, or write me directly to let me know what you did or didn't like about this book—as well as what we can do to make our books stronger.

Please note that I cannot help you with technical problems related to the topic of this book, and that due to the high volume of mail I receive, I might not be able to reply to every message.

When you write, please be sure to include this book's title and author as well as your name and phone or fax number. I will carefully review your comments and share them with the author and editors who worked on the book.

Fax: 317-581-4666

E-mail: feedback@quepublishing.com

Mail: Greg Wiegand
             Que
             201 West 103rd Street
             Indianapolis, IN 46290 USA

INTRODUCTION

INTRODUCING HOME NETWORKING

It was not very many years ago that being the first family on your block to purchase a computer was a big deal. Given the low cost of new computers and the constant advancement in technology, it's not uncommon today for a family to have two or even three computers. It's hard to get rid of a computer that only a few years ago cost you thousands of dollars. Nobody wants to throw away that kind of an investment. But who wants to keep using a computer that doesn't have the latest hardware features or a huge hard drive or DVD player? Home networks allow new life to be given to the older computers. A home network squeezes more out of your dollar by leveraging your investment in your current computer resources by allowing you to share a large hard drive with other computers on the network. A network also lets everyone in the family have access to a shared printer. This way you can still have your shiny new computer with its ultra sleek flat screen monitor and everyone else in the family can have a piece of your computer's huge hard drive without getting in your way.

Of course, home networks are about more than salvaging older computers. A home network is a collection of two or more computers that can communicate and share data and resources with one another. It can provide some practical and fun benefits. For example, a home network will enable you to access your data and work from any room in the house where you have a computer connection. This frees you to work in front of the TV, in the kitchen, or in your bedroom. It can help support a small home business or provide a lot of entertainment by supporting network computer games where two or more players can go head to head against one another.

Working Without Wires

To build a home network you must provide a way for your computers to communicate. Until recently this meant running cables between computers. Although not necessarily a complicated task, running cables between computers can involve a good amount of work, especially if you need to run them inside walls or behind heavy furniture.

Today there are a number of different ways that you can connect your computers. These include installing traditional Ethernet computer cabling, piggybacking network communications over your home's existing power or telephone cabling, and wireless network communication. Of all these options, wireless shows the most promise for home networking. With wireless you don't have to worry about running cable and you are not forced to limit the location of your computers to rooms with phone outlets or walls with power outlets. Wireless home networking provides for a clean and easy network installation that enables you to connect to computers located just about anywhere.

Broadband: Surfing the Internet in the Fast Lane

Today just about any home with a computer is connected to the Internet. A home network lets you share this connection with every computer on the network. When the Internet connection is a high-speed, always-on broadband cable or DSL connection, this shared access is lightning fast and instantaneous.

The sharing of a broadband Internet connection among all the computers on your home network means that everyone in the family will be able to surf without tying up the phone line or waiting for Web pages to take forever to load over dial-up connections. Of course, each computer on your home network should be protected by a software and/or hardware firewall to prevent intruders from gaining access to your home network without compromising your family's access to the World Wide Web.

WHAT YOU NEED TO BEGIN

It is the mission of this book to provide you with all the information and instruction that you'll need to set up and configure your own home network from the ground up, including how to set up shared Internet access. This book will emphasize broadband cable and DSL Internet access as well as wireless networking because these are the current state-of-the-art technologies and are quickly gaining widespread acceptance. However, other technologies such as dial-up Internet access and Ethernet networking will be covered as well to make sure that this book touches all the bases.

This book will use Microsoft's newest operating system, Windows XP Home Edition, as the basis for all examples. Windows XP is Microsoft's latest and most powerful home operating system. However, most of the information provided in this book can be applied to other Microsoft operating systems including Windows 98, 2000, and Me. Windows XP is significantly more powerful and user-friendly than any of its predecessors and has been designed by Microsoft from the ground up to provide you with the ultimate computer and home networking experience.

To initiate this experience you will need at least two computers, one of which should be running Windows XP Home Edition, along with the appropriate networking hardware and software to build your network as outlined in Chapter 1, "Home Networking Basics."

Additionally, if you do not already have an Internet connection you'll want to get one set up. This will preferably be a high-speed cable or DSL connection. You'll also want to get a personal firewall to protect your home network from would-be intruders on the Internet. Windows XP Home Edition provides a basic built-in firewall. However, as this book will explain, you may want to look to any of a number of third-party hardware and software alternatives.

HOW THIS BOOK IS ORGANIZED

Chapter 1 provides a starting foundation for the rest of the book. It explains how home networks operate and outlines the various broadband and wireless technologies that are currently available. Chapter 2, "Getting Your Hands Dirty: Assembling Your Network Hardware," provides a review of how to assemble a completely wireless network as well as how to add a wireless access point to an existing Ethernet, phoneline-based, or powerline-based home network. The advantages and disadvantages of each of these technologies will be examined. You'll also learn how to perform all the steps required to get your computers connected to your home network.

Chapter 3, "The Softer Side of Network Setup," explains the steps required to configure the software portion of your home network including software drivers, TCP/IP, and network client installation.

Chapter 4, "Putting It All Together," takes the home network that you learned how to build in Chapters 2 and 3 and shows you how to organize it into workgroups and tune it for better performance.

Chapter 5, "Sharing Precious Disk Space," presents a thorough discussion of how to configure Windows XP to share disk resources.

Chapter 6, "Maximizing Your Printer Investment," tells you everything that you need to know to install and share a printer over your home network.

Chapter 7, "Battening Down the Hatches," explains how to secure a wireless network, provides a review of Windows XP security, and shows how you can use it to make your home network more secure.

Chapter 8, "Going Online," provides instruction on setting up a cable or DSL high-speed Internet connection. You'll learn different ways that you can share this access with your entire home network and how to protect your home network using personal firewalls.

Chapter 9, "Remote Access: Don't Leave Home Without It," explains the ins and outs of setting up and using remote access to enable you to access your home network and its resources when you are on the road. This chapter also provides additional information on the remote access capabilities of wireless home networks.

Chapter 10, "Just When You Thought Your Work Was Done," provides a whole list of topics that will help you to better administer your home networking including how to manage system resources, view log files, monitor network activity, manage user accounts, and troubleshoot problems including broadband and wireless issues.

Appendix A, "Windows XP NET Commands," provides a list of Windows commands that you can use to perform basic networking tasks from the Windows command line including their syntax and a brief explanation of their purpose.

Appendix B, "TCP/IP Basics," provides a quick TCP/IP primer that covers all the basics of TCP/IP as they relate to home networking.

Appendix C, "A Tour of TechTV," provides a brief introduction to TechTV and a quick look at its many TV shows.

HOW TO USE THIS BOOK

This book is organized into ten chapters and three appendixes and is designed to be read sequentially from start to finish. Chapters 1 through 4 provide the basics of getting your home network up and running. If you want, you can begin to jump around after these four chapters. If you want to continue setting up your home network, you should read Chapters 5 and 6, which provide instruction on how to share disk and printer resources. Read Chapter 7 if you want to learn how to apply advanced security on your network. If you cannot wait to start surfing on the Internet, you might jump to Chapter 8 and learn how to set up a high-speed cable or DSL Internet connection. If you are going to spend a lot of time on the road and still want to be able to access the resources on your home network, you should read Chapter 9. Finally, if you are curious about learning how to apply more detailed administrative control over your home network or if you are in need of some troubleshooting assistance, you'll want to read Chapter 10.

If you like to work from the command line instead of the Windows graphical user interface or GUI, you should check out Appendix A where you will find a list of helpful Windows networking commands and their syntax. If you need to brush up on TCP/IP or are feeling a little rusty, you might want to skip ahead and read Appendix B where you'll find a refresher.

The glossary provides a handy list of terms that you can reference at any point during your reading to refresh your understanding of a term and its meaning.

CONVENTIONS USED IN THIS BOOK

Commands, directions, and explanations in this book are presented in the clearest format possible. The following items are some of the features that make this book easier for you to use:

- **Commands that you must enter**—Commands that you need to type are easily identified by special **bold monospace** format. For example, to view IP configuration information (IP address, subnet mask, and default gateway), the command is displayed like this: `IPCONFIG`. This tells you that you need to enter this command exactly as it is shown.

- **Other commands**—Commands that you are not expected to type are listed as plain `monospace` text.

- **Glossary terms**—For all the terms that appear in the glossary, you'll find the first appearance of that term in the text in italic along with its definition.

- **Notes**—Information related to the task at hand, or "inside" information, is offset so as not to interfere with the task at hand and to make it easy to find this valuable information.

- **Tips**—Here you'll find pieces of information not necessarily essential to the current topic but that offer advice, or help you to save time.

CHAPTER 1

HOME NETWORKING BASICS

Home networks tie all your computers and their disk drives and printers together and provide you with the flexibility of accessing your data from anywhere in your house. Home networks also provide the ability to share a single Internet connection with any computer in the house, letting you surf anywhere that you have a computer without having to worry whether or not somebody else is already online. The purpose of this chapter is to introduce you to home networking and provide an overview of its many components and to explain how they all work together.

Here is what you'll learn:

- Examining the advantages of building your own home network
- Comparing home networks to their corporate counterparts
- Examining wireless networking technologies
- Comparing always-on high-speed Internet access options
- Reviewing the networking features built into Windows XP Home Edition

TODAY'S HOME NETWORK

Local area networks are no longer found only in corporations and government agencies. They are everywhere, in the smallest companies, schools, and even homes. Home networks have been around for a number of years in the form of file and printer sharing networks. A couple of years ago Internet connection sharing was added to the mix, allowing all the computers connected to a home network to share the same dial-up connection, albeit slowly, to the World Wide Web.

Major new developments have begun to improve the quality of home networking. Networks can still share resources and an Internet connection but with the introduction of broadband and wireless technology they can now help you surf the Web, even from the convenience of your backyard at previously unheard of speeds.

Peer-to-Peer Networks

Home networks are built using a peer-to-peer networking model where every computer connected to the network is considered equal to every other computer on the network. There are no designated clients and servers. Each computer has the ability to share its own resources and to access the shared resources of other computers. In addition, each computer maintains responsibility for its own security instead of depending on a central security server to authenticate and validate user logins.

Each computer on a home network is an independent system responsible for itself and its own resources while also having the ability to access the resources of other networked computers and devices.

How Do Home Networks Make Your Life Better?

By interconnecting your computers into a home network you enable the ability to share the data stored on each computer's hard disk. This is known as file sharing. *File sharing* makes it easy to move large files between computers and eliminates sneakernet. *Sneakernet* is a tongue-in-cheek term for simply putting data on a floppy disk and walking over to another computer. Sneakernet is slow and subjects your data to situations where it can be lost, damaged, or even stolen.

A home network helps you to leverage an investment made in a nice color printer by allowing you to share access to it with every other computer on the home network. This means that you do not have to purchase a new printer for each family member nor do you have to quit working at your computer in order for someone else in the family to submit a print job to your printer.

One of the most popular capabilities of a home network is the ability to allow every computer to connect to the Internet simultaneously using one Internet account and connection. This is known as *Internet Connection Sharing* or ICS. ICS eliminates the cost of signing up for multiple Internet accounts with your *Internet Service Provider* or ISP. It also means that you won't have to quit working every time someone wants to surf the Internet. They'll be able to do it from any computer in the house.

Home networks are also capable of providing remote access. *Remote access* allows you to connect to your home network and access your data when you are on the road. This is a great benefit if you find yourself out of town ready to give a presentation that is sitting on your computer at home. Another benefit that the kids will love is the ability to play computer games over the home network. *Networking gaming* allows you to play specially designed network computer games in which you can play not just against the computer but also against your family and friends.

Understanding the Roles of Computers on Networks

On a *peer-to-peer* network all computers act as both clients and servers. When a computer shares a resource such as a file on a disk drive or its local printer with other computers on the home network, it is acting like a server. A *server* is a networked computer that allows other computers to access its resources. However, when this same computer is later used to access a resource located on a computer on the home network, it acts like a client. A network *client* is a computer that accesses and uses resources provided by computers acting as network servers.

Each computer on a client/server network, in contrast, has a predetermined role. Certain computers are set up to act as servers and the rest operate as clients. Operating systems commonly used as network clients include Windows 95, 98, Me, NT Workstation, and 2000 Professional. Windows NT Server, Windows 2000 Server, Advanced Server, and Datacenter Server are designed to provide server services on large networks.

 NOTE Although Windows XP Home Edition and Professional have replaced all other Microsoft desktop operating systems as Microsoft's primary desktop operating systems, Microsoft is still developing its new server operating systems.

Comparing Peer Networks to Server-Based Networks

As you might expect, administering a client/server-based network is considerably more complex than administering a peer-to-peer network. That's why corporations require dedicated network administrators whose sole function is to keep the network up and running. Putting a client/server network in the home would be a big case of overkill.

As you'll learn as you go through this book, a small peer-to-peer home network will provide all the networking infrastructure that you'll need to create a complete home network. Peer-to-peer networks are capable of providing many of the same features found on client/server-based networks. These features include

- Sharing files and folders located on hard disks
- Sharing printer resources
- Sharing access to the Internet

- Providing remote access to the network and its resources
- Communicating with network devices and appliances

Peer networks also have a number of features that differentiate them from client/server networks. Client/server networks centralize the responsibility for network security on specific servers known as domain controllers. Domain controllers contain a database of users who are permitted to access network resources and policies to enforce security restrictions for every user on the network. In contrast, peer networks implement a decentralized security model where every computer is responsible for its own security. A peer network's overall security is then governed by the security implemented on each of its member computers.

Unfortunately not all Microsoft operating systems have the same security features. In particular Windows 95, 98, and Me all allow anyone with physical access to the computer to log in and access network resources. In contrast, a home network comprised of computers running only Windows NT, 2000, and XP operating systems can be made significantly more secure because these operating systems can be set up to require a user to provide a valid username and password before access is granted to the computer or the network. In addition, these more secure operating systems can provide different levels of access to different users, giving more experienced or trusted family members administrative privileges while limiting less experienced family members and children to only the resources that they require.

 To learn more about Windows XP security see Chapter 7, "Becoming Your Own Network Administrator."

CUTTING-EDGE NETWORKING TECHNOLOGIES

Two new technologies are changing the way that new home networks are built and how they operate: wireless and broadband. Wireless home networks are not constrained by physical cable. This makes them much easier to set up and work with. This also means no more cables running across the floor and no more crawling around the attic or basement trying to feed cables through your walls.

Broadband provides fast Internet connections and eliminates slow, shared Internet access provided by 56k modems. Broadband also provides significantly better support for Internet technologies such as streaming audio and video.

Advances in Wireless Technology

Prior to the arrival of wireless home networking products, your ability to set up a home network was limited by the physical constraints of working with network cable. In most cases this meant running cables between computers, over floors, behind furniture, and down the halls. If you were really aggressive, you might have tried to run the cables through your walls.

Another option was to purchase home networking kits that allowed you to build a home network using the telephone wiring already installed in your house. Phoneline networks allow you to connect computers in any room that has a telephone jack. This technology limits the locations where you can connect your computer.

Powerline home networking allows you to build a home network using the existing electrical wiring in your house. Since every room in the house usually has at least one power outlet, this option provides more flexibility. However, as of the writing of this book, powerline home network products were not yet ready and may already be doomed to failure thanks to the arrival of wireless home networking technologies, which have exploded upon the scene.

Though a bit pricey at first, wireless home networking hardware has continued to drop in price to the point where it is now competitive with other home network products. A wireless home network is just that, one built using hardware that can communicate by sending data over radio waves. Wireless technology allows you to set up a home network without regard for most physical constraints. In fact, in most circumstances you'll find that even in the largest house you can set up a home network that is capable of letting you connect to it from anywhere inside the house or even outside, provided you don't stray too far away.

How Does Wireless Networking Work?

Wireless networks move data around by transmitting them over radio waves. This is the same type of technology used by the military since WWII. The wireless technologies involved in home networking use spread-spectrum technology. Spread-spectrum is a wideband radio frequency that uses more bandwidth by spreading signals out over a number of different frequencies in order to create a stronger, clearer signal.

You'll find two types of spread-spectrum technologies used in wireless home networking. These are

- **Frequency hopping**—Constantly switches between 75 1MHz subchannels to create a communications connection.
- **Direct Sequence**—Switches between 14 overlapping 22MHz channels to create a communications connection.

Both the sender and the receiver must be synchronized in order for them to be able to communicate.

Wireless Networking Options

Given recent improvements in price and in product availability, wireless networking is ready to emerge as the preferred technology for home networking. Sounds too good to be true, doesn't it? Well it is true. However, like any new technology wireless home networking has its own set of issues. Perhaps the biggest problem facing people ready to begin building a wireless home network is figuring out which type of wireless network is the right

wireless technology to choose. There are several to choose from, each with its own distinct set of advantages and disadvantages and there are lots of compatibility issues to contend with. The available options include

- **Bluetooth**—A technology that lets you wirelessly connect a computer to up to 7 other computer devices, eliminating the need for physical cables and allowing computers to communicate with one another.
- **HomeRF**—A technology that lets you build a wireless local area network capable of supporting data, voice, and multimedia.
- **802.11x**—A family of very popular wireless networking technologies, each of which lets you build a wireless local area network. However, not all of these technologies are compatible.

Each of these wireless technologies is outlined in the sections that follow. As you read about them, take special note of their capabilities, speeds, and their compatibility with each other.

In the end some of these technologies may die off while others live on. Unfortunately it's still too early to say for sure how things will turn out. Therefore one of the goals of this book is to provide those who choose to set up a wireless network with enough information to be able to make an informed decision as to which wireless home network technology is best for them.

Bluetooth Personal Area Networks

Bluetooth is a wireless technology used to create personal area networks. A *personal area network* or *PAN* is a small network that spans an area the size of a room and connects computers to wireless devices as depicted in Figure 1.1.

 Bluetooth is named after Harald Blaatand, a Viking king who ruled Denmark from 940-981 A.D. History remembers him as the sponsor of a number of remarkable bridges.

Bluetooth began as a cable replacement technology that was designed to facilitate communications between a computer and its peripheral devices. Examples of Bluetooth-enabled devices include

- Keyboards
- Mice
- Printers
- Speakers
- Digital cameras
- Portable MP3 players
- Digital video recorders

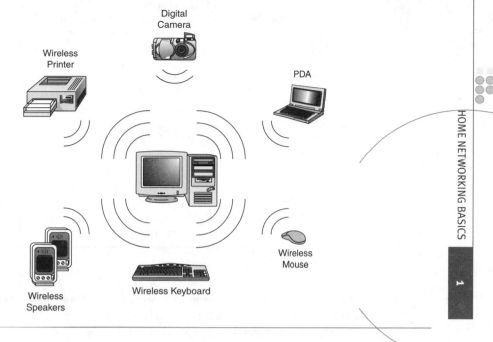

Figure 1.1

Bluetooth personal area networks support up to 7 wireless connections within a 30 foot radius.

The current version of Bluetooth is 1.1. It has grown somewhat from this initial concept to include a number of additional technologies including:

- Using it to connect a laptop to a Bluetooth-enabled mobile phone in order to share data and provide an Internet connection
- Using it to connect two computers together
- Using it to transfer data between a computer and a PDA without a cradle

While Bluetooth can be used to support communications between two computers, it was not designed to support a local area network. However, it can connect with them, so you could set up one or more Bluetooth PANs in various rooms of your house in addition to a local area network.

As a cable replacement technology, one of Bluetooth's missions is to provide an effective alternative to infrared. Infrared has been used to support wireless communications between PCs for many years. For example, Microsoft supports infrared communications as a substitute for a parallel or serial direct connection between two computers. You can set up an Infrared connection using Windows XP's New Connection Wizard, which is found on the Network Connections folder.

NOTE Infrared is a wireless technology commonly found in TV and appliance remote controls that can transmit data at a rate of up to 4Mbps within a range of 6 feet. However, a direct line of site is required between the two communicating devices making it a difficult technology to implement. Nevertheless, a number of infrared-based devices have been sold including keyboards and mice.

NOTE You can learn more about infrared by visiting the Infrared Data Associated or IrDA at www.irda.org. The IrDA is a consortium of technical companies that develop official infrared standards.

How Bluetooth Works   You can create a Bluetooth PAN by installing a Bluetooth USB or PC card in your PC or laptop and then purchasing Bluetooth- enabled appliances. Bluetooth supports the creation of ad hoc peer-to-peer networks over distances of less than 30 feet. Every Bluetooth device has a unique 48-bit number that identifies it. In order for the device to join a PAN, its PIN number must be supplied. Bluetooth can support up to 7 simultaneous communicating devices.

Bluetooth PANs operate in the unlicensed 2.4GHz radio spectrum. This is the same area of the spectrum in which devices such as wireless phones and microwave ovens operate. Bluetooth employs frequency-hopping spread spectrum or FHSS technology, hopping over 79 frequencies 1600 times per second. This rapidity helps to minimize interference with other technologies that share the 2.4GHz radio frequency. Bluetooth networks deliver a top speed of 1Mbps, which is fine for many peripheral devices but slow for communications between computers.

While frequency hopping provides a degree of security by making it difficult for all but the most technically inclined to eavesdrop on its communications, Bluetooth also employs 128-bit encryption. Data encryption encodes data before it is transmitted so that only the receiver can decode it. Bluetooth also employs the use of PIN numbers to prevent an unknown device from simply joining your PAN. However, if you work in an environment where security is not a big concern you can disable the use of PINs, thus allowing any Bluetooth-enabled device that comes in range to automatically join the PAN. Even if you require the use of PINs, however, your PAN can be penetrated if someone steals one of your wireless devices. Bluetooth authenticates devices and not people (e.g., anyone who gets their hands on your device can access to your PAN).

Bluetooth's Prospects   The Bluetooth standard is developed by the Bluetooth SIG (Special Interest Group), which represents a consortium of IT companies. Its members include companies like 3Com, Microsoft, IBM, Intel and Motorola. Although Bluetooth has been talked about for a number of years it has yet to achieve widespread use. However, Bluetooth does now seem to be gaining some momentum as Bluetooth-enabled products are finally coming to market. IBM, 3Com, and Toshiba are just a few of a growing number of companies now selling Bluetooth USB and PC Card adapters. In addition, Bluetooth-enabled devices are beginning to appear. For example, Epson now sells a Bluetooth Printer

Adapter that you can attach to the parallel printer port of most Epson Ink Jet printers to turn them into wireless printers. Sony has added Bluetooth support to its DCR-IP7 camcorder and Ericsson has added Bluetooth support to its T68 mobile phone. You'll also find Bluetooth cards for your Palm PDA. The recent emergence of these and many other products does seem to have positioned Bluetooth as a viable consumer product.

 NOTE For more information check out the official Bluetooth Web site at www.bluetooth.com.

However, Bluetooth still has a few obstacles to overcome. Microsoft failed to provide native support for it in Windows XP. So if you are running Windows 98 or Me, you'll find that your computer won't be able to communicate with your Bluetooth devices after upgrading to Windows XP. This does not mean that Microsoft will not provide an upgrade that will add Bluetooth support to Windows XP or that Bluetooth vendors won't supply the necessary software with their own products.

Another obstacle to Bluetooth is that many hardware developers have long been selling wireless solutions based on other wireless standards and have a lot of time and money invested in them. For example, Logitech, who is a member of the Bluetooth SIG, still sells wireless keyboards, mice, and trackballs using its own proprietary technology that it calls Palomar.

HomeRF Networks

HomeRF is one of two technologies competing to become the dominant wireless local area network communications standard for home networking. The other competitor is the 802.11x family for wireless standards, which will be covered next.

The HomeRF Working Group introduced HomeRF in 1998. Version 1.0 supported a top transmission speed of 1.6Mbps and a maximum range of 150 feet. This provided adequate support for Internet connection sharing but proved lacking when it came to moving around MP3s and downloading streaming audio and video.

HomeRF 1.0 was the first wireless home networking solution to hit the market and despite its initial high cost it enjoyed some early success. However, a competing standard known as 802.11b soon arrived on the scene sporting an 11Mbps transmission speed. As a result most hardware vendors switched over to the 802.11b standard.

How HomeRF Works   Like Bluetooth and 802.11b, HomeRF operates in the unlicensed 2.4GHz frequency range. While this range is rather crowded, HomeRF detects interference on a particular frequency. It then adjusts itself to ensure that no 2 consecutive hops will occur at that frequency. This makes HomeRF a better performer than 802.11b when residing in areas that contain other devices that operate in the 2.45GHz range (e.g., Bluetooth PANs, mobile phones, microwave ovens, etc.).

Recently introduced HomeRF 2.0 has 10Mbps transmission rates. In addition it provides for:

- *Quality of Service* or QoS, which is a technique used to guarantee bandwidth required by certain applications including voice and multimedia. This helps to ensure clear phone calls and smooth-playing video and audio.
- Support for up to 4 wireless voice telephone conversations and up to 8 handsets. It also supports caller ID and call waiting and forwarding.
- Interference immunity using intelligent frequency hopping

HomeRF 2.0 is designed to support data, voice, and entertainment over the same network. It employs frequency hopping spread spectrum or FHSS technology and provides security features that include the ability to require a network password before allowing a device to join the network and 128-bit encryption. A HomeRF network can host up to 127 devices.

Unlike the competing 802.11x family of wireless technologies, users of HomeRF have a clear migration path because version 2.0 is backward compatible with version 1.0. HomeRF is used to build peer-to-peer networks where every computer is connected to the network using a HomeRF network adapter as depicted in Figure 1.2. No intermediary access point is required, which helps keep the cost of building and later upgrading the network down. Despite this, the cost of HomeRF products is still high because of its small market share and lack of vendor support.

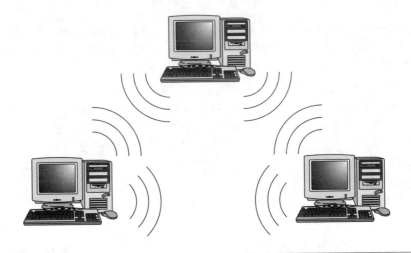

Figure 1.2

HomeRF networks allow computers to communicate directly with one another at distances of up to 150 feet.

HomeRF-based networks support Microsoft Internet connection sharing or can be used with wireless HomeRF gateways to create shared Internet access.

HomeRF's Future   Clearly, HomeRF is in a delicate position given the 802.11x family of wireless networking standards current market dominance and stronger vendor support. However, HomeRF advocates argue that HomeRF is better suited than 802.11x for the home users while 802.11x is better suited for the business world. 802.11x's lack of prioritization support for audio and video makes it less valuable to the home user. HomeRF advocates also believe that the rise of broadband will drive sales and help it achieve a much stronger market presence. This vision has been clarified bwy AT&T who joined the HomeRF Working group in January 2002. This support from a market heavyweight brings new hope that HomeRF may have a bright future in helping to deliver broadband Internet and telephone services.

The HomeRF Working Group believes that HomeRF's cordless phone and multimedia streaming support will attract broadband carriers, in addition to AT&T, and help to quickly spread its acceptance. HomeRF has also begun an aggressive European push. In late 2001 the HomeRF European Working Group was established and now promotes HomeRF to the European marketplace. Plans for HomeRF 3.0 are also in the works and include the promise of 20Mbps transmission speeds with enhanced DVD-quality support for audio and video.

The question is whether or not all these recent developments are enough to make HomeRF a major player again in home networking. It may be that HomeRF 2.0 has delivered too little too late given that 802.11a wireless networking products are now on computer store shelves. This standard provides for up to 54Mbps transmission speeds and some vendors actually have 72Mbps implementations. This kind of speed more than offsets HomeRF's support for prioritized audio and video transmissions. In addition, the 802.11x family of wireless networking standards suffers with compatibility issues as well.

Unlike 802.11x, HomeRF is aimed strictly at the home user. As a result you can expect easier installation and setup (although the setup of 802.11x is not very difficult either). You can expect to be guided through the setup of a HomeRF network by a wizard that will initiate everything from network access to file and printer sharing. In addition, at least one HomeRF vendor, Proxim (www.proxim.com), provides support for a virtual modem, which allows you to share your modem with any networked computer. This is something that is not available on most home networks. Proxim also sells USB and PC Card HomeRF network adapters as well as a HomeRF wireless gateway, which makes short work of setting up shared cable or DSL Internet access.

NOTE   To learn more about HomeRF check out the HomeRF web site located at www.homerf.org.

802.11x Wireless Networks

By now you should have a pretty good idea that 802.11x is a family of *wireless local area networking standards* or *WLANS* that support wireless networking. Unlike HomeRF, 802.11x wireless networking is targeted at both home and corporate networks.

There are currently 4 802.11x standards as outlined in Table 1.1.

TABLE 1.1—A COMPARISON OF 802.11X WIRELESS NETWORKING STANDARDS

Standard	Speed	Frequency	Comments
802.11	2MB	2.45GHz	Not widely deployed due to low transmission speeds
802.11b	11MB	2.45GHz	Heavily deployed in home and corporate networks
802.11a	54MB	5GHz	Currently available but not backward compatible with 802.11b although many vendors are promising dual support for 802.11a and 802.11b by late 2002
802.11g	54MB	2.45GHz	Backward compatible with 802.11b but not available until late 2002

Of these standards, 802.11b and 802.11a are currently available. 802.11 was too slow and never really caught on and the first 802.11g wireless products are not going to be ready until late 2002.

802.11b has been the dominant wireless technology since 1999 for both home and corporate networks. 802.11a and 802.11g are both poised to expand this market dominance. Unlike HomeRF, 802.11x wireless networking products have enjoyed strong vendor and consumer support and are probably the best choice today for building a wireless home network. There are plenty of 802.11x wireless products already available in your local computer store. 802.11b products are very competitively priced and while 802.11a is more expensive, you can expect prices to fall as it gains market share.

All of the 802.11x standards use spread-spectrum technology, sending data over a collection of alternating frequencies. However, they do not all operate at the same radio frequency creating some compatibility and migration issues and making the choice of which one to select difficult. For example, 802.11a is not backward compatible with 802.11b but 802.11g promises to be. However, 802.11a is available now and 802.11g is not going to arrive for a while. On the other hand, a number of vendors are promising to deliver dual-mode wireless equipment that can support both 802.11a and 802.11b hardware around the same time that 802.11g arrives.

The problem that you face with these standards is knowing which one to start with. Unfortunately, at least for now, there is no best answer. Each of these standards and their advantages and disadvantages are examined more fully in the sections that follow.

802.11   802.11 was approved in 1997 by the IEEE 802.11 committee. It defines a wireless networking standard that uses the 2.4GHz radio frequency. 802.11 provides network security in the form of the *wired equivalent privacy* or *WEP* protocol. WEP encrypts or encodes data before transmitting it to the receiving computer in order to prevent it from being read by a computer other than the designated receiving computer.

NOTE The IEEE (Institute of Electrical and Electronic Engineers) is an independent standards body that is responsible for defining a number of networking standards including Ethernet and wireless networking.

802.11 provided for two types of operation, ad hoc and infrastructure. In ad hoc mode, two or more computers equipped with 802.11 network adapters can communicate with one another directly in much the same manner that HomeRF networks communicate. 802.11 ad hoc networks, as their name implies, are usually set up as temporary networks and are not generally used to create permanent networks.

Infrastructure networks add another component to the mix in order to establish and manage the network. This component is delivered in the form of a wireless access point or gateway. Figure 1.3 depicts a home network created using a wireless access point. The access point serves as a hub for network communications and can control which computers are allowed to join the network.

Figure 1.3

Using an access point to establish an 802.11x-based wireless home network.

While an access point can be used to set up a standalone home network, it is more common to see them used as a way of adding wireless network support to an existing wired network. When used this way the access point is connected to the existing network and then functions as a bridge by providing network access to wireless clients as depicted in Figure 1.4.

If you already have a home network and want to add one or more wireless connections to it, then an access point is the way to go. On the other hand, if you are setting up a home network from scratch, then you should consider purchasing a wireless gateway. A wireless gateway performs a number of roles on a home network as depicted in Figure 1.5. First of all it connects every computer with a wireless network adapter into a network. It also connects a home network to a cable or DSL modem, thus providing for shared Internet access.

In addition, these devices also provide built-in firewall services and provide protection for your entire home network from Internet intruders.

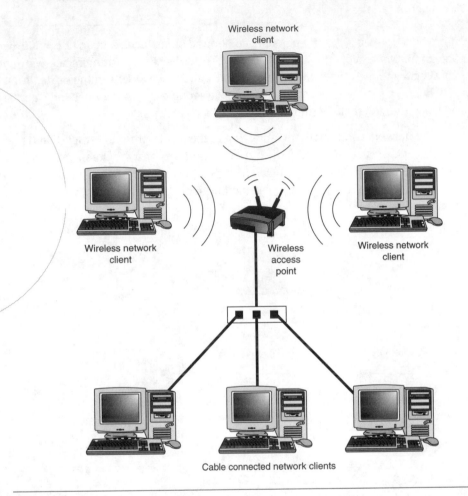

Wireless network
client

Wireless network
client

Wireless
access
point

Wireless network
client

Cable connected network clients

Figure 1.4

Using an 802.11x access point to add support for wireless networking to an existing local area network.

For more information on how to work with a wireless access point or gateway, see Chapter 8 "Going Online."

802.11 defines two different and incompatible ways of transmitting data. These are

- **FHSS (Frequency Hoping Spread Spectrum)**—Switches transmissions over 75 1MHz subchannels

- **DSSS (Direct Sequence Spread Spectrum)**—Switches between 14 overlapping 22MHz channels

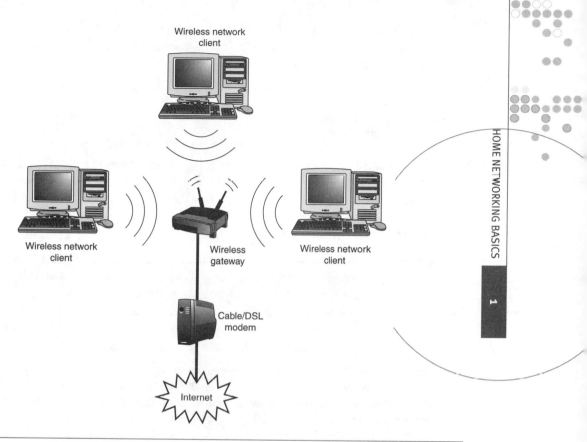

Figure 1.5

Using a 802.11x wireless gateway to set up shared Internet access on a home network.

Unfortunately, by defining two different means of transmitting data, 802.11 created some confusion and concerns about incompatibility issues among vendors and consumers. 802.11 operated with a maximum transmission speed of 1 to 2Mbps. This is very slow compared to standard Ethernet, which is capable of 10Mbps. Because of these factors and competition with HomeRF version 1.0, which at the time provided 1.6Mbps transmission speeds, 802.11 never really took off.

802.11b   The introduction of 802.11b in 1999 sparked the beginning of the widespread deployment of wireless networks. 802.11b operates in the 2.45GHz radio frequency. By providing for wireless networks that provided 11Mbps transmission speeds and a range of up to 150 feet (indoors), 802.11b immediately attracted strong vendor support.

802.11b automatically backs off its speed when interference is detected in order to ensure clear communications. The 2.45GHz radio frequency is also occupied by a number of other electronic devices including microwave ovens and portable telephones. Therefore, 802.11b is susceptible to interference from any of these kinds of devices and may result in slower transmission speeds.

802.11b, also known as *WiFi* (which stands for *Wireless Fidelity*), transmits data using Direct Sequence Spread Spectrum or DSSS. It provides security in the form of WEP and supports encryption levels up to 128-bits.

Some vendors have extended their implementation of 802.11b to include 152-bit encryption. Make sure that you look for these vendors' products if high levels of encryption are important to you.

One missing feature in 802.11b is the ability to prioritize the transmission of audio and video such as the capability found in HomeRF networks. Despite this, 802.11b has remained the dominant wireless networking technology for both corporate and home networks. This is due in part to the fact that HomeRF only recently began to run at 10Mbps while 802.11b has been doing it for years.

Between the recent arrival of 802.11a and the pending arrival of 802.11g, 802.11b is certain to be eventually supplanted, although it may still hang around for a while as people try to figure out whether 802.11a or 802.11g is the way to go. In addition, 802.11b currently enjoys a strong price advantage over 802.11a and provides a less inexpensive way to get a wireless home network up and running now. That network can then be upgraded later, once the smoke clears around 802.11a and 802.11g.

802.11a 802.11a is a 54Mbps wireless networking standard. It operates in the 5GHz radio frequency, which unfortunately makes it incompatible with 802.11b. As of the writing of this book 802.11a wireless network adapters and access points were beginning to appear in computer stores. 802.11a gateways are certainly not far behind and may be available as you read this.

Some 802.11a hardware vendors have engineered a "Turbo Mode" which increases transmission speeds up to a theoretical 72Mbps. If speed is important to then, make sure that you look for these products. However, you may have to pay a little extra for them.

The 5GHz radio frequency is a lot less crowded than the 2.45GHz radio frequency. This makes 802.11a a lot less subject to interference.

802.11a products were introduced at prices about double that of 802.11b products. However, 802.11a provides a lot of muscle for this price, with transmission speeds up to 5 times as fast as 802.11b. Prices are bound to come down as more people buy products based on this standard.

In theory 802.11a can maintain its 54Mbps transmission speeds at distances of up to 60 feet. After that it drops back and can support a range of approximately 120 feet, but at half its normal transmission speed. It will continue to drop back as the distance increases eventually falling all the way down to 6Mbps and subsequently to no transmission once the distance exceeds the range of the device. This maximum range will vary and is affected by environmental factors.

 NOTE No wireless networking standard actually operates at its maximum speed. In fact, it is typical that they run at about half their stated theoretical speeds. There are a number of reasons for this including interference and physical barriers. Also, turning on encryption slows things down a bit by adding additional processing requirements to every data packet that is sent out.

While 802.11a does not provide prioritized support for audio and video like HomeRF networks, its increased transmission speeds more than offset this missing capability. 802.11a's major disadvantage right now is its incompatibility with 802.11b. However, a number of vendors have indicated that dual-mode products will eventually be delivered that can support both standards and assist in the migration of 802.11b to 802.11a. This should be of major importance to corporate IT departments that may have hundreds or even thousands of wireless clients to migrate. However, for an individual with a home network consisting of 2 or 3 computers, the process of migrating is usually much simpler.

Another problem that 802.11a faces right now is that 802.11g is on the way and 802.11g will provide backward compatibility with 802.11b, which will make things easier for existing 802.11b users. However, if you are building a new home network from scratch and want to set up the fastest network possible, then you have to think a bit harder. The fast track is to purchase all-new 802.11a hardware. Or you can wait for 802.11g and then give both technologies a chance to battle it out and see which one is winning before committing. In this case, a minimal investment in 802.11b might be preferable just to get started.

802.11g   By delivering speed comparable to 802.11a, while also providing backward compatibility with 802.11b, 802.11g offers enough reasons to make you pause before rushing out to purchase 802.11a equipment.

802.11g was approved by the IEEE in November 2001 and should begin to make its presence known in late 2002. It operates in the 2.45GHz radio frequency. Its main advantage is that it provides a very clear upgrade path for 802.11b users and 802.11g products will almost certainly be marketed at prices comparable to 802.11a products.

The question that remains to be answered about 802.11g is whether or not it will suffer much from the same disadvantage that HomeRF has suffered by arriving late to the dance and allowing competing technologies to get a head start. Unfortunately, only time will tell.

What's in Store for 802.11x   Today, the 802.11x wireless networking standards are leading the way in wireless home networking. However, the bottom line is that it is still too early to tell which way things will turn out. You can save money by building a home network today using 802.11b and worry about upgrading later. You can also simply go with 802.11a. Alternatively, you can wait a while and see what happens with 802.11g. Even when 802.11g arrives on the scene it will probably take a while for it to battle it out with 802.11a.

Even as current standards vie for supremacy, new 802.11x standards are being developed that will eventually replace them. Recognizing the importance of providing for the prioritization of audio and video, the IEEE is developing the 802.11e standard. In addition, 802.11h is being defined and will provide tweaks designed to improve operation in the 5GHz frequency range.

The Arrival of High-Speed Internet Access

The arrival of always-on high-speed Internet access has changed everything. Gone are the days of listening to dial tones as your modem attempts to establish a connection to your ISP. Now all you have to do is open your Internet browser and off you go.

For the home user, this powerful new access comes in either of two forms:

- **Cable**—Internet access provided by your local cable company. While capable of speeds over 1Mbps, speeds of 300Kbps to 500Kkbps are more common.
- **DSL**—Internet access provided by your local telephone company that provides similar speed to that provided by cable Internet access.

Both cable and DSL provide the same basic capabilities and will cost you about the same. Although both the technologies are rapidly becoming available just about everywhere, there are still places where one or the other may not be available yet.

With a price that is usually only somewhere around $10 - $20 more per month than dial-up Internet access, cable and DSL services are a solid deal. Especially when you compare the 40Kbps – 44Kbps connection speeds that the typical dial-up connection can provide to a 300Kbps to 500Kbps cable or DSL connection. If you have not tried either of these types of Internet access, then do so. Once you see how fast things go you'll never want to go back to your dial-up connection again.

Cable and DSL access is especially important to families with home networks that have been set up to share their Internet connection. There is just no comparison between 2-3 people trying to access the Internet at the same time using a shared dial-up connection versus a shared high-speed connection. With the high-speed connection you may hardly notice each other.

The next few sections will delve more deeply into cable and DSL and explain more about how these technologies work and compare to each other.

Cable Versus DSL

Cable and DSL offer services that are competitively similar. Both provide always-on high-speed Internet access and both interface with your home network in the same manner. How this works is that you'll end up with a cable or telephone connection to a cable or DSL modem, which you'll then connect to your home network. You can do this in a number of ways including connecting the modem to a wireless Internet gateway. The connection between the cable or DSL modem and the gateway will be made in the form of an

Ethernet connection using an RJ-45 CAT-5 cable which comes packed with your modem. The type of Internet access, cable or DSL, won't matter as far as your home network is concerned.

 CAT-5 is the standard cabling for a home Ethernet network while RJ-45 refers to the connector. More information on Ethernet and cabling is presented in Chapter 2, "Getting Your Hands Dirty: Assembling Your Network Hardware."

Cable and DSL provide the same set of services. However, there are differences between the two technologies. Cable Internet access is provided via the same coaxial cable that you currently use to receive cable TV access. DSL on the other hand is delivered via a telephone line. Cable modems support cable connections and DSL modems support DSL connections. The two types of modems are not compatible.

Cable connections are asymmetric in nature, meaning that they can download a lot faster than they can upload. Fortunately most Internet communications are asymmetric. For example, clicking on a link on a Web page involves transmitting very little information whereas downloading streaming audio and video requires a lot more communications bandwidth.

Unlike cable, there are a number of different types of DSL. However, of these only one type is applicable to the home user. This is *ADSL*, which stands for *Asynchronous Digital Subscriber Line*. Like cable, DSL connections provide more communications bandwidth for downloading data than for uploading it.

When it comes to ordering cable Internet access all that you have to do is contact your local cable company and see if it offers the service. Ordering DSL can be a little more difficult because you'll lease it from a local ISP and not from the telephone company. There are a number of places that you can go to see if DSL is offered in your area. One option is to call your local telephone company and see if it provides DSL access and then ask for the name of an ISP with whom the telephone company jointly provides the access. Another is to call up the local ISPs in your area and find out if any can provide DSL access. A third option is to check out one of the following Web sites that provide information where DSL access is available.

- www.dslreports.com
- www.getconnected.com
- www.thelist.com

Unlike cable, which does not have any distance restrictions, the quality of a DSL Internet connection depends on your proximity to the telephone company's central office. A central office is simply a junction where the telephone company manages telephone and data communications. There are thousands of such offices spread out around the country. You'll need to be located within 3 miles of one of these offices to be able to receive DSL service. Unlike cable access, the farther you are from your central office the slower your

connection will be. Keep this in mind if both cable and DSL access are available in your area and you are trying to decide which one to sign up for.

One other difference between cable and DSL is that a cable connection is actually nothing more than a connection to a local area network that your cable company has set up in your neighborhood or community. As a shared connection, it will slow down as more of your neighbors go online. However, while DSL represents a direct connection between your house and the telephone company, things can still become congested back at the central office where all the Internet connections for your area must share the telephone company's pipeline to the Internet.

Leverage the Power of the Internet with Shared Access

Home networks allow you to move your data quickly from computer to computer with minimal effort. They also make sharing disk space and printers a snap. In addition, there is one other critical resource that can be shared, Internet access. By sharing Internet access you only need to pay your ISP one monthly fee in order to allow your entire family to surf the Internet. This can save you big bucks over time. When combined with an always-on high-speed Internet connection it feels like each member of the family has their own dedicated Internet service. Many people find that Internet connection sharing alone provides more than enough justification for setting up their own home network.

Protecting Yourself with a Personal Firewall

Whenever you connect to the Internet you are accessing a global network that contains almost unlimited resources. However, many people fail to realize that this network connection goes both ways. In other words, just as you can reach out and connect to Internet resources, people on the Internet can reach in and touch your home network. That is unless you put up a wall, actually a firewall, to stop them.

In many ways Microsoft's operating systems seem to be designed without security in mind. When connected to a network they, by default, respond too easily when prompted for information and unless you have taken steps to lock things down, are only too willing to allow access to your data. However, Microsoft has been slowly working towards tightening things down with each new version of Windows. Windows XP, for example, is the first Microsoft operating system to provide a built-in personal firewall. However, it's a limited implementation and lacks many of the features found in more seasoned third-party software. There are two types of personal firewalls, hardware and software. A hardware-based personal firewall is usually included in Internet connection devices called Internet Gateways or Ethernet routers and are capable of protecting your entire network as depicted in Figure 1.6.

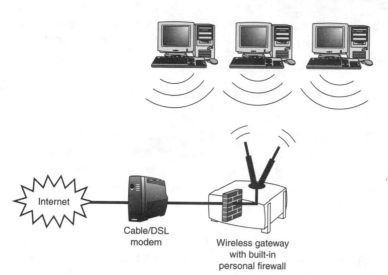

Internet

Cable/DSL
modem

Wireless gateway
with built-in
personal firewall

Figure 1.6

Most wireless gateways also double as a personal firewall, protecting your home network from Internet intruders.

As an alternative to hardware firewalls, you can install a software-based personal firewall on each of your network computers. Examples of software-based personal firewalls include ZoneAlarm, BlackIce, or McAfee. They can be used as a second line of defense on your computers just in case an intruder makes it past the hardware firewall or as a primary means of defense on home networks that do not have an Internet gateway.

 See Chapter 8, "Going Online," for more on broadband, Internet connection sharing, gateways, and firewalls.

Anytime you connect to the Internet you are opening up an avenue from which someone on the Internet can try to launch an attack. The attacker may be a teenager playing practical jokes or someone looking for your Quicken and Microsoft Money files. Both dial-up and always-on high-speed Internet connections can be considered exposures. However, high-speed connections are far more dangerous because they leave your computer open to attack any time that you turn it on. Unlike dial-up connections where your ISP assigns you a random IP address, most cable and DSL connections retain their IP address assignments for long periods of time, allowing an intruder that has identified your computer to return over and over again in order to attempt to gain entry. And since cable and DSL connections are fast, the intruder is able to work faster.

Large corporations have long protected their computer networks using firewalls and security experts. However, the recent explosion in cable and DSL has led to the development of personal firewalls that are specifically designed to protect the home user without requiring you to become a security professional. When properly implemented, a personal

firewall can make your computer or home network look and act as if it were invisible by ignoring all attempts at network communication that do not originate from your computer. No home network with a shared Internet connection should be without one.

INTRODUCING THE MICROSOFT FLAGSHIP OPERATING SYSTEM — WINDOWS XP

Windows XP is the name of a new collection of operating systems developed by Microsoft. Microsoft has developed two new Windows XP operating systems targeted at desktop users. Windows XP Home Edition is targeted at home consumers whereas Windows XP Professional is targeted at corporate users, software developers, and computing professionals. Although both operating systems are based on the same code set, there are a number of differences, perhaps most importantly in the area of security, where Microsoft believes corporate users have higher security requirements. Windows XP Home Edition has been customized with the home user in mind whereas Microsoft has built Windows XP Professional for corporate and technical users. In fact, Windows XP Home Edition cannot even participate as a client in Windows domains, which precludes a more complicated network setup.

Windows XP Home Edition represents Microsoft's most recent and most advanced operating system designed for the home consumer. Windows XP Home Edition will be used for the procedures and examples presented in this book. However, Windows XP is by no means a hard requirement for building your own home network or sharing a broadband Internet connection. When it comes to home networking, Windows 98 2nd edition and Windows Me both have everything that you need to get the job done. If you're still using one of these operating systems, then your screens may look a little different but the steps involved in setting things up are essentially the same as in Windows XP.

Windows XP represents a merger between the Windows NT/2000 line of operating systems and the Windows 95/98/Me line of operating systems. Although its base code has been developed from the Windows NT/2000 kernel, many of its new features and capabilities have been developed by modeling key functionality of Windows Me code. It is Microsoft's intention that Windows XP Home Edition and Windows XP Professional replace all previous versions of its home operating systems.

Although Windows 98 and Windows Me provided users with many enhancements and features not found in Windows 95, neither represented as significant a change as was the jump from Windows 3.X to Windows 95. However, the jump to Windows XP Home Edition should be regarded as another major leap for home operating systems.

Windows XP Home Edition's hardware requirements will give you a good indication of just how different the operating system is from Windows 95, 98, and Me. These hardware requirements are outlined in Table 1.2.

TABLE 1.2—WINDOWS OPERATING SYSTEMS' HARDWARE REQUIREMENTS

Operating Systems	Processor	Memory	Hard drive
Windows 95	386	4MB (8MB Recommended)	40MB
Windows 98	486DX 66	16MB (24MB Recommended)	175MB
Windows Me	Pentium 150	32MB	480MB
Windows XP Home Edition	Pentium 233	64MB (128MB Recommended)	

The official Windows operating system hardware requirements listed in Table 1.1 are true minimum requirements. To effectively use an operating system to do any real work you need to make sure that your hardware surpasses these requirements in each of these categories. Windows XP's 128MB of recommended memory is one such example as 64MB will allow installation, but performance is likely to be inadequate.

Redesigned Graphical User Interface

The look and feel of Windows operating systems takes a major leap forward with Windows XP. Its graphics are much more colorful and attractive and you have greater control over a number of user interface features such as whether you must log in in order to access computer resources. In addition, changes have been made to just about every dialog box, menu, and icon.

A Cleaner Install Process

Odds are if you are going to be installing Windows XP yourself, that you'll be performing an upgrade of a current operating system. Windows XP does an excellent job of transferring your configuration settings during the upgrade to Windows XP. Windows XP also provides an advanced plug-and-play capability that supports all the latest hardware technologies including enhanced USB and IEEE 1394 support as well as support for a number of new wireless networking devices.

One of the first things that you notice when installing Windows XP is that it installs more easily than other Microsoft operating systems. This is due in part to the addition of a new installation feature known as Dynamic Update. Dynamic Update uses your current operating system's Internet connection to determine whether or not Microsoft has provided any updates that should be downloaded and applied during your upgrade to Windows XP. Updates may include software drivers, security fixes, and other compatibility updates for your hardware and software.

Application Compatibility

One of the limitations of the Windows 2000 line of operating systems was a partial incompatibility with some Windows software that was originally designed for Windows 95, 98, and Me. Microsoft has addressed this issue by ensuring that Windows XP is compatible with the top 1,000 most popular software programs that run on Windows 95, 98, and Me. In fact, most currently available Windows programs should be able to run on Windows XP.

Notable exceptions include antivirus programs, backup programs, and some system utility programs.

In the event that you have an application that still won't run on Windows XP, Microsoft has provided an answer by providing a new *Program Compatibility Wizard* to the operating system. You can start this wizard by clicking Start, All Programs, Accessories, and then Program Compatibility Wizard. After selecting the program that you want to configure you see a dialog box like the one shown in Figure 1.7. From this screen you select the operating system that the program was designed to run on. Windows XP will then use this information to set up and run the program in an environment that emulates the specified Windows operating system.

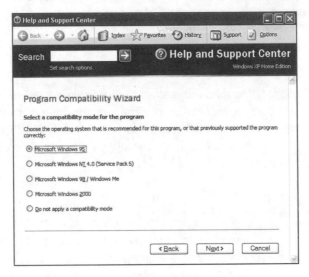

Figure 1.7

You can use the Program Compatibility Wizard to set up the execution of applications that were designed to run on other versions of Microsoft operating systems.

Fast User Switching

Windows 95, 98, and Me operating systems allow users to access system resources without requiring proof of who they are. Nor do these three operating systems provide a means of limiting user access to local resources such as files, folders, and printers. Windows NT and 2000 both provide a strong security model that by default implements a strong user authentication process. The tougher security requirements of Windows NT and 2000 are appropriate for corporation users for whom the operating systems were intended, but are often overkill for home users.

Because ease of use is usually more important than security to home users, Microsoft allows you to turn off or on the requirement of supplying the Windows XP with a username and password. Windows XP Home Edition allows users to access the computer resources by default. In addition, this version of Windows XP defaults to Fast User

Switching mode. Fast *User Switching* allows two or more users to share a computer without having to log on and off. For example, if one of the kids is working on a paper for school but then receives a phone call, you can start a new session and check your e-mail without having to log the child off and close any open files. Microsoft has incorporated terminal server features into Windows XP, which allows the operating systems to switch between users' active sessions by storing inactive sessions in memory.

To let a family member use Fast User Switching to perform a quick task while you are using the computer you select Start, Log Off and then Switch User as shown in Figure 1.8. Alternatively, you can log off before turning over control of the computer but this will close all of your open applications and files.

Figure 1.8

Fast User Switching makes sharing a single computer easier and faster by eliminating the need to close your open applications and log off when another family member needs to use the computer for a minute.

Redesigned Start Menu

One of the most noticeable changes in Windows XP's new GUI interface is the Start Menu, which gives Windows a totally new look and feel. The Windows XP Start Menu, shown in Figure 1.9, now displays the following options:

- Your five most commonly used programs
- Your default Internet browser
- Your default e-mail application
- Links to the My Documents, My Pictures, and My Music folders
- A Link to the Windows Control Panel
- Help and Support, Search and Run options
- An All Programs option that provides a cascaded listing of all your applications
- Log Off and Turn Off Computer options

By adding more intelligence into the Windows Start Menu Microsoft has made it easier to access the programs you are likely to use most often while reducing most of the clutter that previous versions of Windows' Start Menus could accumulate. Microsoft has also decided to assume that everyone uses the Internet and e-mail and has therefore set up static links to these applications on your Start Menu.

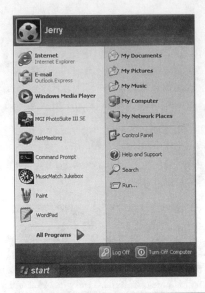

Figure 1.9

Microsoft has streamlined the Windows Start Menu to present you with the applications that you use most often.

A Reorganized Taskbar

Microsoft has also changed the way that multiple open instances of the same application are added to the Windows taskbar. In previous versions of Windows each instance of an open application was added as a separate taskbar icon. In Windows XP a single icon that displays the number of active instances now represents multiple instances of the same icon. If you click on the icon, as shown in Figure 1.10, you see each instance displayed. This feature, like the changes made to the Windows Start Menu, is designed to streamline the GUI and reduce desktop clutter, giving you as much desktop real estate as possible to work with.

Figure 1.10

Reorganizing the way application icons are added to the Windows taskbar gives you more room on the Windows desktop.

More Functional Folders

Microsoft has also made it easier for you to keep track of your data by improving the way that Windows displays the files you open and how you view folder contents. As Figure 1.11 shows, Windows XP can now group files by file type. In the case of Figure 1.11, all compressed subfolders within the folder are displayed first, then all regular subfolders, then all Rich Text Documents, and finally all text files.

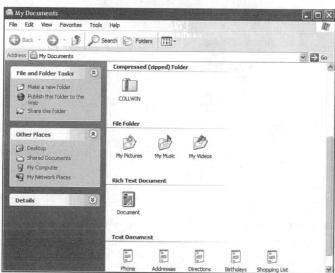

Figure 1.11

By grouping files by type Windows XP helps improve presentation and makes it easier for you to locate your files.

In earlier versions of Windows you had to group files of the same type into their own subfolders if you wanted to view them as a group. This new feature not only improves the presentation of your files but also saves you the effort of creating a subfolder hierarchy to manage the type.

Windows Task Manager

The Windows XP Task Manager, shown in Figure 1.12, will be new to Windows 95, 98, and Me users but should be old hat to Windows NT and 2000 users. However, Windows XP's version of the Task Manager has been significantly enhanced compared to Windows NT and 2000 versions of the Task Manager.

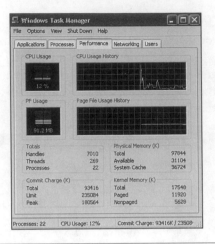

Figure 1.12

Windows XP's Task Manager provides quick access to real-time status information about the operation of Windows, its application, and the network.

Better Multimedia Support

Windows XP introduces Windows Media Player 8, which allows you to view audio and video content. With Windows Media Player 8 you can play CDs and DVDs. You can listen to Internet radio and view online video. Windows Media Player also features built-in Jukebox support and can communicate with many portable devices. In addition to playing multimedia content you can use the Windows Media Player to create it as well. For instance, it provides features that allow you to burn new audio CDs.

Windows XP also features the Windows Movie Maker, which allows you to create home movies using video capture hardware and to perform basic editing features. In addition, Windows XP provides expanded support for a number of new digital devices, providing greater hardware compatibility than any other Windows operating system.

Better Reliability

Because Windows XP is based on the Windows NT/2000 kernel it inherits a significantly more secure foundation than it would have had it instead been modeled after the Windows 9.x kernel. The inherited advantages of Windows XP are too numerous to cover in this book but a partial list includes the NTFS file system protected kernel mode operation and an advanced security system, which includes security permissions and policies.

 If you'd like to learn more about ins and outs of Windows XP, check out Que's *Special Edition Using Microsoft Windows XP, Home Edition*, ISBN # 0789726270.

Windows XP continues to add to the stability of Windows operating systems by adding supports for the following features:

- **Windows Update**—This is a feature that first appeared with Windows 98. It allows you to tell Windows to check the Windows Update Site for any updates applicable to your computer. These updates include new software drivers, security fixes, and application updates. Windows XP has extended its use of the Windows Update feature so that it now looks for updated drivers anytime you add a new piece of hardware.

- **Driver Roll Back**—Anytime you update a software driver Windows XP automatically saves a copy of the previous driver so that you can restore it in the event that the new software driver causes problems.

- **System Restore**—This is a Windows XP feature that allows you to restore the computer to a previous state in the event that a problem occurs. Your personal data is protected and is not affected by the restore option. Windows XP automatically creates restore points daily. In addition it creates them whenever you install a new software application or change a software driver.

Driver Roll Back works with all hardware devices except for printers. Fortunately a poorly written printer driver is unlikely to prevent the proper operation of your computer in the same way that a poorly written NIC or video driver might.

Enhanced Hardware and Software Support

Windows XP inherited most of its hardware support directly from Windows 2000. However, Microsoft has supplemented this with enhancements to USB and IEEE 1394 support. Microsoft has also added support to Windows XP for hundreds of new hardware devices that are lacking in Windows 2000.

Microsoft migrated Windows Me's support for *Windows Image Acquisition* or WIA into Windows XP. Windows XP uses WIA when working with digital cameras and scanners to transfer images. It provides a better interface than did Windows 2000's TWAIN support. Windows XP also supports a number of new wireless networking devices and is ready to support the next generation of high-resolution monitors.

Networking Advancements

Windows XP sports a number of powerful networking features that will assist you in setting up your home network. Windows 98, Me, and 2000 support some of these features. However, some are entirely new. Each of these Windows XP networking features is listed here:

- **Home Network Wizard**—This wizard automates much of the work involved in setting up your home network. You still have to install hardware and its software drivers. However, this wizard does most of the remaining work including setting up file, folder, and printer sharing. The wizard also helps you to set up a shared Internet connection and a personal firewall to protect your network from Internet intruders.

- **Network Bridging**—*Network bridging* is a new Windows feature that allows you to combine a number of different network media such as a traditional Ethernet network and a wireless network into a single network segment.

- **Internet Connection Sharing**—*Internet Connection Sharing* or *ICS* allows you to share a single Internet connection with all the computers on your home network. If you have dial-up Internet access, this means you only need one telephone online and one Internet account. If you have cable or DSL access, this feature will allow you to provide your entire family with high-speed Internet access.

- **Internet Connection Firewall (ICF)**—This personal firewall is integrated directly into Windows XP. It provides dynamic packet filtering so it can inspect all incoming data packets from the Internet. Any data packets that did not originate from your home network are automatically rejected. In addition, the firewall protects your computer from the port scans run by Internet intruders as they seek out new victims. ICF operates with dial-up, cable, and DSL connections.

- **Universal Plug and Play**—Universal Plug and Play allows Windows XP to automatically discover devices on the network and configure itself to communicate with them. For example, if you have a cable or DSL Internet connection with an Internet gateway or router or a network attached printer, Windows XP should detect and configure access to these devices with zero effort on your part. Universal Plug and Play promises to deliver even more home networking benefits in the near future as new network-aware appliances such as intelligent toasters, refrigerators, and other devices are introduced.

CHAPTER 2

GETTING YOUR HANDS DIRTY: ASSEMBLING YOUR NETWORK HARDWARE

This chapter provides you with the background required to design and assemble your own home network. You'll learn how to work with and install network hardware. You will also learn about different ways to connect everything. By the time you have completed this chapter you should know the type of network that you want to build and be ready to go out and purchase the hardware that you will need to make it happen.

Here is what you'll learn:

- How to work with and install different types of network equipment
- How to set up a home network
- How to examine the advantages of wireless network
- How to compare wireless networks to their cabled counterparts

WHAT YOU'LL NEED TO GET STARTED

Before you roll up your sleeves and start assembling your home network you'll need to decide which of the types of networks that you'll see in this chapter is best for you and your home. Once you know which type of network you will be building you'll be able to go out and purchase the hardware that you will need to get started.

As I stated in Chapter 1, "Home Networking Basics," this book is written based on Windows XP Home Edition (although you can still apply it to other Microsoft operating systems or a mixture of different operating systems). So, if you have not already done so, now might be a good time to upgrade your computers to Windows XP. To upgrade to Windows XP your computers will need to meet Windows XP's minimum hardware requirements, which as stated in Chapter 1, are a 233MHz or better processor, 64MB of memory, and a 1.5GB or larger hard drive.

Explaining the steps involved in installing Windows XP Home Edition is beyond the scope of this book. If you'd like to learn about it, check out Que's *Special Edition Using Microsoft Windows XP Home Edition* by Robert Cowart and Brian Knittel (ISBN # 0789726270).

Loading Windows XP or any Microsoft operating system on a computer that just meets the operating system's minimum hardware requirements is not a good idea. These requirements are usually just enough to boot the computer and don't leave a lot left over for running your applications and getting any real work done. At a minimum you'll probably want to run Windows XP Home Edition on a system that has 128MB of memory and a 2.5GB hard drive.

NETWORKING OPTIONS

For you to get all your computers talking to one another on a home network you must somehow connect them. This means providing some sort of a *network medium* to carry data between each computer. A network medium consists of several items including *network adapters*, which are devices that connect your computers to the network, and the path over which network data will be transmitted over the network.

Today there are four common network media for creating home networks, each of which is actually very similar in the way that they operate. The difference between them is the way that wiring or lack of wiring is used to connect everything. These four options are outlined here.

- **Wireless**—A home network that operates without any wiring. All data is transmitted over short-range radio frequencies. There are two primary wireless LAN technologies competing in the home marketplace. These are HomeRF and the 802.11x family of wireless networking standards. Transmission speeds vary among these technologies and can range from 1.6Mbps up to or exceeding 54Mbps.

- **Ethernet and Fast Ethernet**—A home network that requires you to provide your own physical cabling over which all network data is transmitted. Ethernet networks transmit data at 10Mbps speeds and Fast Ethernet networks operate at 100Mbps.

- **Phoneline**—A home network that you can set up that operates by transmitting data over your telephone lines using a technique know as *frequency-division multiplexing,* or *FDM,* where network signals are sent at a different frequency than voice communications. Phoneline networks operate at 10Mbps.

- **Powerline**—A home network that you can set up that operates by sending data through the electrical current in your home's electrical wiring. Powerline networks use a technique known as *orthogonal frequency-division multiplexing or OFDM* to send network data over different frequencies. Powerline networks operate at 14Mbps.

> There is a fifth option of setting up your home network known as a hybrid network. A *hybrid* network is a network that consists of a combination of two or more types of network media. For example, you might decide to set up your home network as a traditional Ethernet network but also add a wireless access point to allow a laptop connection from anywhere in your home. Although it would be overkill, you could even set up a home network that combines all four types of network media.

Wireless represents the easiest way to go of all the networking options. It does not require any cable, there is little concern for physical barriers, and the price of wireless networking equipment is not too much higher than its wired competition.

Having been around the longest, Ethernet is the least expensive option and works fine if all your computers are located close to one another or if you are comfortable with network cable installation. If you already have a home network, then chances are it is based on Ethernet. Consider purchasing an 802.11x wireless access point and also some wireless 802.11x adapters and going with a hybrid home network. This will protect your current investment while giving you the flexibility to grow your network without the constraints that a standard Ethernet network can pose.

If you do not want to go wireless and cannot bear to tackle the task of installing a cabled Ethernet network, there are always the alternatives of phoneline and powerline networking. However, as of the writing of this book powerline has yet to make its debut and like phoneline, you'll be limited as to where you can create new network connections. Overall, discounting its slightly higher price, 802.11x-based home networks are currently the most convenient and flexible home networking option. As such, they'll be the focus of much of the rest of this chapter.

NETWORKING STANDARDS

A network standard is a defined collection of rules for how all computers must operate in order to connect to and operate on a particular type of network.

Different standards apply to different types of networks. The Institute of Electrical and Electronics Engineers or IEEE is an internationally recognized standards body that is responsible for defining a number of LAN standards. Table 2.1 lists the IEEE LAN standards that are applicable to home networking.

TABLE 2.1—IEEE LOCAL AREA NETWORK STANDARDS

Standard	Description
802.3	Carrier sense with multiple access and collision detection (10Mbps Ethernet)
802.u	Fast Ethernet (100 Mbps Ethernet)
802.11	1Mbps Wireless Networking with Carrier operating in the 2.45 GHz frequency range
802.11b	10Mbps Wireless Networking with Carrier operating in the 2.45 GHz frequency range
802.11a	54Mbps Wireless Networking with Carrier operating in the 5 GHz frequency range
802.11g	54Mbps Wireless Networking with Carrier operating in the 2.45 GHz frequency range
802.15.1	Developed in conjunction with the Bluetooth SIG, this standard defined the Bluetooth version 1.1 standard

One of the advantages that 802.11x wireless standards is that the IEEE defines them. The IEEE has been around a lot longer than the organizations that define standards for competing networking technologies. When the IEEE talks hardware, vendors and technical enthusiasts listen.

The IEEE 802.3 networking standard defines Ethernet networking and the IEEE 802.u standard defines Fast Ethernet. Fast Ethernet is the 100Mbps version of Ethernet that operates just like regular Ethernet except that it's a heck of a lot faster. The rest of the standards in Table 2.1 define wireless networking standards. If you are interested, you can learn more about the IEEE networking standards by visiting www.ieee.org.

Absent from Table 2.1 are the standards that define HomeRF, phoneline, and powerline networks. The HomeRF Working Group defines HomeRF standards. You can learn more about them at www.homerf.org. Networking standards for phoneline networks are defined by the Home Phoneline Networking Alliance or HomePNA. You can learn more about the HomePNA by checking out www.homepna.org. The HomePlug Powerline Alliance sets the standards for powerline networking. You can learn more about the HomePlug Powerline Alliance by checking out www.homeplug.org.

Dry as they may be, well-defined networking standards are critical and are constantly evolving. One of the best ways to stay on top of things is to keep your eye on the standard body's Web site whose network technology you have chosen to work with.

NOTE There is a competing powerline network technology known as Passport. Passport is an older technology and only supports a transmission rate of 50–350Kbps. Make sure when you are purchasing your powerline networking equipment that you are not purchasing Passport networking hardware.

SETTING UP YOUR NETWORK BACKBONE

Now that you know a little about the types of networks that you can set up and the standards that govern them, let's take a closer look at each type of network and see how they work and how you assemble them.

Wireless Home Networks

The main advantage of wireless networking is that it gives you the ability to build a home network without the hassles of installing cables or being forced to locate all your computers near telephone or electrical outlets. However, unless you are running a laptop computer using its internal battery, it is impossible to escape a connection to a power outlet, thus at least partially negating wireless's advantage over powerline. The primary disadvantage of wireless networking is its cost, which is a little higher than all the other networking technologies.

Wireless networks operate using radio waves to transmit data instead of physical wiring. Radio waves have the ability to penetrate or bounce around just about any obstacle making wireless networking a good choice for situations where it is inappropriate or inconvenient to run cable. For example, if you live in an old home that has some historic significance, then you probably do not want to knock holes in your walls to run cable from room to room. Likewise, if you have small children, you probably don't want to leave cable lying on the floors along the sides of your walls.

Wireless home networks can be created using either HomeRF or one of the 802.11x wireless standards. Today 802.11x is the better of these two options and will therefore be the focus of the rest of this book's coverage of wireless networking. Regardless of which 802.11x standard you choose for your home network, they all operate using the same basic technology and are constructed in the same manner.

Setting Up a Wireless Network

If you are setting up a wireless home network from scratch, the best way to begin is to purchase a wireless Internet gateway. A typical wireless Internet gateway provides a number of network services, including:

- **Multi-port 10/100Mbps switch/hub**—This feature allows you to connect computers wired with Ethernet connections to your home network.
- **Built-in access point**—This feature allows up to 253 computers with compatible wireless network adapters to connect to your home network.

- **Internet connection sharing**—This feature allows you to connect the wireless Internet gateway to a cable, DSL, or dial-up modem and use it to establish an Internet connection that can be shared by the entire network.

- **Personal firewall service**—This feature protects your home network from Internet intruders by hiding your computers from the Internet and blocking all unsolicited network traffic.

- **Print server**—This feature allows you to attach a printer to the Internet gateway's parallel port and then share it with the rest of the network.

If you do not care about connecting your home network to the Internet, then you can save a few dollars and build yourself a wireless 802.11x home network using an access point instead of a wireless gateway. An access point will allow you to set up a totally wireless home network but will not include other features found on Internet gateways including Internet-related services, a built-in print server, or a multi-port switch/hub. These services could, however, still be provided by individual network computers. For example, any networked Windows XP computer with an Internet connection or printer can always share it.

When you go shopping for your Internet Gateway you may come across wireless devices advertised as wireless broadband routers. These devices provide the same functionality as wireless Internet gateways.

Figure 2.1 depicts a wireless home network built using an Internet gateway.

To set up a wireless network you'll need to decide which wireless standard you are going to use and then purchase the following components:

- A wireless Internet Gateway or access point
- Wireless network adapters for each computer

There is a second way to set up a wireless network without the use of a wireless access point. This is known as an ad hoc network. An *ad hoc* wireless network consists of computers fitted with wireless PC cards. There is no access unit. Therefore, the computers must be in close proximity to one another, usually within the same room. Ad hoc wireless networks are convenient if you travel a lot and need to set up a network in a hotel room or similar environment where network cable would not be an option.

There are only a few steps involved in assembling a wireless home network. First, get a wireless Internet gateway and place it in a centralized location within your home or the area of your home where you plan to set up your network. Try to place the device away from other appliances that may cause interference such as microwave ovens or wireless telephones. Next, physically install wireless network adapters in each of your computers as described a little later in this chapter. You will then need to install the software portion of your network and configure your computers as outlined in Chapters 3 and 4.

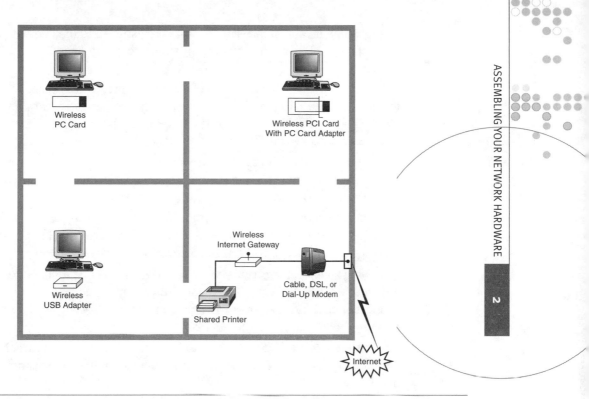

Figure 2.1

An Internet gateway can be used to create a wireless home network and provides an extra bonus in the form of Internet connection sharing and a built-in print server.

Once you have completed the software setup and configured each of your computers for network access you'll be poised to complete the following tasks:

- Share disk drives and folders
- Share printers
- Share Internet access
- Configure your Internet gateway

NOTE For more instruction on sharing disk resources see Chapter 5, "Sharing Precious Disk Space." To learn how to share your printer read Chapter 6, "Maximizing Your Printer Investment." Read Chapter 8, "Going Online," to find out how to share an Internet connection.

Because each vendor's products will differ somewhat in their implementation it's impossible to specifically outline the steps involved in administering all Internet Gateways. However, there are some tasks that you are going to want to perform. These tasks include

- Changing the default administrative password assigned to the Internet gateway or access point. This way you can prevent others from logging in and making changes.

- Building a MAC address table that will be used to prevent computers other than the ones you own from accessing your wireless Internet gateway or access point. This will prevent a neighbor or someone passing by with a laptop computer from being able to connect to your home network.

- Cloning the MAC address assigned to one of your computers to the gateway if you previously used that MAC address to set up your broadband connection. This eliminates the need to register another MAC address with the ISP.

- Upgrading the firmware installed on the wireless gateway or access point. This way, if the manufacturer of your Internet gateway or access point provides new enhancements or fixes, you can stay up to date.

- Specifying any IP settings supplied by your ISP that may be required to set up your Internet connection. If your ISP assigned you a static IP address or you have a DSL connection that uses PPP over Ethernet, you'll need to specify this information in order to set up shared Internet access.

- Administering DHCP and its pool of IP addresses. This allows your wireless Internet gateway or access point to manage the assignment of IP addresses on your home network.

- Defining TCP/IP ports that should be allowed to communicate through your Internet gateway. By default the built-in personal firewall features of your Internet gateway will prevent any Internet connection that was not initiated from your home network. However, if you are running a personal Web or FTP service on one of your computers, you'll need to open the ports specified by the service (in this case ports 80, 20, and 21) in order to allow people on the Internet to access the computer's services.

- Specifying computers via their MAC addresses that should not be able to use the network's shared Internet connection. In addition to using MAC addresses to prevent unauthorized computers from being able to connect to your home network, you can define a list of MAC addresses that specify which of your network computers are and are not permitted to use the network's shared Internet connection.

- Enabling or disabling remote administration of your Internet gateway. By default, Internet gateways can only be administered by a computer on your local area network. However, if the gateway is connected to the Internet, you can enable the ability to administer it over the Internet.

- Administering WEP security and selecting the appropriate encryption level to employ on your network. By enabling encryption you force all computers to encode all the data that they send out over your home network, permitting only the destination computer to decrypt or decode it. The higher the encryption level the tighter your security will be. However, setting higher encryption levels will add additional processing requirements and will slow things down just a bit.

A MAC address is a 48-bit address assigned to networking devices that uniquely identifies each device. You can determine the MAC address of any computer's network adapter by opening the Windows command prompt and typing **IPCONFIG** and looking for a line of output similar to the following:

```
Physical Address. . . . . . . . . : 00-A0-CC-53-46-7A
```

Because the MAC address is guaranteed to be unique, all you have to do is type it into your wireless Internet gateway or access point and then use it to allow or deny network access.

Wireless Internet gateways and access points are administered using your Internet browser. To interact with and administer your wireless Internet gateway or access point you need to have at least one working network connection. In other words, you need to complete the physical installation of the network adapter on at least one computer and then configure its network settings in order to be able to manage your wireless Internet gateway or access point.

You'll probably need to use version 4 or higher of Internet Explorer or Netscape Communicator in order to interact with your wireless Internet gateway or access point.

You can administer the wireless Internet gateway or access point by opening your browser and typing its URL and pressing enter. The exact URL that you'll need to type will be supplied with your wireless Internet gateway or access point and varies among manufacturers. You'll be prompted to supply an administrative ID and password, which will also be supplied with your wireless Internet gateway or access point. You'll then be able to manage your device. Make sure that you address each of the previously listed options in order to properly configure your wireless Internet gateway or access point according to its documentation.

If you are unable to reach your wireless Internet gateway or access point using your Web browser, try pinging it from the Windows command prompt. PING is a network command that can be used to test connectivity between two network devices. To use it just type **PING**, add a space, and then type the IP address assigned to the wireless Internet gateway or access point and press enter. If the command fails, go back and double-check to make sure that you set everything up correctly. If the command succeeds, then make sure you are using a supported version of your Internet browser and then try again. If you are still having problems, read the section that covers troubleshooting wireless networking in Chapter 10, "Just When You Thought Your Work Was Done."

Ethernet Home Networks

If you are not ready to jump into the world of wireless networking, then you can always go with an Ethernet-based network. Ethernet is tried and true and is the oldest and most mature home networking technology. It's also the least expensive.

Ethernet networks come in two flavors: regular Ethernet and Fast Ethernet. Regular Ethernet supports transmission speed up to 10Mbps while Fast Ethernet networks can operate at a theoretical 100Mbps. Of course, you'll pay more for Fast Ethernet. In addition, you'll find plenty of combo products that automatically adjust themselves to run on either a 10 or 100Mbps network.

To set up an Ethernet-based home network you'll need the following components:

- A 10, 100, or 10/100Mbps combo Ethernet network card for each computer (PCI, PC card, or USB)
- CAT 5 twisted-pair cables with RJ-45 connectors
- A 10 or 100Mbps hub/switch

Figure 2.2 depicts a typical Ethernet network consisting of four computers.

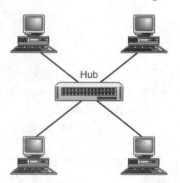

Figure 2.2

Ethernet-based networks provide a tried-and-true cabled alternative to wireless networks.

Ethernet has two advantages over other types of home networks. First, it is very well understood by companies that produce home networking hardware. When you visit your local computer store you'll notice that Ethernet networking products are represented by as much as a 4-to-1 ratio over all the other networking options combined. However, this is beginning to change as wireless technologies gain market share. Ethernet's other advantage is that it is less expensive to implement than other network technologies.

Another feature of Ethernet is that it's the only one of the network options listed previously that can be expanded to 100Mbps.

Ethernet's main disadvantage for home networking is that it requires the use of external network cabling. If all your computers are in the same room or are in adjacent rooms, you may be able to get away with running the cable along the walls. Otherwise, Ethernet cabling can get a little ugly when you try to run your cables into another room or down the hall.

If you are building a new house, you might want to consider arranging for the builder to pre-install your network cabling inside your walls. This way, all that you'll have to do to plug a computer into the network is to connect to a small wall outlet.

If you are going to set up an Ethernet network, make sure that you purchase 10/100Mbps network adapters. These adapters are able to sense the speed of their network connection and automatically configure themselves as appropriate. This way, if you later decide to upgrade to a 100Mbps Fast Ethernet network, the only thing that you'll have to do is replace your 10Mbps hub with a 100Mbps hub. The price of 10/100Mbps cards is a few dollars more but in the long run it will be worth it.

Of course, you can always skip standard Ethernet and just build a 100Mbps Fast Ethernet home network.

Ethernet Hardware

The twisted-pair cabling used in today's Ethernet networks is known as Category 5 or CAT 5 cable. You can find CAT 5 in any computer store. CAT 5 cable is similar to common telephone cables except that it has eight instead of four wires and the small plastic connectors at each end of the cable, known as RJ-45 connectors, are slightly larger than the telephone wire counterparts.

Each computer or network device connected to an Ethernet network requires an Ethernet network adapter. Ethernet adapters can be internal adapter cards, PC cards, or USB connectors. Your choices are limited by the type of connection your computer accepts and by your personal preference. Installing adapters is covered a little later in the chapter.

Ethernet networks that use CAT 5 twisted-pair wiring also require a network device known as a hub that connects the entire computer on the network together. The hub is a very important piece of equipment on an Ethernet network. Ethernet hubs typically operate at 10Mbps, although the 100Mbps variety is available at a higher price. Figure 2.3 shows the Linksys 5-port Workgroup hub. This little hub lets you connect up to five computers to build a small home network. It also has an additional port called an uplink port. If you find your home network growing past five computers, you can later purchase a second hub and chain the two hubs together via the uplink ports to expand your network to as many as ten computers. With some hubs, the uplink port is shared with an adjacent port and may limit the amount of computers that can be connected at the same time. Check the documentation of the device to be sure.

NOTE Hubs are the most basic connectivity devices to use with a standard Ethernet network, but you will also encounter other devices with additional features and, of course, additional cost, that function as the central connection for the network. Manufacturers use a variety of names for such devices. These may include residential or Internet gateways, switches or switching hubs, and router or cable/DSL router. Any such device can be used to connect a small home Ethernet network.

Figure 2.3

The Linksys 5-port Workgroup hub lets you build a home network of up to five computers and can be connected to another hub to grow your network as required.

To assemble your Ethernet network you must install or attach an Ethernet network adapter for each computer to be connected to the network. You can then connect each computer to the network using CAT 5 cable by inserting the RJ-45 connection on one end of the cable to the network adapter and the other end into the hub.

Most Ethernet hubs include a set of indicator lights that help assist you in diagnosing network connection and communication issues. By examining the hub you can tell if a computer has a good connection and whether it is sending or receiving information. The Ethernet hub acts as a single point of failure. If the hub should lose power or fail, the entire network will cease functioning.

Phoneline Networks

Phoneline networks are designed to use the telephone wiring already installed in your house. Phoneline networks use a technique known as frequency-division multiplexing, or FDM, to send network signals over your phone wires at a different frequency from that used to carry voice communications. Phoneline networks operate at 10Mbps.

With phoneline networks you don't have to worry about installing cabling, and phoneline networks cost only slightly more than Ethernet networks. Phoneline networks, however, are limited to a maximum transmission speed of 10Mbps and they require a phoneline in every room where a computer is to be connected to the network as depicted in Figure 2.4.

If you want to put a computer in a room that does not have a telephone outlet, then you either need to change your plans, pay the phone company to install a new line, or create a hybrid home network that includes both phoneline and a wireless or powerline connection.

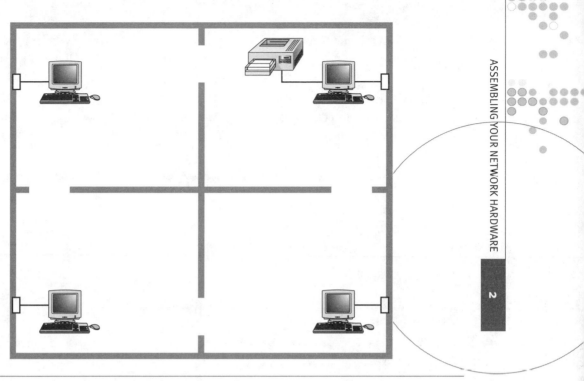

Figure 2.4

A phoneline network takes advantage of the telephone wiring already in your home.

To set up a phoneline network you'll need the following components:

- A phoneline network adapter for each computer to be connected to the network
- A standard telephone cable for each computer
- A telephone outlet in every room where you want to make a network connection

You'll first need to buy a phoneline home networking kit. These kits include everything that you'll need to network two computers together. Then purchase an additional phoneline network adapter for each additional computer that you have. You'll find that your phoneline home networking kit will provide you with everything that you'll need and will guide you through the process of setting up your own home network step by step.

Powerline Networks

Powerline networks leverage the convenience of the wiring provided by your home's electrical system. To create a powerline network you purchase powerline network adapters and power cords and connect your computers to the electrical outlets in your house. Because every computer requires power this means that you can set up a network connection anywhere that you can turn on a computer as demonstrated in Figure 2.5.

Powerline networks use a technique known as orthogonal frequency-division multiplexing or OFDM to send network data over different frequencies. One major advantage of powerline networks is speed. Powerline networks will operate at 14Mbps, which makes them faster than all other home networks except for those built using Fast Ethernet.

The disadvantage of powerline networks is that because the technology is new there will be less of a selection for some time. Although the goal of powerline networks is to be as inexpensive as phoneline networks, it may take some time for its prices to reach the same level.

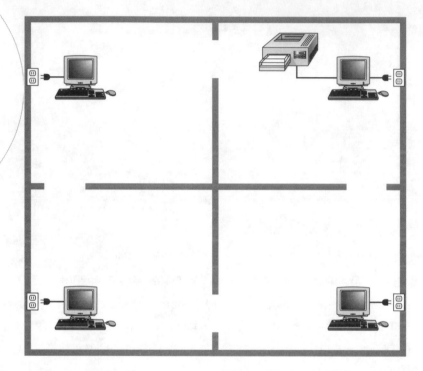

Figure 2.5

A powerline network takes advantage of the telephone wiring already in every room in your home.

To set up a powerline network you'll need to purchase the following components:

- A powerline network adapter for each computer to be connected to the network
- A powerline power cable, which should be supplied with each powerline network adapter
- A power outlet in every room where you want to make a network connection

Like phoneline networking, all that you'll need to get started building a home network based on powerline networking is a powerline home networking kit and an additional phoneline network adapter for each computer that you have. You should expect to install and run a network application on each of your computers. This application runs a wizard that steps you through the entire network setup process.

Adding Wireless to an Existing Home Network

If you already have a home network that is working well and satisfying your needs, there is no point in replacing it just because you also want to add one or more wireless network clients. All that you'll need to do is purchase a wireless access point and wireless network adapter cards for each new wireless connection and then connect the wireless access to your home network. For example, Figure 2.6 depicts a hybrid wireless/Ethernet home network.

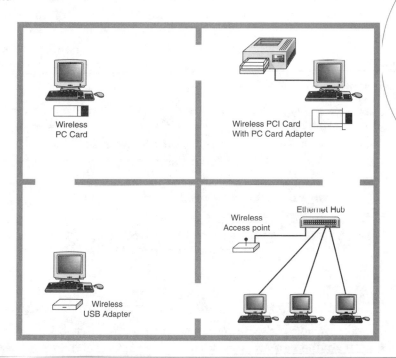

Figure 2.6

A hybrid home network consisting of wireless and Ethernet components.

As you can see in Figure 2.6 all that was required to add wireless clients to the network was to connect the wireless access point to the network hub, switch, or Internet gateway. This connection is made using a CAT 5 RJ-45 Ethernet cable that can be supplied with the wireless access point.

If your home network is based on phoneline or powerline instead of Ethernet, the easiest way to set up a hybrid network is to purchase a bridge. For example, a number of phoneline manufacturers sell Ethernet to phoneline bridges. These devices connect a phoneline network to another network using a CAT 5 RJ-45 Ethernet cable. All that you'll have to do is plug your wireless access point into the bridge's Ethernet point.

NOTE Another option for creating a hybrid network is to install one network adapter for each type of network connection into a single computer running Windows XP Home Edition and then use Windows XP Home Edition's new network bridging feature. To do this first install both network adapters and then open the Network Connections folder. Select the network adapters that you want to use to create the bridge. Then right-click and select Bridge Connections. This will set this computer up as a bridge, allowing it to receive data from one side of the bridge and to forward it on to the other side.

NETWORK HARDWARE

Up to this point you have learned about the basic steps required to set up and configure your home network's backbone. Now let's look at what it takes to install network adapters on your computers so that you can connect them to your new home network. A *network adapter*, also known as a *Network Interface Card* or *NIC*, is a piece of hardware that connects to your computer and the network. Regardless of which type of network you choose to build, network adapters will always be required.

There are scores of available network adapters manufactured by companies such as Linksys, NetGear, D-Link, and SMC. There are specific types of adapters for specific types of needs. For example, there are adapters specifically designed to operate on wireless, Ethernet, phoneline, and powerline networks. Within these categories are many subcategories of network adapters including PCI, ISA, PC Card, and USB. Let's take a look at the different types of network cards and then see how they are installed.

NOTE For simplicity's sake I will use Linksys network adapters in my examples throughout this chapter. You can learn more about Linksys network adapters by checking out www.linksys.com.

Buying a Compatible Network Adapter for Your PC

It doesn't matter from which manufacturer you purchase your network adapter cards, as long as you purchase the right type of card for your computer and for your network. For example, for a laptop computer you will need to purchase a PC card. The type of network that you are going to build will determine the specific type of PC card that you will need.

Desktop Network Cards

There are a number of different types of network adapters available today. Desktop computers always support internal network adapters. These are network cards that you insert into an open expansion slot inside your computer.

If you have a computer that's a few years old, you may find that there are two different types of expansion slots on your computer's motherboard. These are ISA and PCI. ISA is the older of the two technologies. It is slower and cannot transmit data as fast. Network connections pass a lot of data so you'll want to use a PCI network adapter. For example,

Figure 2.7 shows the Linksys EtherFast 10/100 Network Adapter. This particular adapter is designed to connect a computer to either a 10Mbps or a 100Mbps Ethernet network.

Figure 2.7

The Linksys EtherFast 10/100 Network Adapter inserts into a desktop computer's PCI slot and can connect a computer to either a standard Ethernet or Fast Ethernet network.

Laptop Network Cards

Laptop computers do not use the same type of network adapters as their desktop counterparts. Laptops are too small to house the types of network cards used in desktops. Instead, laptops use PC cards.

PC cards, also known as *PCMCIA cards*, are no bigger than a couple of credit cards stacked on top of one another. These compact network cards are designed to slip into small expansion slots on the sides of laptop computers. Figure 2.8 shows the Linksys WPC11 - Instant Wireless Network Adapter PC Card.

Figure 2.8

The Linksys WPC11 - Instant Wireless Network Adapter PC Card inserts into the PC Card expansion slot on the side of your laptop and can connect a computer to a standard 802.11b wireless network.

NOTE If you have a docking station to which your laptop connects, then you may be able to connect the laptop to your home network by inserting a desktop network adapter in the laptop's docking station. Check the documentation that came with the docking station to see if it supports this type of configuration.

USB Network Adapters

If your desktop computer or laptop is less than a few years old, then chances are pretty good that you have at least one USB port on your computer. If so, then you also have the option of connecting your computer to your home network using a USB network adapter.

For example, Figure 2.9 shows the Linksys WUSB11 - Instant Wireless USB Network Adapter. The advantage of this type of network adapter is its ease of installation. You don't have to worry about opening your computer's case. Just connect it to an open USB port and supply the CD that came with the network adapter when Windows XP Plug and Play asks you to do so.

Figure 2.9

The Linksys WUSB11 - Instant Wireless USB Network Adapter makes setting up network access a snap by providing an external USB connection.

Buying the Right Network Adapter for Your Network

Now that you know about the different types of network adapters that you can purchase you need to make sure that you purchase the right type of network adapter for your network. For example, if you are connecting a laptop computer to a wireless home network, you will need to purchase either a wireless PC card or a wireless USB network adapter.

Wireless Network Adapters

If your home network is going to be wireless, then you'll be happy to know that you'll find a number of wireless network adapters including the Linksys Instant Wireless Network PC Card (shown in Figure 2.8).

This little network adapter looks just like a regular PC card adapter except that it contains an extra antenna portion that makes the card about an inch longer than a typical PC card.

If you prefer USB, Linksys also makes a Wireless USB network adapter. In addition, Linksys and many other network card manufacturers also make Wireless PCI adapters, which allow you to use a Wireless PC card in a desktop computer. For example, the Linksys Instant Wireless PCI adapter shown in Figure 2.10 lets you use the Linksys Wireless PC Card.

Figure 2.10

The Linksys Wireless PCI Adapter lets you use your Linksys Instant Wireless Network PC Card to provide wireless access to any desktop computer.

Ethernet Versus Fast Ethernet Network Adapters

Network adapters like the Linksys EtherFast 10/100 Network Adapter (shown in Figure 2.7) support two different types of Ethernet networks. A traditional Ethernet network operates at speeds up to 10Mbps. In recent years Fast Ethernet has appeared, offering 100Mbps transmission rates. Until recently the cost of Fast Ethernet made it an expensive choice for use on a home network. However, as its popularity has grown the price of Fast Ethernet components has fallen.

Ethernet and Fast Ethernet network components are not compatible, meaning that you cannot combine Ethernet and Fast Ethernet components on the network and expect then to communicate with one another. In other words, you must build either a 10Mbps Ethernet home network or a 100Mbps Fast Ethernet home network. There are two main differences between the two networks, cost and speed. A 10Mbps home network is fast and will probably provide all the speed that you will desire. A 100Mbps Fast Ethernet network costs a little more may be overkill on home networks. However, given that the cost of building a Fast Ethernet network is now not that much more than building an Ethernet network, it's really just a matter of personal preference.

techtv tip

If you are really into computer gaming or think that you will be transmitting large amounts of data or graphic files, then a Fast Ethernet network is probably the way to go. Its extra bandwidth will let you move your data around faster with less wait time. Given relatively small cost difference between the two I'd go for it and get Fast Ethernet.

You can always start with an Ethernet network and upgrade to a Fast Ethernet network later. To migrate from Ethernet to Fast Ethernet all that you have to do is replace all the Ethernet components on your home network with Fast Ethernet components.

When you purchase your Ethernet network adapters you'll see that you have three choices:

- **10 Mbps network adapters**—These cards connect your computer to a 10Mbps Ethernet Network.
- **100 Mbps networks adapters**—These cards connect your computer to a 100Mbps Ethernet Network.
- **10/100 Mbps network adapters**—These cards can connect your computer to either a 10Mbps or 100Mbps Ethernet network. The card is automatically configured to run on whichever type of network is present.

10/100Mbps network adapters costs a few dollars more than the other network adapters but provide an upgrade flexibility that usually makes their purchase a good investment.

Phoneline Network Adapters

Home networks that use phoneline technology require phoneline-compatible network adapters. For example, Figure 2.11 shows the Linksys HomeLink Phoneline Network Card, which allows you to connect a desktop computer to your phone network. These network cards usually provide two connectors: one to allow you to connect the card to a telephone jack and the other to allow you to continue phone service in the room by connecting your telephone into the second connector.

Figure 2.11

The Linksys HomeLink PhoneLine Network Card provides a PCI connection to phoneline networks.

Of course, there are phone adapters for just about every type of computer including phoneline PC cards and phoneline USB network adapters. The easiest way to get started with a phoneline network is to purchase a phoneline networking kit. Phoneline network kits include everything that you need to connect two computers into a home network. You can then purchase additional add-on phoneline cards for each additional computer that you own.

Powerline Network Adapters

Powerline networks are a new technology. In fact, as of the writing of this book powerline networking hardware was not available. Version 1.0 specifications for this new technology were released on July 26, 2001 allowing manufacturers to begin developing powerline network products. The first of these products is expected to be available before the end of 2002.

You can expect to find powerline network adapters from many of the same companies that provide phoneline hardware including NetGear and Linksys, both of which are also members of the HomePlug Powerline Alliance.

Rolling Up Your Sleeves and Installing Your Network Adapters

Depending on the number and types of computers that you have, you may need to purchase and install several different types of network adapters. To assist you with this chore the process for installing PCI, PC card, and USB adapters is outlined here.

Installing a PCI Network Adapter—Desktop

If you have a PCI network adapter, you'll have to manually install the card into an open expansion slot. This means opening your computer's case and getting into the bowels of your PC. Don't be intimidated; the following process outlines the steps that you'll need to complete the installation yourself.

1. Turn off the power to your computer and unplug it.
2. Remove the computer case.
3. Remove the metal slot cover from one of the computer's available PCI expansion slots.
4. Insert the PCI Ethernet adapter into the slot and screw it in as shown in Figure 2.12.
5. Replace the computer case.
6. Power on the computer.
7. Windows XP Plug and Play will recognize the new device and may prompt you to supply the CD that contains the software driver that came with the network adapter.
8. Follow the instructions as presented on the screen.

Figure 2.12

Installing an internal PCI network adapter requires a certain degree of comfort in working inside the internals of your computer. Used by permission of T.J. Lee and Lee Hudspeth.

Most computer warranties prohibit you from opening your computer's case and installing new hardware. Doing so may violate the remainder of your warranty and can result in the manufacturer's refusal to provide you with service in the event a problem occurs. Unless you are experienced in installing computer hardware, have someone else install your PCI network adapters. Often you can get the technicians at the store where you purchase computer hardware to install it for you.

Installing a PC Card Network Adapter—Laptop

If you are connecting a laptop using a PC card, then you'll find installing the network adapter to be a little easier as outlined in the following steps.

1. Power off your laptop.
2. Insert the PC card in an open PC Card slot on the side of the laptop.
3. Power on the laptop.
4. Windows XP Plug and Play will recognize the new device and may prompt you to supply the CD that contains the software driver that came with the network adapter.
5. Follow the instructions as presented on the screen.

Installing a USB Network Adapter

The fastest of all the installation options is the USB network adapter because it does not require a reboot of your computer. The USB install process is outlined here.

1. Turn on your computer.
2. Connect the USB network adapter to the USB cable that was supplied with the adapter.
3. Connect the other end of the USB cable to an open USB port on your computer as shown in Figure 2.13 or to your USB hub if you have one.

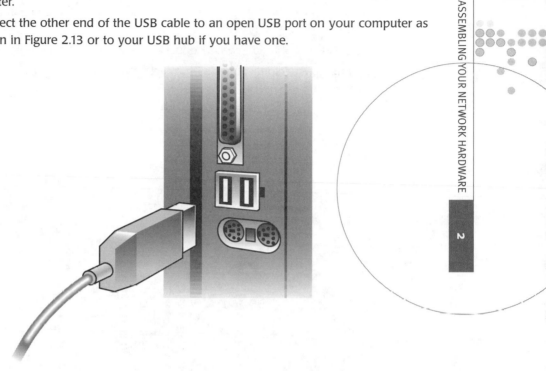

Figure 2.13

Installing a USB network adapter is as simple as plugging it in. Used by permission of T.J. Lee and Lee Hudspeth.

4. Windows XP's Plug and Play will automatically detect the device and may prompt you to supply the CD that contains its software driver.
5. Follow the instructions as presented on the screen.

PUTTING IT ALL TOGETHER

Once you have decided on the type of network that you are going to set up (for example, wireless, Ethernet/wireless hybrid, Ethernet, Fast Ethernet, phoneline or powerline) you'll need to set up all your hardware. This will include installing adapter cards and then connecting everything together using a wireless Internet gateway, wireless access point, cables and hubs, your phone lines, or power lines.

When everything is physically in place the next step is to run the Windows XP Network Setup Wizard on each of your computers as explained in the chapters that follow. The wizard will assist you in performing the following network configuration tasks:

- Configuring network adapters (covered in Chapter 3)
- Assigning network names to your computers (covered in Chapter 4)
- Setting up the sharing of your disk drives and printers (covered in Chapters 5 and 6)
- Configuring a shared Internet connection (covered in Chapter 8)
- Setting up a personal firewall to protect your Internet connection (covered in Chapter 8)

CHAPTER **3**

THE SOFTER SIDE OF NETWORK SETUP

Windows XP Home Edition provides a complete set of home networking tools. Although Windows XP draws on features of Windows Me, its most direct descendant is Windows 2000, from which it inherits a rich set of networking tools including support for TCP/IP, automatic IP addressing, virtual private networking, and Internet connection sharing. Windows XP Home Edition has made improvements to these and virtually every other Windows networking feature making them run faster and more reliably.

Here is what you'll learn:

- How Windows XP Plug and Play works
- How to install a network adapter driver
- How to install a network protocol
- How to configure TCP/IP settings
- How to examine network clients and services
- How to remove network adapters, protocols, clients, and services

HOME NETWORKING WITH WINDOWS XP

Once you know the type of network that you are going to set up (for example, wireless, Ethernet/Fast Ethernet, phoneline, or powerline), you have to physically install your network adapters and connect everything (unless of course you are going 100 percent wireless). Then you'll need to install the following software components:

- **A Network adapter software driver**—Provides the operating system with the ability to communicate and control the network adapter.

- **Network protocols**—These protocols transport data over the network, using established sets of rules and standards. There must be a single common protocol running on every network computer. You'll have several to choose from but you want to make sure that you go with TCP/IP.

- **Network client software**—Allows a computer to access network resources such as network printers and disk drives. Without this software everything would be connected but none of your computers would be able to connect to and use any shared network resources.

- **Network services**—This is the software component that allows a computer to share its resources. Without this piece of software there's no point to setting up your own network. After all, you are building this thing so that you can share resources among your computers.

If you are going to set up a hybrid home network using wireless and Ethernet, then all you'll have to do is plug a wireless access point into your Ethernet hub or switch. Otherwise you'll need to set up one of your computers with two network adapters. For example, if you created a home network using Ethernet and phoneline, then one adapter would be an Ethernet network adapter and the other would be a phoneline network adapter. Each of the network adapters will have its own software adapter, which you'll have to install. Otherwise you won't be able to use Windows XP to set up a network bridge and connect both parts of your home network.

If you have not finished the physical setup of your home network hardware, now is the time to do so. The rest of this chapter assumes that your computers are running Windows XP and that your hardware is in place and ready to go.

Remember that even though Windows XP is the example used throughout this book, you can still apply just about everything that you'll read to Windows 98, Me, and 2000.

WORKING WITH WINDOWS XP PLUG AND PLAY

Ever since the introduction of Windows 95 and Plug and Play, Microsoft has been working with hardware manufacturers to improve the way that computer hardware is installed and configured. Windows 95's initial implementation of Plug and Play left much to be desired.

However, Microsoft has continued to refine it. You'll find that the Windows XP implementation of this technology is very effective.

Plug and Play is both a software and hardware specification. It is designed to provide an operating system with the ability to automatically detect and configure new hardware. For Plug and Play to work and properly install your hardware, your Windows XP computer will need the following components.

- A plug-and-play system BIOS
- A plug-and-play operating system
- Plug-and-play hardware
- Plug-and-play software drivers

Plug-and-Play BIOS

BIOS is software stored in read-only memory on your computer's *motherboard* or main circuit board. The plug-and-play BIOS is automatically loaded when your computer is first turned on and is responsible for a number of functions including:

- Performing a Power On Self Test (POST)
- Performing a check of system resources
- Detecting new hardware
- Managing hardware configuration

Any computer with enough CPU and horsepower to run Windows XP should have a plug-and-play BIOS. BIOS information is usually displayed at system startup and you will see a message stating that your system's BIOS is plug-and-play compatible. For example, you may see statements such as "Initialization of Plug and Play loads" or "PNP Init Complete."

Plug-and-Play Hardware Detection

Windows XP Plug and Play looks for new hardware on a number of occasions, including

- During the initial installation of Windows XP
- Each time you start Windows XP
- Whenever you run the Add New Hardware Wizard
- Whenever a PC card or USB device is inserted

Purchasing plug-and-play network adapters will make the setup of your home network a lot easier. Fortunately just about every network card sold today is plug-and-play compatible. All that you have to do to install a plug-and-play device, such as a network adapter, is physically connect the device to your computer. If you are using a PCI card, it should be detected the next time you turn on your computer. PC Cards and USB devices should be recognized as soon as they are inserted, thus launching Windows XP Plug and Play. When everything works like it is supposed to, the only thing that you should have to do is provide either the diskette or CD-ROM that contains the device's software driver.

Unless you are trying to use old hardware, you shouldn't have any trouble with the software portion of network setup. As part of Windows XP's Plug and Play detection and hardware configuration of your network adapter, you'll find that Windows XP will automatically install a default set of networking software for you and even help configure it. So if you're ready, let's get started.

BEHIND EVERY GOOD NETWORK ADAPTER IS A GOOD SOFTWARE DRIVER

Every network adapter comes with a floppy disk or CD-ROM that provides copies of its software drivers for various operating systems. In addition, a diagnostic utility is usually included to assist you in testing the network adapter should you suspect it is defective.

Locating Your Network Adapter Software Driver

Because Windows XP is a new operating system you may find that a Windows XP software driver is not included with your network adapter. Windows XP ships with a large number of software drivers and you may find a driver for your network adapter on the Windows XP CD-ROM. You can also check the download or support area on the card manufacturer's Web site for a Windows XP software driver. If you cannot find one, you can e-mail the vendor for advice on how to proceed or replace the network adapter with another one. Another option is to try to install the network adapter's Windows 2000 software driver. In most cases this driver will work fine, although you'll have to reply to a warning message when you install the software driver giving Windows XP permission to use it.

Network adapter manufacturers are constantly improving their software drivers by fixing program bugs and adding new features. They post these new software drivers on their Web sites, making them available for free download. It's a good idea to double-check and make sure that you are installing the most current software driver for your network adapter.

Understanding How Software Drivers Operate

Figure 3.1 shows you how the network adapter's software driver extends the operating system's control over the network adapter. After physically connecting the network adapter, which can be an internal PCI card, a PC card, or an external USB device, Windows XP Plug and Play will autodetect it and prompt you to supply the disk or CD containing its software files. Windows XP then retrieves the network adapter's software driver, saves it to the hard disk, and registers it in the Windows XP Registry. Windows XP then uses the software driver to communicate with and control the network adapter.

NOTE The Windows XP *Registry* is a special database where the operating system stores critical operating system, hardware, software, and application settings. Windows XP relies on the data stored in its registry to control and manage all computer operations.

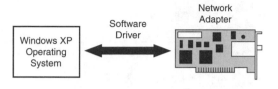

Figure 3.1

Your network adapter's software driver extends Windows XP's control over the network adapter and is the glue that binds your hardware and software together.

Installing Your Network Adapter's Software Driver

Windows XP includes advanced plug-and-play support. This means that the operating system should automatically be able to detect any newly installed hardware device and step you through its installation process, including the installation of its software driver. To help ensure that this process goes as smoothly as possible, make sure that you purchase Windows plug-and-play compatible hardware.

However, if you already have an older network adapter, you may find that Windows XP does not properly discover it. In this case Windows XP provides you with the Add Hardware Wizard to assist you with installing and configuring the network adapter. You can run the wizard and tell it to try and find the newly installed adapter or you can tell it that you want to manually install the device.

The following procedure outlines the steps required to install a network adapter when Windows XP Plug and Play does not automatically detect it. This procedure assumes that you have already installed the network adapter but that Windows XP has not detected it.

1. Click the Start button on the Windows XP taskbar. The Windows XP Start menu appears.
2. Select Control Panel. The Windows XP Control Panel appears.
3. Click Printers and Other Hardware.
4. Click Add Hardware in the See Also panel on the upper-left side of the dialog box. The Add Hardware Wizard appears as shown in Figure 3.2.
5. Click Next to start the hardware setup process. The wizard will scan your computer looking for new hardware. In a few moments the screen shown in Figure 3.3 will appear, giving you two options: Yes, I Have Already Connected the Hardware and No, I Have Not Added the Hardware Yet. Select the first option and click Next.

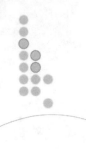

Figure 3.2

The Add Hardware Wizard will take you step-by-step through the software installation portion of your network adapter's installation.

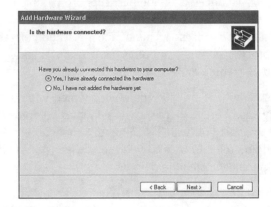

Figure 3.3

The wizard wants to double-check and make sure that you have connected your new hardware.

6. The wizard displays a list of all currently installed hardware on the computer as shown in Figure 3.4. You can troubleshoot an existing device by selecting it and clicking Next. Because we are trying to add a new network adapter, you should select Add a New Hardware Device and click Next.

7. The wizard displays the following two options:

- Search For and Install the Hardware Automatically (Recommended)
- Install the Hardware that I Manually Select from a List (Advanced)

The second option lets you select from a list of known hardware manufacturers or supply a floppy disk or CD-ROM that contains the device's software driver. Select the option to perform a manual install and click Next as shown in Figure 3.5.

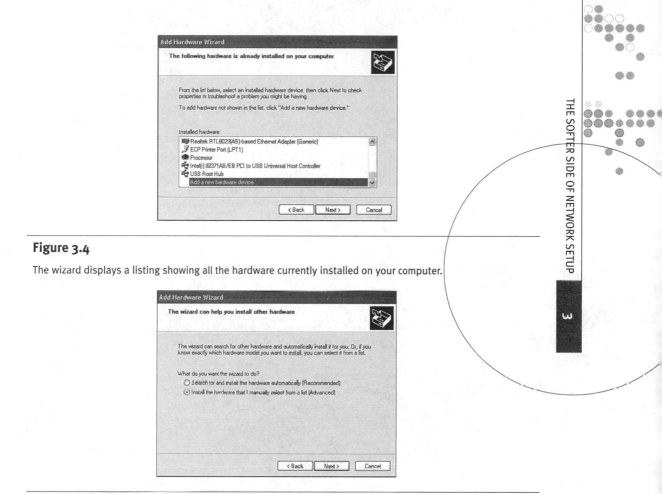

Figure 3.4

The wizard displays a listing showing all the hardware currently installed on your computer.

Figure 3.5

Selecting the option to manually install your software driver.

8. The wizard prompts you to select the type of device that you are installing. Scroll down and select Network adapters as shown in Figure 3.6 and then click Next.

9. The Select Network Adapter dialog box appears as shown in Figure 3.7. If the manufacturer of your network adapter appears in the manufacturer list, select it. This displays a list of network adapters made by the manufacturer. If your network adapter is in the list, select it and click Next. If either your network adapter's manufacturer or network adapter is not listed, click Have Disk and you'll be prompted to supply the disk or CD-ROM that came with the network adapter to provide Windows XP with your network adapter's software driver.

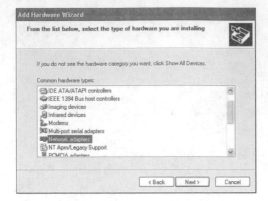

Figure 3.6

Tell the wizard that you are installing a network adapter.

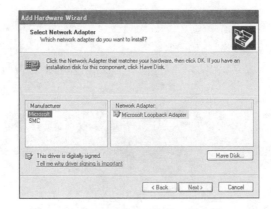

Figure 3.7

Supplying the wizard with specific information about your network adapter.

 NOTE If you supply a software driver that has not passed Microsoft's certification tests, you'll receive a message that says that the software driver that you are installing has not passed the Windows logo test and that continuing the installation could be dangerous for your system. This does not mean that the software driver won't work or that it will harm your computer. It does, however, mean that problems could occur. If this is a Windows 2000 software driver, then things will probably work fine but you should upgrade to a Windows XP software driver as soon as one becomes available.

10. The wizard copies the software files for your network adapter to the computer hard disk and displays a confirmation dialog box. Click Finish.

Repeat this procedure for every Windows XP computer on your home network.

Note that you did not have to restart your computer to begin using your newly installed network adapter. This is one area where Windows XP is much better than Windows 95, 98, and Me, and is an important feature that is all too easily overlooked.

Windows XP Network Settings

Windows XP makes a number of assumptions when it installs a network adapter. In doing so it installs and configures a number of network software components. These software components include

- **The network adapter's software driver**—Software that lets Windows XP control your network adapter.
- **A network protocol**—A set of standards and rules that allow the computer to communicate with other network devices and computers.
- **A network client**—Software that lets your computer access network resources.
- **Network services**—Software that lets a Windows XP computer share its resources with other computers on the network.

Although each Windows operating system installs its own set of default network software, every Windows operating system since Windows 98 installs similar components that enable Windows 98, Me, 2000, and XP computers to interoperate on the same network with minimal effort on your part.

You've already learned about the importance of the network adapter's software driver. Most of the remainder of this chapter is dedicated to explaining Windows XP's remaining software components.

If you installed Windows XP Home Edition as an upgrade (an upgrade, not a dual-boot installation) on another Windows computer and that computer was already connected to a network, then Windows XP will retain many of the previous operating system's settings. These settings may include any previously installed network protocols, clients, and services.

SORTING THROUGH LOCAL AREA NETWORK PROTOCOLS

A network protocol is a set of rules and procedures for communicating and exchanging data over a network. Windows networks operate using a number of different networking protocols. These protocols can be thought of as operating at three different logical layers as depicted in the following three-layered model shown in Figure 3.8.

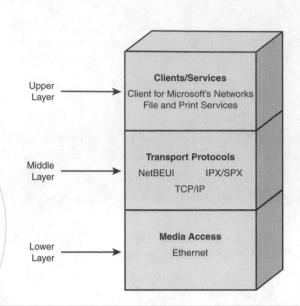

Figure 3.8

Windows-based networks use a number of protocols, each of which provides a different type of functionality.

Protocols operating at the bottom level of this networking model:

- Are known as hardware protocols or access methods
- Specify how network data is transported over the network
- Determine how data is exchanged between any two network devices or computers
- Determine how improperly formatted data is handled

Protocols operating at the middle layer of this networking model:

- Are known as software protocols or transport protocols
- Specify how network hardware communicates
- Determine how network data is organized into packets and sent across the network
- Depend on the services provided by lower-level protocols

Protocols operating at the upper layer of this networking model:

- Determine how the operating system and its software will communicate
- Depend on the services of middle-layer protocols

A home network consists of a number of protocols, each of which has a specific function and all of which must work together.

Access Methods: Bottom Level of Networking Model

The lowest-level protocol that will run on your home network is the *access method*. Access method protocols determine:

- The format in which data is to be transmitted over a network
- When computers and network devices are permitted to transmit network data
- How data collisions are handled

Access method protocols are implemented based on the selection of network adapters. They are loaded on your computer when the software driver for your network adapter is installed. There are a number of competing access methods including

- **Ethernet**—This is the current standard for local area networks and is the only viable choice for a home network.
- **Token Ring**—This is an older protocol pioneered by IBM, which has lost favor in recent years.
- **FDDI**—This access method applies to fiber-optic networks and is not appropriate for home networking.

The selection of your type of network, and therefore, of your network cards, determines the selection of your network's access method.

Transport Protocols: Middle Level of Networking Model

Although you really do not have a choice in the type of low-level protocol or access method that your network will use, you do have a lot more flexibility in selecting which middle-level protocol or transport protocol you'll run on your network.

Actually you can run two or more protocols at the same time on your home network If you have a need. However, when you use multiple protocols you use up more of your network's bandwidth and place a greater demand on your network computer processors. An important part of tuning your network and keeping it running at full speed involves removing any unnecessary protocols from your computers. As you learn in just a few minutes, there is really only one protocol that you need to run anyway.

You have three transport protocols to choose from when setting up your network. They are

- **NetBEUI**—A simple protocol that is easy to install and that requires no maintenance. This protocol is good for small networks but does not support Internet access.
- **IPX/SPX**—This is a very sophisticated protocol developed by Novell for the NetWare networks. However, it has lost much of its luster in recent years and has, for the most part, been replaced by TCP/IP.

- **TCP/IP**—This is the protocol of the Internet. It's also the default protocol installed by Windows XP whenever a network adapter is installed and most likely is the only protocol that you need to run on your home network.

Windows XP Home Edition supports all three of these protocols. Each protocol has a separate and distinct set of rules and standards that makes it incompatible with other protocols, meaning that it can only communicate with other computers running the same protocol. Of the three protocols, the only one that you need to use is TCP/IP. It is the only one of these protocols that supports Internet and local area network communications.

NetBEUI: The Little Protocol That Could

NetBIOS Extended User Interface, or *NetBEUI*, is a small but fast protocol developed by IBM and Microsoft in the mid-1980s. It is faster than TCP/IP and IPX/SPX and requires a small amount of memory overhead on each computer. It was designed to support small department-sized networks with no more than 50 computers. NetBEUI is a simple self-configuring protocol that requires no administrative overhead after its initial installation. Its major drawback is that it lacks support for routing.

The best use for NetBEUI is to help troubleshoot a failed attempt to set up a home network. If after installing your hardware and setting up your home network, nothing seems to be working, you can install NetBEUI on every network computer and see what happens. If things begin working and your computers can now see one another, then you'll know that there is nothing wrong with your network adapters, wiring, or basic configuration. Most likely the problem lies with the configuration of TCP/IP.

A *router* is a hardware device that connects two or more networks. Larger corporations usually divide their networks into small networks or subnets and then connect everything with routers. By dividing a larger network into a number of small subnets you are able to isolate network traffic to specific subnets and reduce the overall demands on the total network. Routers are designed to allow network traffic to flow from one subnet to another but only allow network data to pass through if it's specifically addressed to another subnet. IPX/SPX and TCP/IP both support routing between subnets.

As I have already stated, NetBEUI does not require any configuration or administration on your part. You simply install it and it works. Microsoft Windows 95 loads NetBEUI as its default network protocol. NetBEUI is a good protocol for a home network. However, ever since Windows 98, Microsoft has replaced NetBEUI with TCP/IP as the default protocol for Microsoft operating systems. One reason for this is the almost universal acceptance that TCP/IP has achieved in recent years. Another is that even if you run NetBEUI, you are still going to need to load TCP/IP to connect to the Internet.

NOTE Microsoft discourages the use of NetBEUI as a home networking protocol. In fact, it does not even list NetBEUI as an available protocol. However, you will find it buried on the Windows XP Home Edition CD-ROM in \VALUEADD\MSFT\NET\NETBEUI.

The following procedure outlines how to install NetBEUI and can also be used as a general procedure for installing other network protocols, although each protocol installs a little differently.

1. Click Start and then select My Network Places. The My Network Places dialog box appears as shown in Figure 3.9.

Figure 3.9

The My Network Places dialog box is the focal point where you'll manage most of your computer's network configuration.

2. Click View Network Connection in the upper-left pane. You'll see a dialog box displaying an icon representing your Local Area Connection as shown in Figure 3.10.

3. Right-click the Local Area Connection icon and select Properties. The Local Area Connection Properties dialog box appears as shown in Figure 3.11. This dialog box displays a list of all currently installed network clients, services, and protocols. As you can see, TCP/IP is already installed on this computer.

Figure 3.10

Viewing your local area connection.

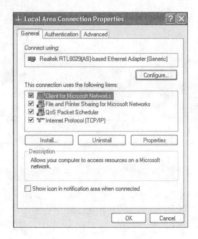

Figure 3.11

Examining currently installed clients, services, and protocols.

4. Click Install. The Select Network Component Type dialog box appears as shown in Figure 3.12.

5. Select Protocol and click Add. The Select Network Protocol dialog box appears as shown in Figure 3.13.

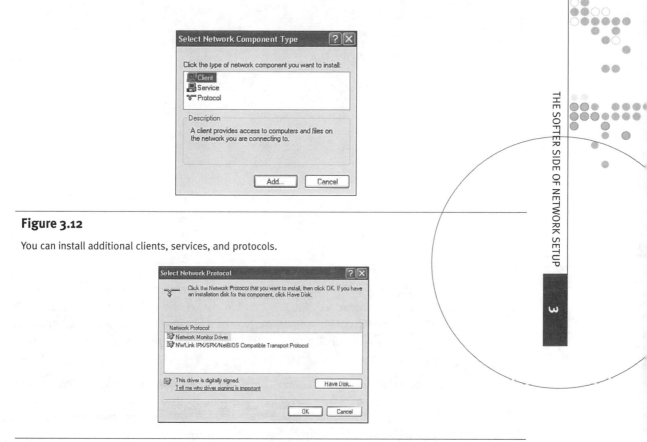

Figure 3.12

You can install additional clients, services, and protocols.

Figure 3.13

Viewing a list of available protocols.

6. NetBEUI is not displayed. It is located on the Windows XP Home Edition CD-ROM. To Select it click Have Disk. Type **X:\VALUEADD\MSFT\NET\NETBEUI** when prompted to supply the location of the protocol (X: represents your CD-ROM drive) and click OK.

7. The Select Network Protocol dialog box appears displaying NetBEUI as an entry. Select the NetBEUI Protocol entry and click OK as shown in Figure 3.14.

8. Windows XP installs NetBEUI and then displays a dialog box asking for permission to restart your computer. Until the computer is restarted, the new protocol will not be available to the system. Click Yes to restart your computer.

 As long as you are using TCP/IP you do not need to run any other protocols and should remove them. This will free up resources on your computer and reduce your network traffic.

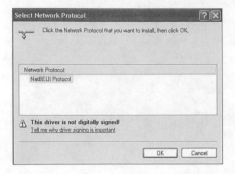

Figure 3.14

You can install NetBEUI after locating it on the Windows XP Home Edition CD-ROM.

IPX/SPX: NetWare's Proprietary Protocol

IPX/SPX is a proprietary protocol developed by NetWare for its Novell network operating system. Microsoft implements IPX/SPX under the name of *NWLink IPX/SPX/NetBIOS Compatible Transport Protocol*. As a proprietary protocol only NetWare is permitted to make changes to it, as opposed to TCP/IP where thousands of different people and organizations participate in the protocol's development.

Novell developed this protocol based on the Xerox XNS protocol. IPX/SPX has been the default network protocol on all NetWare networks up to version 4.X. However, starting with NetWare 5.X, Novell began making TCP/IP its default protocol. Therefore, it's a pretty safe bet that, like NetBEUI, IPX/SPX's days are numbered.

IPX/SPX is a little slower than NetBEUI. But like TCP/IP, it runs well on networks that have been divided into multiple subnets. Its major drawback is that it is not supported on the Internet. IPX/SPX is sometimes used on corporate networks to connect computers to older NetWare networks. Although it can certainly serve as the main transport protocol on your home network, you'll find that you'll still need to run TCP/IP to connect to the Internet.

Even if you choose not to install IXP/SPX on your home network, you may find that it sneaks its way onto your computer. This can happen because a number of network-based computer games use IPX/SPX and will automatically install it on any computer where you install the game. There is no harm in this. However, if you ever decide to uninstall your network games(s) you should also remember to uninstall IPX/SPX as well. After all, it consumes valuable computer resources and adds unnecessary traffic to your home network.

TCP/IP: The Protocol of the Internet

As I stated earlier, TCP/IP is probably the only transport protocol that you'll need to run on each computer on your home network. TCP/IP is the protocol of the Internet. It was designed to run on the Internet and only found its way to local area networks at a later date. For years it has been the choice of large corporate networks. However, Microsoft has now embraced it as the transport protocol of choice for all networks, large and small.

TCP/IP was created in 1969 as part of the Department of Defense's *ARPAnet* network. ARPAnet was an early wide area network designed to survive a nuclear attack. It was designed to be able to suffer from multiple failures and keep on operating.

TCP/IP is actually a large suite of related protocols that work together. A list of TCP/IP protocols includes:

- **ARP**—A protocol used to locate the hardware addresses of network computers using their IP address
- **DHCP**—A protocol that automatically assigns IP configuration data to network computers
- **FTP**—A file transfer protocol used to transport files
- **ICMP**—A protocol that reports on packed delivery errors
- **RARP**—A protocol used to locate a network computer's IP address when using its hardware address
- **SMTP**—An electronic mail transfer protocol
- **Telnet**—A protocol that supports remote terminal access
- **UDP**—A protocol similar to TCP except that it does not provide the guaranteed delivery of data

TCP/IP is slower than NetBEUI and IPX/SPX. It also requires more configuration than either of these two protocols. This might make TCP/IP seem inappropriate for small home networks; however, Microsoft has worked hard to make using TCP/IP much easier on any size network.

TCP/IP is the default protocol for Windows XP and for all other Microsoft operating systems since Windows 98. It is automatically installed and configured during the network adapter installation process. Microsoft has done much to simplify and automate the installation and configuration of TCP/IP. Windows XP includes an automatic IP address assignment feature that has actually been around since Windows 98, which allows every Windows XP computer to automatically configure its TCP/IP settings. This feature enables Windows XP to prepare your computer to participate on any network.

TCP/IP uses IP address to identify computers on a network. Every computer must have a unique IP address that belongs to the same logical network, in order for everything to work.

If you are not already familiar with TCP/IP addressing, then you should take a look at Appendix B, "TCP/IP Basics," before continuing with the rest of this section. This appendix will provide you with a basic review of TCP/IP and how it works. As you may already be aware, TCP/IP is a very complex topic. If you'd like to learn more about it, check out *Special Edition Using TCP/IP* from Que.

When a Windows XP computer connected to a home network starts up it will automatically assign itself a temporary IP address on a Class B network of 169.254.0.0 with a subnet mask of 255.255.0.0. No additional configuration is required for you to set up your peer network. The TCP/IP network address of 169.254.0.0 is a special reserved network address. No company or organization connected to the Internet is permitted to use it.

NOTE If you are going to have Windows 95 or Windows NT Workstation 4.0 systems attached to your home network, then you will have to manually configure these operating systems to participate on your 169.154.0.0 network. Neither of these operating systems provides for its own automatic IP address configuration. You can assign any IP address in the range of 169.254.0.1 to 129.254.0.254 to these computers. Just remember to assign a subnet mask of 255.255.0.0 to each computer. Make sure that you start the computers that you manually configured first. Windows computers that implement automatic IP addressing check to make sure that an IP address is not in use on the network before assigning it to themselves. If you turn on a Windows 95 or NT computer that has an IP address that has already been self-assigned by another computer, an IP address conflict will occur. The Windows 95 or NT computers will not be able to operate on the network and you'll either have to assign a new address to the Windows 95 or NT computer or restart the conflicting computer in order to allow it to reassign itself a different IP address.

If you prefer, you can manually configure the TCP/IP address settings on your Windows XP computer instead of allowing Windows XP to do it for you as outlined in the following procedure. It's up to you. If you decide to manually assign the IP address of some of your Windows XP computers, remember to assign them an IP address between 169.254.0.1 and 169.254.0.254 and to assign them a subnet mask of 255.255.0.0.

1. Click Start and then select My Network Places. The My Network Places dialog box appears.
2. Click View Network Connection in the upper-left pane.
3. Right-click the Local Area Connection icon and select Properties. The Local Area Connection Properties dialog box appears.
4. Click Internet Protocol (TCP/IP) and click Properties. The Internet Protocol (TCP/IP) Properties dialog box appears as shown in Figure 3.15.
5. Select Use the Following IP Address. Type an IP address in the range of 169.254.0.1 and 169.254.0.254 in the IP address field. Type 255.255.0.0 in the Subnet mask field. For now leave the Default gateway field blank. Likewise leave the DNS fields at the bottom of the dialog box clear.

For more information on these fields see "Setting Up Shared Internet Access with an Internet Gateway" in Chapter 8, "Going Online."

6. Click OK. Click Close when returned to the Local Area Connection Properties dialog box.

Figure 3.15

Manually configuring the TCP/IP settings on a Windows XP computer.

It is easy to tell what your TCP/IP configuration settings are if you manually configure them. However, they are not so apparent if you allow Windows XP to automatically configure them. You can view your computer's TCP/IP configuration by executing the IPCONFIG command from the Windows command prompt.

The Windows command prompt is a text-based interface that allows you to communicate with the operating system by typing in text commands and reviewing command text output.

If you are a Windows 95, 98, or ME user, then you may be used to working with the WINIPCFG command. This command provides the same information as the IPCONFIG command does on Windows NT, 2000, and XP.

The following procedure outlines the use of the IPCONFIG command to view your computer's TCP/IP settings.

1. Open the Windows Command prompt by clicking Start, All Programs, Accessories, and then Command prompt.

2. Type **IPCONFIG** and press enter to view the TCP/IP configuration settings for the computer local area connection as demonstrated in Figure 3.16.

3. To view additional TCP/IP configuration settings or to view other network connections type **IPCONFIG /ALL** and press Enter.

4. When done reviewing the results of the IPCONFIG command type **EXIT** and press Enter to close the Windows command prompt.

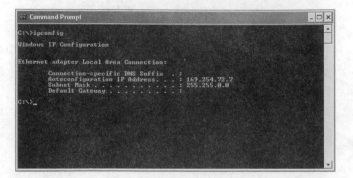

Figure 3.16

Using IPCONFIG to view Windows XP's TCP/IP configuration settings.

To learn more about working with the IPCONFIG command refer to Appendix A, "Windows XP Net Commands."

Network Client: Upper Level of Networking Model

The third level of network protocols determines how the operating system and its applications will communicate. These protocols are provided in the form of network clients. For home networks running Microsoft's operating system, the required client is the Client for Microsoft Networks. The Client for Microsoft Networks provides Windows XP with the ability to access and use network services. It is automatically installed by default by Windows XP when your network adapter is installed.

A standalone computer not connected to a network has access to its own resources, which include its printers and local disk drives. When connected to a local area network the computer must run a network client to be able to access network resources. The network client acts as a redirector. A *redirector* intercepts requests to access hardware resources and determines where the resource resides. If the resource is local to the computer, the request is permitted to process normally. However, if the request is for a network resource, the redirector steps in and redirects the request out over the network.

ENABLING NETWORK SERVICES

Protocols allow your Windows XP computer to communicate over the network. A network client lets it access network resources. Network services allow Windows XP to share local resources with other computers on the network.

By default Windows XP automatically installs these services in the form of *File and Printer Sharing for Microsoft Networks* when your network adapter is installed. However, it is important to understand that installing file and print sharing does not automatically make all your local disk drives and printers available to other computers on the network. Instead, you must configure access to your shared resources manually on a device-by-device basis.

This gives you complete control over what is and what is not shared over your home network.

 To learn more about how to configure shared access to your disk and print resources, see Chapter 5, "Sharing Precious Disk Space," and Chapter 6, "Maximizing Your Printer Investment."

UNINSTALLING NETWORK ADAPTERS, PROTOCOLS, CLIENTS, AND SERVICES

In the event that you ever want to remove your computer from your home network, you'll want to uninstall its network adapter, protocols, clients, and services. There is no point to running any of these components if they are not going to be used. Each one requires a small percentage of your computer's resources and will create an unnecessary drain.

To remove all the networking components from one of your computers first remove the hardware component and then perform the following procedure.

1. Click Start and then select My Network Places. The My Network Places dialog box appears.
2. Click View Network Connection in the upper-left pane.
3. Right-click the Local Area Connection icon and select Properties. The Local Area Connection Properties dialog box appears.
4. Select the desired client, service, or protocol and click Uninstall.
5. Click Yes when prompted to confirm the Uninstall.
6. If prompted to restart the computer, click Yes.

CHAPTER **4**

PUTTING IT ALL TOGETHER

In the previous chapter you learned how to complete the assembly of a home network by configuring software. However, there is still plenty of work left to do. For example, you still have to set up the sharing of your disk and printer resources. As a precursor to these tasks you'll need to perform some additional network configuration to get your home network into top shape.

Here is what you'll learn:

- How to assign names to your computers
- How to organize your home network into workgroups
- How to enable file and print sharing
- How to tune Windows XP for better performance on your network

ACCESS PRIVILEGES

Windows XP Home Edition automatically creates two user accounts during its installation. They are the:

- **Owner**—An administrative-level account with the ability to execute any command, modify any file or folder, manage other user accounts, install new software, and configure any Windows XP feature.

- **Guest**—An account with very limited access. A person using the guest account can log in and run most applications but cannot perform any configuration, software installation, or account management.

In addition to these two accounts, Windows XP also prompts you to create new user accounts during its installation process. Each of these new accounts is then given the same level of administrative privileges as the Owner account. If you choose not to create any new accounts during the installation of Windows XP Home Edition, then you will automatically be logged on as Owner whenever you turn on your computer.

After its installation, Windows XP Home Edition also enables you to create additional user accounts. When you create a new account you can assign it either of the following levels of authority.

- **Administrative**—This assigns administrative level privileges over all the resources on the computer to a user account.

- **Limited**—This assigns the user account enough privileges to perform most day-to-day work. However, users with these accounts will not be able to install new applications, alter the computer's configuration settings, or access other users' files.

 To learn more about Windows XP Home Edition security read Chapter 7, "Becoming Your Own Network Administrator."

To complete most of the procedures found in the remainder of this book, it is assumed that you will be logged in using a user account with administrative-level privileges. Microsoft recommends that you create and assign user accounts with limited access to all users and that you give users who occasionally require administrative privileges a second account with instructions to use it only when necessary.

 The reason for using an account that has limited access when performing normal day-to-day work is to prevent a virus or similar program from running amok on your computer. If you accidentally download one of these programs from the Internet and it tries to run under the covers, it will be limited to whatever access privileges you have. If you happen to be logged in with administrative privileges, then the program can do a lot more damage.

I recommend holding off until you have read Chapter 7 before you start creating user accounts. This way you can complete the setup and configuration of your network before letting the rest of the family loose on your home network.

OVERVIEW OF NETWORK CONFIGURATION

In Chapter 2, "Getting Your Hands Dirty: Assembling Your Network Hardware," and Chapter 3, "The Softer Side of Network Setup," you learned how to assemble and build your own home network. In this chapter you'll learn how to organize the computers on your home network. You'll also learn some additional ways that you can tweak each Windows XP network computer's performance over and above the standard default Microsoft network configuration.

In order for your network to operate smoothly and efficiently each computer on the network must have a unique computer name. A computer name can be as many as 15 characters long.

A computer name cannot contain any of the following characters:
: ; " ⟨— —⟩ + * = \ ? | ,

In addition to its name, each computer must also be assigned to a workgroup. Workgroup assignment provides a way to logically organize the computers on your home network into groups. Computers that are part of the same workgroup can share their resources more easily.

Another important administrative task that you may want to perform on some of your network computers is the allocation of resources between application and network performance. By default every Windows operating system gives preference to running applications. This gives the person sitting in front of the computer the fastest possible response time. Windows gives you the option of switching priority over to background processes. By assigning greater priority to background processes, you configure the computer so that it can better service network requests. For example, if you set aside a particular computer for everyone in the family to use to store files or to use as a print server, you'll probably want to configure this computer for better network performance.

On a home network most of your computers will probably be set up to share some of their local resources. However, you may also have one or more computers that will not be sharing their resources. For these machines, you can disable file and printer services, freeing up a small portion of system resources.

See the sections "Configuring File and Print Sharing" and "Configuring Windows XP for Peak Performance" to learn about these settings.

If you have any computers with two or more disk drives, then you may want to tweak their virtual memory settings. Virtual memory lets a computer simulate physical memory by mapping out a special area on a local disk drive to which it can copy the contents of a portion of memory when the amount of available physical memory begins to run low.

SETTING UP YOUR COMPUTER AND WORKGROUP NAMES

Computers on a home network must be assigned unique computer names. These names can be up to 15 characters in length and should provide a useful description of the computer. You might assign each computer a name based on its owner or on its function. For example, you might give your computers names such as FamilyPC, FamilyPrintSvr, and DadsPC.

Microsoft networks support two organizational structures; workgroups and domains. Domains are used on large networks that employ a sophisticated client/server architecture. Workgroups, on the other hand, are well suited for home networks. Typically, a small home network will have just one or two workgroups as demonstrated in Figure 4.1.

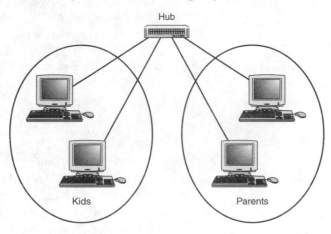

Figure 4.1

A home network with computers assigned to two workgroups.

The network shown in Figure 4.1 is organized into two workgroups: kids and parents. This way, when one of the children clicks the View workgroup computers option on the My Network Places dialog box, he or she just sees the computers in his or her own workgroup.

Membership in a workgroup makes it easier to find other computers in the same workgroup and to access their shared resources. Workgroup membership does not preclude the ability to access computers in other workgroups, it just saves you an extra couple of mouse clicks.

You are prompted to provide a Windows XP computer's name during the installation of the operating system. However, you may change a computer's name or workgroup membership at any time. There are a couple of different ways to change a Windows XP computer's name and workgroup membership.

One way to change your computer's name or workgroup is from the System Properties dialog box as outlined in the following procedure.

1. Click Start and then right-click My Computer and select the Properties option from the context menu that appears. The System Properties dialog box appears.

2. Click the Computer Name property sheet as shown in Figure 4.2.

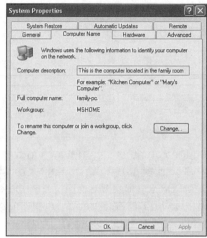

Figure 4.2

You can change your Windows XP computer's name or workgroup membership from the System Properties dialog box.

3. The following three pieces of information are displayed on this property sheet.

- **Computer description**—An optional description of the computer
- **Full computer name**—The name currently assigned to the computer
- **Workgroup**—The computer's current workgroup assignment

You can change the computer's description directly from this page by typing a new description in the Computer description field.

4. To change either the computer's name or workgroup membership click the Change button. This opens the Computer Name Changes dialog box as shown in Figure 4.3.

5. To change the computer's name, type a new name in the Computer name field. To change the computer's workgroup membership, type a new workgroup name in the Workgroup field. Click OK.

 By default Microsoft suggests adding all Windows XP computers to a workgroup named MSHOME. However, you can name your workgroups anything you want. If you type in a workgroup name that does not already exist, a new one will be created.

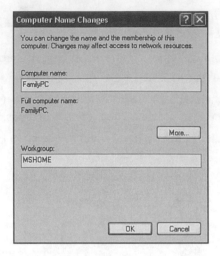

Figure 4.3

Changing your computer's name or workgroup.

6. If you only changed the computer's name, then in a few moments you'll see a Windows prompt that tells you that the computer must be restarted for the change to take effect. Click on OK to close the prompt. If you changed the computer's workgroup, then instead you'll see a Windows prompt welcoming you to the workgroup as shown in Figure 4.4. Click OK to close this prompt.

Figure 4.4

If you change your computer's workgroup membership, you'll see a Windows prompt welcoming you to the workgroup.

7. Click OK when returned to the System Properties dialog box. You'll then be prompted to restart your computer. Click Yes.

Another way to change your computer name or workgroup membership is by running the Network Setup Wizard as described in the following procedure.

1. Click Start, All Programs, Accessories, Communications and then Network Setup Wizard. The Network Setup Wizard appears displaying its welcome screen. Click Next.

2. To learn more about setting up a home network click the Checklist for creating a network link. Otherwise click Next.

3. The next screen, shown in Figure 4.5, asks you to choose one of three options:

- **This computer connects directly to the Internet**–The other computers on my network connect to the Internet through this computer. If you select this option, the wizard will install Internet connection sharing or ICS on your computer. You will learn more about ICS in Chapter 8, "Going Online."

- **This computer connects to the Internet through another computer on my network or through a residential gateway**–Select this option if you already have shared Internet access set up on your network using another Windows XP computer or an external Internet Gateway appliance.

- **Other**–If you do not yet have Internet access set up for your network, choose this option.

 For more information on Internet Gateways see Chapter 2, "Getting Your Hands Dirty: Assembling Your Network Hardware" and Chapter 8, "Going Online."

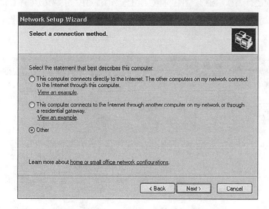

Figure 4.5

The Network Setup Wizard collects information from you about your network.

For now, choose Other and click Next.

4. The next screen, shown in Figure 4.6, presents you with three additional options. They are

- This Computer Connects to the Internet Directly or Through a Network Hub. Other Computers on My Network also Connect to the Internet Directly or Through a hub.

- This Computer Connects Directly to the Internet. I Do Not Have a Network Yet.

- This Computer Belongs to a Network that Does Not Have an Internet Connection.

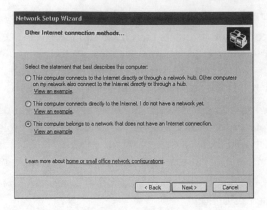

Figure 4.6

Giving the Network Setup Wizard more detailed information about your network.

We'll go over setting up your network to connect to the Internet in Chapter 8, so for now select the third option. To see a graphic depiction of this option click the View an Example link that follows this option. The image shown in Figure 4.7 will appear. Close this image and then click Next.

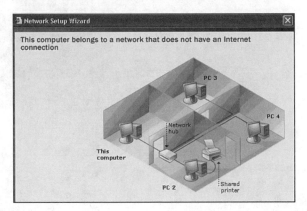

Figure 4.7

The wizard presents a graphic depiction of the specified option.

5. The next screen, shown in Figure 4.8, lets you change your computer's description and name. Change these entries as desired and then click Next.

6. The wizard next prompts you to change the name of your computer's workgroup as shown in Figure 4.9. By default, the wizard suggests MSHOME but you can change it to anything you want. Click Next.

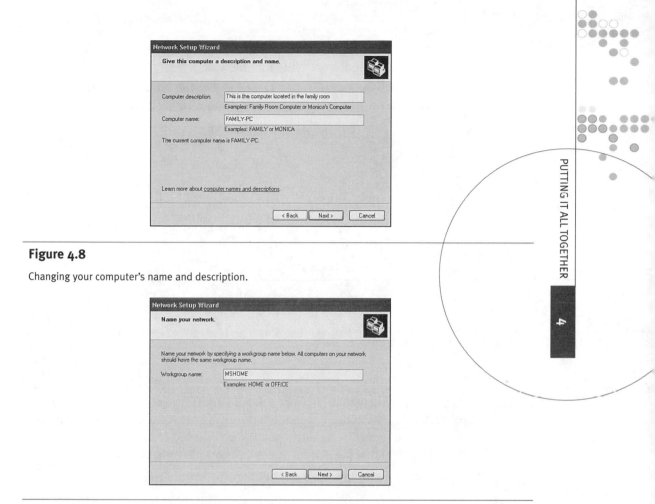

Figure 4.8

Changing your computer's name and description.

Figure 4.9

Changing your computer's workgroup membership.

7. The wizard announces that it is ready to apply any changes that you have made. It displays a list of information that it has collected from you. Review the list for accuracy and then click Next.

8. The wizard makes the changes that you supplied to your computer's configuration. It then displays the following screen, shown in Figure 4.10, giving you the chance to create a Network Setup Disk.

   Your options are

   - **Create a Network Setup Disk**—Tells the wizard to guide you through the process of creating a new Network Setup Disk.

   - **Use the Network Setup Disk I Already Have**—Tells the wizard to present you with instructions for using the Network Setup Wizard.

- **Use My Windows XP CD**—Tells the wizard to provide you with instructions for using the Windows XP CD to run the wizard.

- **Just Finish the Wizard; I Don't Need to Run the Wizard on Other Computers**—Tells the wizard to end without creating a Network Setup Disk.

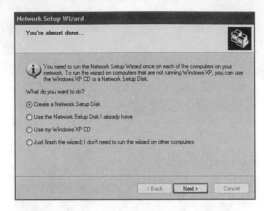

Figure 4.10

You can create a Network Setup Disk and use it to change the network configuration on all your other computers.

If you choose to create a Network Setup disk, just follow the instructions that are presented. If you choose either of the next two options and click Next, then you'll see instructions specific to each option. If you choose to just finish the wizard and click Next, then the final wizard screen appears allowing you to click Finish.

9. Click Yes when prompted to restart your computer.

You can use a Network Setup Disk on the rest of your network computers. The disk will work on Windows 95, 98, Me, NT, and 2000 computers. To run it from a disk, insert the disk into a computer floppy drive and click Start, Run and then type **a:netsetup**.

CONFIGURING FILE AND PRINT SHARING

For a computer running Windows XP to share its folders, disk drivers, and printers with other computers on a home network the File and Printer Sharing for Microsoft Networks must be installed and enabled. By default, Windows XP automatically installs and enables this service. You can verify this using the following procedure.

1. Click Start and then right-click My Network Places and select Properties from the context menu that appears. The Network Connections dialog box appears.

2. Right-click the icon representing your local area connection and select Properties. The properties dialog box for your local area connection will appear.

3. Look for File and Printer Sharing for Microsoft Networks In the list of install network components in the middle of the dialog box and make sure that it has been selected.

If you do not see the File and Printer Sharing for Microsoft Networks in the list of installed network components, then it is not installed. To install it click Install and select Service when prompted. Then click Add and select it from this list of network services that will be presented.

The act of enabling the File and Printer Sharing for Microsoft Networks service does not mean that all the printers and disk drives on your computer are now accessible to other computers on your home network. It only means that the service that facilitates resources sharing is active. To share a particular resource, you must select it and then configure it as shared.

 Check out Chapter 5, "Sharing Precious Disk Space," to learn how to share a folder or entire hard drive over your home network. To learn all about setting up and sharing your printer, read Chapter 6, "Maximizing Your Printer Investment."

CONFIGURING WINDOWS XP FOR PEAK PERFORMANCE

By default Windows XP Home Edition configures itself to provide the best possible response to the person sitting in front of its monitor and keyboard. For a standalone computer (for example, one that is not connected to a network and sharing its printer and folders) this makes good sense. This may also make sense for a computer on your home network that is seldom accessed over the network. However, if you have a network computer that is frequently accessed by the entire family, then you may want to tune it so that it allocates more of its resources in favor of better network response time.

There are several ways that you can tweak a Windows XP computer for better network performance as listed here:

- **Processor scheduling**—Adjusting the amount of processor time allocated to local programs and background services.
- **Memory usage**—Adjusting the amount of memory allocated to local programs and System cache.
- **Virtual memory**—Moving the paging file on a computer with more than two disk drives to the drive that does not store the Windows XP files in order to provide faster disk access time.

As you can see, configuring a Windows XP system for better performance is really just a matter of helping it to properly allocate resources correctly. Because the default settings are best for computers that will not get accessed a lot by other network computers, you

only have to tweak the computers that you expect your family will access a lot. For example, if you have a computer with a really large hard drive that you know will be accessed constantly, you'll probably find that you can speed things up a bit using the procedures that are outlined in just a minute.

A local program is an application that is used when sitting in front of the computer where it resides. Examples include programs such as Microsoft Word and Excel. Setting processor and memory settings to favor local programs ensures that the owner of the computer gets the best possible performance.

Computers that share their local resources over the network are providing a service. The best example of such a background service is the File and Printer Sharing for Microsoft Networks. By configuring processor and memory for better network performance, the computer is able to provide faster response time to network users. The price of this response time is a slower response time for the local user.

Windows XP performance settings are configured from the Performance Options dialog box, which you can access using the following procedure.

1. Click Start and then right-click My Computer and select Properties from the context menu that appears. The System Properties dialog box appears as shown in Figure 4.11.

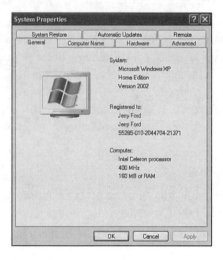

Figure 4.11

The General property sheet on the System Properties dialog box displays information about the computer and its resources.

2. Click the Advanced property sheet.

3. Click Settings, which is located in the Performance section at the top of the property sheet. The Performance Options dialog box appears.

4. Select the Advanced Properties sheet as shown in Figure 4.12.

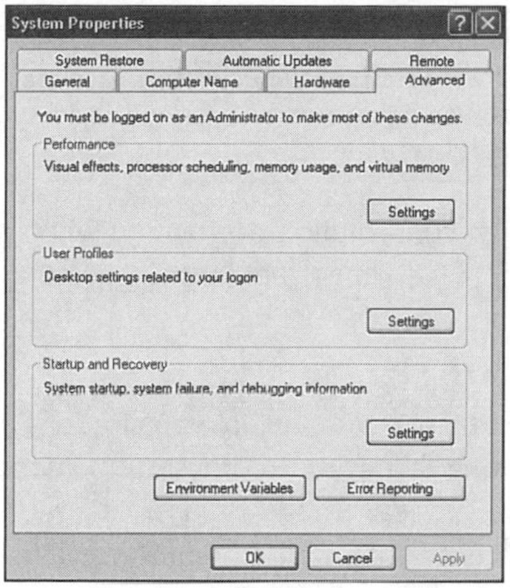

Figure 4.12

The Advanced Properties sheet enables you to configure your computer for better network performance.

Tweaking Processor Performance

By default every Windows XP system is set up to allocate processor scheduling in favor of local applications programs. This setup provides better performance for the computer's owner. However, if you are willing to give up a little local response time, you can configure the computer to allocate more of its CPU's attention to servicing requests from network users by selecting the Background services option in the Processor scheduling section on the Performance Options dialog box's Advanced Property sheet. This will allow the File and Printer Sharing for Microsoft Networks service to provide faster file and printer services.

Configuring Memory Allocation

As important as processor speed is to a computer's performance, memory is regarded as an even more important resource. By selecting the System cache option in the Memory usage section of the Performance Options Advanced properties sheet you are telling Windows XP to increase the amount of system cache, which better supports the servicing of requests from network computers.

Adjusting Virtual Memory

Windows XP requires a minimum of 64MB of memory just to start up and run. Microsoft strongly recommends a minimum of 128MB of memory. If you install Windows XP Home Edition on a computer with 128MB of memory you'll find that even when your computer is completely inactive, the operating system is using over 60MB of memory.

Given Windows XP's high consumption of memory when simply idling, it is easy to see why memory management is so important for this operating system. One of the best ways to improve the performance of this operating system is to add more memory to your computer. However, this is not always practical.

If you like to load up and work with multiple applications at the same time, then it does not take Windows XP long to run out of physical memory. To be able to keep running when memory begins to run low, Windows XP uses a technique known as virtual memory to supplement the amount of physical memory installed on your computer with additional storage space mapped out on your disk drive. This enables Windows XP to load and run programs that require more memory than is available.

Windows XP uses virtual memory (for example, a mapped out portion on your hard drive) to move pages of data stored in memory when they have not been used for a while in order to free up that memory for new storage. Later if some of the data that has been moved to the hard drive is needed, it is paged back in. The processing of moving chunks of data to and from virtual memory is known as paging and the area on the hard drive where the pages are moved is called the pagefile.

By default Windows XP creates one paging file. It places this file on the same hard drive where the Windows XP source files are stored. Windows XP access this drive a lot to get to its own source files. Placing the pagefile here places additional access requirements on this drive and can create a point of congestion and slowdown when requests of operating system files occur simultaneously with paging activity.

If your computer has more than one hard drive you can make things run faster by moving the pagefile to the other disk drive. Because both the paging file and the systems files are highly used resources, moving them to separate drives spreads out the processing load and speeds up processing. In fact, if you have a third or fourth disk drive, you can spread the pagefile over all your hard drives (except for the one that contains your Windows XP source files) and make things run even more efficiently.

Virtual memory is configured from the Virtual memory dialog box, shown in Figure 4.13, which you can access by clicking the Change button in the Virtual memory section on the Performance Options Advanced properties sheet.

The following procedure demonstrates how to move the pagefile to another hard drive on a computer that has a second hard drive.

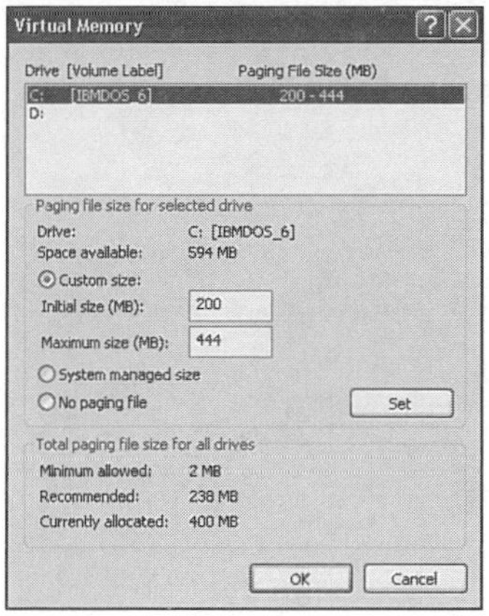

Figure 4.13

Configuring your computer's virtual memory.

Configuring Virtual Memory

1. Click the Change button in the Virtual memory section of the Performance Options property sheet. The Virtual memory dialog box appears.

2. You should see an entry for each hard disk drive on your computer in the Drive section at the top of the dialog box. Click the hard drive that does not contain the Windows Source files (in this case it's the D drive).

3. Select the Custom size option in the middle of the page. This enables the Initial size and Maximum size fields. Type a value in the Initial size field that is at least as large as the Initial size value for the current pagefile. Type a value in the Maximum size field that is at least as large as the Maximum value for the current pagefile.

4. Click Set. This tells Windows XP to set up a new pagefile.

5. Click on the original pagefile and then select the No paging file option.

6. Click Set. This tells Windows XP to delete the original pagefile.

7. Click OK to Close the Virtual Memory dialog box. Click OK to close the System Properties dialog box.

8. Reboot the computer when prompted.

CHAPTER 5

SHARING PRECIOUS DISK SPACE

By now you have all the information that you need to get a home network up and running. However, in order for a home network to provide any real value you have to set it up to share your data, printer, and Internet connection. In this chapter you learn everything that you need to know in order to set up shared folders and disk drives. This allows you to access your data from any computer on your home network regardless of where it is actually stored.

Here is what you'll learn:

- How to turn a folder or hard drive into a network resource
- How to access network drives
- How to map a network drive
- How to provide access to shared resources
- How to monitor who's accessing your shared resources

SHARING INFORMATION

Except for sharing an Internet connection and perhaps sharing a nice color printer, a home network has no more important function than allowing information to be easily shared. This information sharing can occur in numerous ways, including

- Allowing everybody in the family to share files stored on their own computer
- Allowing everybody to centrally store files that they want to share on a specific computer

 See Chapter 8, "Going Online" for more about Internet connections and Chapter 6, "Maximizing Your Printer Investment," for more on printers.

Windows XP allows you to decide just how much sharing occurs. Specifically, it allows you to:

- Share all the files located in specific folders
- Share the contents of entire disk drives

techtv tip

Windows XP does not, however, allow you to share individual files. If you want to share a single file, then you have to put it into a folder by itself and share that folder.

Examples of the kinds of things that you may want to share on your home network include

- A folder where your children store their book reports and other homework for your review
- A shared family to-do-list where mom and dad can post weekly chores
- A collection of photos creating a shared family photo album
- Copies of applications that can be loaded directly from over the network in an effort to save disk space on other computers
- A family calendar with important dates, birthdays, and events

Windows XP Home Edition provides three basic types of security for files.

- **Don't Share Them**—Just do not store your personal files on a shared drive or in a folder that is shared.
- **Allow Read-Only Access**—Allows others who access your files from over the network to read them but not to modify or delete them.
- **Allow Full Control**—Allows others who access your files from over the network to read, modify, and delete them.

Windows XP will allow you to share a number of different types of storage devices, including

- Hard disk drives
- Floppy drives
- CD-ROM drives
- CD Read Writable drives
- DVD drives
- Folders
- Zip Drives
- Jaz Drive

Windows XP allows you to share an entire drive or a folder. Sharing a folder means sharing all the files stored in that folder. If the folder includes other folders, then those subfolders are shared as well. When you share a folder on your computer over your home network the folder is referred to as a *shared folder*. Likewise when you share an entire disk drive over your home network it is called a *shared drive*. It is also often called a *network drive*.

Instead of sharing entire disk drives share at the folder level whenever possible. To keep things more secure and make your files easier to manage, try placing the files that you want to share in one or two shared folders. This will make them easier for the rest of the family to find and use.

SETTING UP SHARED DRIVES AND FOLDERS

Whether you decide to share just a folder on your hard drive or the entire drive itself, the process is almost the same. Microsoft does make you go through an extra step when sharing an entire drive to give you a chance to consider the ramifications. Unless you are 100 percent certain that it's safe to open up your whole drive to everyone in the family, you really should restrict sharing to just a folder or two. After all, it does not take much for one of your children to accidentally delete a business report or paper.

The process of sharing a floppy drive, hard drive, CD-ROM drive, Zip drive, and Jaz drive is the same. When a folder or drive is shared its icon changes to reflect its shared status by showing a hand underneath. For example, Figure 5.1 shows a shared floppy drive and a shared folder.

Once a drive or folder has been shared it becomes visible to other computers on the network.

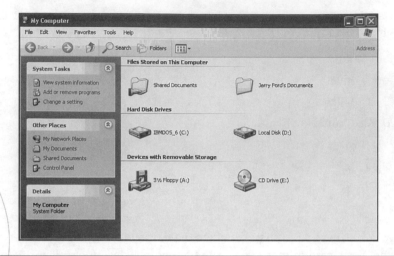

Figure 5.1

The presence of a hand underneath its icon tells you that a drive or folder has been shared.

Sharing a Drive or Folder

As I already stated, the process of sharing a drive or folder is essentially the same. Therefore you can use the following procedure to share either type of resource.

1. Click Start and then My Computer. The My Computer dialog box appears.

2. You can share a disk drive from this folder or you can drill down into a drive to locate a folder that you want to share. Once you have found the resource that you want to share, right-click it and select the Sharing and Security option from the context menu that appears.

If you do not see the Sharing and Security option, then File and Printer Sharing for Microsoft Networks has not been installed or enabled. Refer to "Configuring File and Print Sharing," in Chapter 4, "Putting It All Together," to learn more about working with this service.

3. If you are sharing an entire drive, then the Properties dialog box for that drive appears as shown in Figure 5.2.

   As you can see there is not much to look at here except for the following link:

   `If you understand the risk but still want to share the root of the drive,`
   `click here.`

   This is Microsoft's way of telling you to think twice before sharing your entire drive. To continue, click the link. If you are sharing a folder instead of an entire drive, you won't see this dialog box. Instead the first thing that you will see is the dialog box shown in the next step.

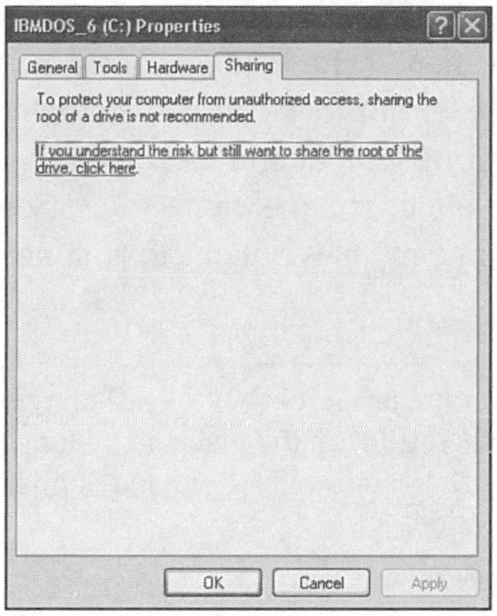

Figure 5.2

Microsoft wants to make sure you understand the risk of sharing disk resources over a network.

4. The Sharing property sheet belonging to the resource appears as shown in Figure 5.3. The middle portion of this property sheet, labeled Network sharing and security, allows you to share the drive or folder. To share the drive or folder click Share this Folder on the Network. This automatically enables the remaining fields in the Network sharing and security section.

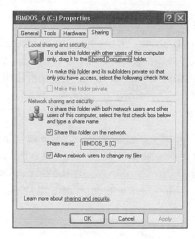

Figure 5.3

Sharing your local C drive.

5. Type the name by which the drive or folder will be visible on the network in the share name field.

6. Windows XP Home Edition provides limited security over a shared drive or folder. You have two options here, either allow everybody on your home network to read the contents of the folder or provide them with full control over its contents. The read option lets everyone look at and view the files stored in this folder but they will not be able to delete or change them. To provide full control select the Allow network users to change my files option. To limit access to read-only leave this option disabled.

At the bottom of the Sharing property sheet is a sharing and security link that you can click to learn more about setting up the disk and folder sharing and the risks involved. When you click this link the Windows XP Help and Support Center appears providing you with tons of information.

7. Click OK.

Now if you open the My Computer folder and go find the drive or folder that you just shared, you should see that its icon now shows that it's a shared resource.

There is one important point about the security that you are applying to your shared drives and folder. This security only affects network users. In other words, anyone who sits down in front of your computer and logs on is not affected by the network security applied to Windows XP's shared resources.

Examining Hidden Shares

The shared drive or folders that you create are only one type of shared resource. There is another known as a hidden share. A *hidden share* is a shared drive or folder that is not visible to network users. In other words, it does not appear in any Windows dialog boxes when browsing the network. Therefore, to access a hidden share you need to know that it exists and what its name is.

You can create a hidden share by adding a $ as the last character of the share name. If you open the My Computer dialog box after creating a hidden share for a drive or folder, you won't be able to tell that the share exists by looking at its icon. You can however, view it by opening the Computer Management console and selecting the Shares view as shown in Figure 5.4.

As Figure 5.4 shows, a hidden share has been created for the A drive on the computer. A hidden share can therefore be used to share drives and files in a somewhat more secure fashion. However, this added security is really just an illusion because anyone who finds out about the share can access it.

Windows XP automatically creates some hidden shares, which it uses to support communication between computers on a network. These hidden shares and their purpose are outlined here.

- **IPC$**—An interprocess communication share that supports the remote administration of network computers

- **PRINT$**—A share created by Windows XP when you set up a shared printer that Windows XP uses to perform printer management tasks

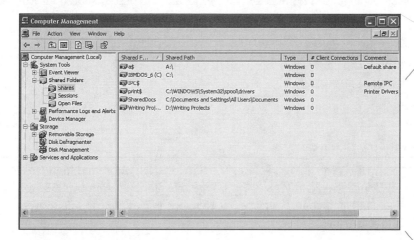

Figure 5.4

Viewing your computer's hidden shares.

Terminating a Shared Drive or Folder

If, after a while, you decide that you no longer want to share a drive or folder on your computer with the rest of the family, then you'll want to tell Windows XP to unshare it. After all, if Junior keeps deleting its contents or filling it up, it's time to take it back.

Unsharing a drive or folder is a straightforward process and is outlined next.

Remember that once you stop sharing a drive or folder, the only way to access it is by logging on to the computer that owns it.

1. Click Start and then My Computer. The My Computer dialog box appears.
2. Right-click the shared drive or folder that you want to stop sharing and select the Sharing and Security option from the context menu that appears.
3. Clear the Share this Folder on the network option.
4. Click OK.

LOCATING NETWORK RESOURCES

OK, so now you know how to set up shared drives and folders on your network. Now let's take a look at how they look to other computers on your home network.

Windows XP provides a number of ways to locate and access shared network drives and folders. These include

- My Network Places
- Internet Explorer
- Windows dialog boxes
- The Run command

My Network Places

The My Network Places folder replaces the Network Neighborhood found in older versions of Windows including Windows NT 4.0, Windows 95, and Windows 98. You can open it by clicking Start and then selecting My Network Places. Figure 5.5 shows a typical My Network Places folder.

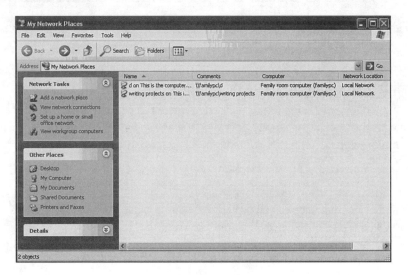

Figure 5.5

The My Network Places folder provides the focal point for most network operations including locating and accessing shared network drives and folders.

The My Network Places folder displays a list of shared network drives and folders. You cannot tell whether or not the shared resource is a drive or folder. You can access it by double-clicking it.

On the upper-left hand of the My Network Places folder is the Network Tasks section where the following tasks can be initiated.

- Add a network place
- View network connections
- Set up a home or small office network
- View workgroup computers

Adding a Network Place

Selecting Add A Network Place starts the Add Network Place Wizard. This wizard assists you in setting up several types of network connections, including

- A connection to an Internet storage provider
- A shortcut to a Web site
- A shortcut to an FTP site
- A connection to a shared network drive or folder

Use the following procedure to set up a connection to a shared network drive or folder on your home network.

1. Click Start and then My Network Places. The My Network Places folder appears.
2. Click Add a Network Place. The Add Network Place Wizard appears. Click Next.
3. The following choices appear as shown in Figure 5.6.
    - **MSN Communities**—A Microsoft service that will provide supplemental Internet storage
    - **Choose Another Network Location**—Allows you to specify a Web site, FTP site, or network resource to establish a connection to

    Select the Choose Another Network Location option and click Next.
4. You are prompted to type the name of an Internet or network address. To create a connection to a drive or folder located on your home network type the resource's UNC address as demonstrated in Figure 5.7 and click Next.

The Universal Naming Convention or UNC is a shorthand way of identifying resources on a computer or network. To specify a UNC address, type \\ followed by the name of the computer where the network resources resides, followed by a \ and the path to the resource. For example, to specify the UNC name of a network drive named *C* on a computer named *FamilyPC* specify *FamilyPC\C*.

5. Next you are prompted to provide a name for the network connection as shown in Figure 5.8. Type a descriptive name and click Next.

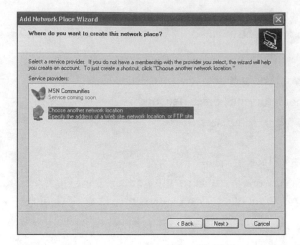

Figure 5.6

You can set up a connection to a network drive or folder by selecting the Choose Another Network Location option.

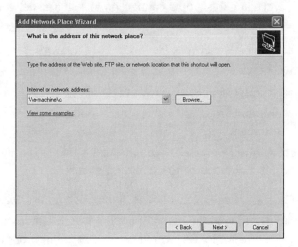

Figure 5.7

Supply the UNC address of the network resource to which you want to connect.

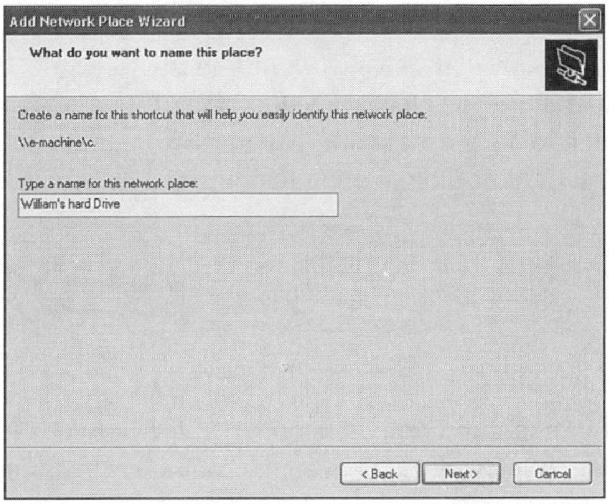

Figure 5.8

Provide a descriptive name for the network resource.

6. The wizard displays a screen stating that it has set up the connection. Click Finish.

When you return to the My Network Places folder you will see an icon for the network connection. Double-click to open it.

You'll find links to the My Network Places dialog box throughout Windows XP. For example, if you open the Windows Explorer (click Start, All Programs, Accessories and the Windows Explorer) you'll see links to your My Documents folder, My Computer, and My Network places. This allows you to drill down and browse your network in much the same way that you are used to doing when you use Windows Explorer to browse the files and folders on your computer.

View Network Connections

The View network connections task in the Network Tasks section of the My Network Places folder displays a list of all your computer network connections. From here you can configure each connection's properties and perform a number of management tasks.

Check out Chapter 3, "The Softer Side of Network Setup," for more information on working with the properties of your network connections. Also look to Chapter 10, "Just When You Thought Your Work Was Done," for information about performing network management tasks.

Set Up a Home or Small Office Network

The Set Up a Home or Small Office Network task in the Network Tasks section of the My Network Places folder starts the Network Setup Wizard. This wizard assists you in configuring your computer to join a network. It can also be used to install and configure Windows XP's Internet Connection Sharing features and its built-in personal firewall.

 To learn more about working with this wizard check out Chapter 3, "The Softer Side of Network Setup," and Chapter 8, "Going Online."

View Workgroup Computers

Selecting the View Workgroup Computers option in the Network Tasks section of the My Network Places folder displays a listing of all the computers that are members of the same workgroup as your computer. In order for a computer to appear in this list it must be configured to be a member of the workgroup and must be turned on. To view all the shared resources belonging to a given computer, all that you have to do is double-click it.

 To learn how to configure your computer's workgroup membership refer to Chapter 4, "Putting It All Together."

NOTE If you attempt to access a workgroup computer and are unable to do so, then it may be that the computer has been turned off. It takes a few minutes for all the computers on your home network to recognize when a computer has been shut down or disconnected from the network.

Internet Explorer

Most people do not realize it but you can usually access any disk or folder on a Microsoft computer or network from any dialog box that allows you to type its address. This includes Internet Explorer. For example, Figure 5.9 shows an opened shared drive on a computer named E-Machine. Notice its UNC address in the IE Address Bar.

Accessing Network Resources from Windows Dialog Boxes

Many Windows dialog boxes allow you to access network drives and folders. Perhaps the best examples of this capability are the Windows XP Open and Save dialog boxes. These dialog boxes are used by many Windows applications to open and save files. They allow you to store and retrieve files on your local drives. In addition, because they provide a link to My Network Places you can also access any available network drive or folder.

Figure 5.10 shows the Windows XP Save As dialog box. On the left side of the dialog box is a list of icons that provide easy access to the places where you will most likely want to store your files. At the bottom of this list is the My Network Places icon. Click it to access the shared network drives and folders on your home network.

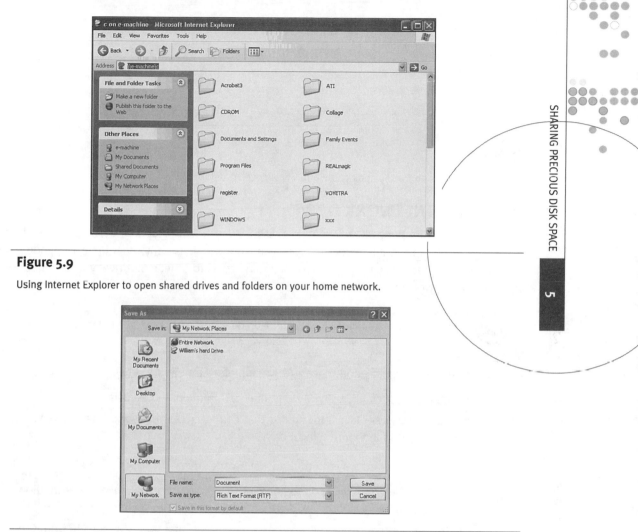

Figure 5.9

Using Internet Explorer to open shared drives and folders on your home network.

Figure 5.10

Using the Windows XP Save As dialog box to store a file on a network drive or folder.

Saving Time with the Windows XP Run Command

The Windows XP Run dialog box, shown in Figure 5.11, offers a quick way to access a network drive or folder. You can open the Run dialog box by clicking Start and then selecting Run.

After typing the UNC address of the drive or folder that you want to access just click OK. A Windows Explorer dialog box will then open and display the contents of the drive or folder. If you do not know the UNC address of the drive or folder, you can click the Browse button and search for it that way.

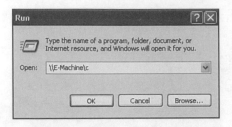

Figure 5.11

The Run dialog box gives you quick access to a network drive or folder by typing its UNC name.

MAPPING A NETWORK DRIVE

You can make network drives look as if they are a local resource by mapping to them. When you map to a network drive you can work with it like any other drive. Depending on how long you are going to need to maintain access to a network drive, you can map to it temporarily or set it up to automatically reconnect every time you log on to your computer.

Each drive that you map slows your logon down just a bit. However, unless you create a bunch of them, you probably won't notice a significant delay.

There are a couple of good reasons for mapping to a network drive.

- Mapping makes accessing a drive that you frequently use easier
- Mapping allows older applications that cannot access network drives to view a network drive as if it were a local drive

There are two different ways to map to a network drive.

- **The Map Network Drive dialog box**—A GUI dialog box that collects information from you about the network drive and then establishes a connection
- **The NET USE command**—A text-based command that you can execute from the Windows XP command prompt to set up a mapped drive

Setting Up a Mapped Drive from the Windows GUI

The easiest way to map to a network drive is from the Windows graphical user interface or GUI. The procedure for doing so is outlined here.

1. Click Start, right-click My Computer and select Map Network Drive. The Map Network Drive dialog box appears as shown in Figure 5.12.

2. Select an available drive letter from the Drive drop-down list. Drive letters already assigned to local drives are not listed. Drive letters already assigned to other network drives are listed and show the name of the drive and machine that owns it.

Figure 5.12

Establishing a network drive connection.

3. Type the UNC address of the network drive in the Folder drop-down list or click Browse to search your network for it.

4. If you want to reconnect the drive mapping each time you log on, make sure that the Reconnect at Logon option is selected. If you clear this option, Windows XP will remove the mapping at the end of your current login session.

5. Click Finish. A dialog box will appear showing all the files and folders stored on the network drive as demonstrated in Figure 5.13.

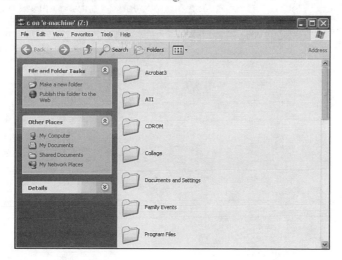

Figure 5.13

Viewing the contents of a network drive.

It is easy to tell which drives are network drives. Just look underneath the network icon. If there is nothing there, it's a local drive. If there is a hand there, it's a shared drive. If there is a network cable, it's a network drive.

Working from the Command Line

If you prefer working from the Windows command line you can use the Windows XP NET USE command to create new network mappings.

1. Click Start, All Programs, Accessories, and then Command Prompt. The Windows XP Command prompt appears.

2. Type `NET USE X: \\computer_name\share_name` and press Enter. In this example, X represents the drive letter that you want to assign to the mapping and the remainder of the command is simply the UNC address of the network drive.

 For more information about working with the NET USE command see Appendix A, "Windows XP Networking Commands."

Disconnecting a Mapped Network Drive

After a while, you may decide that you no longer need to map to a given network drive. In that case you can delete the mapping. After all, if you are not going to be accessing it, you might as well get rid of it and shave off a little time during your logon process. The following procedure shows you how to unmap a network drive.

1. Click Start, right-click My Computer and select Disconnect Network Drive. The Disconnect Network Drive dialog box appears as shown in Figure 5.14.

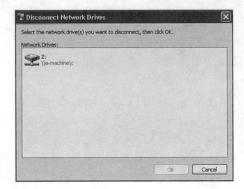

Figure 5.14

Removing a connection to a network drive.

2. Select the drive that you want to disconnect and click OK.

 You can also disconnect a mapped network drive by right-clicking its icon and selecting Disconnect from the context menu that appears.

MONITORING SHARED RESOURCES

Any time you share a drive or folder on your computer and let the rest of the family have access to it you are turning your computer into a kind of file server. This means that when others are accessing your computer's files from over the network you may experience a small performance hit. Under normal conditions this may not be a problem. But what if while working you hear your hard drive start to spin. After a few moments it is still spinning. A few minutes later it is still taking a pounding. Because you are not accessing you hard drive then somebody else is, but whom?

Windows XP allows you to monitor network access to local resources using the Computer Management console. You can access this console by clicking Start, Control Panel, Performance and Maintenance, and then Administrative Tools as shown in Figure 5.15.

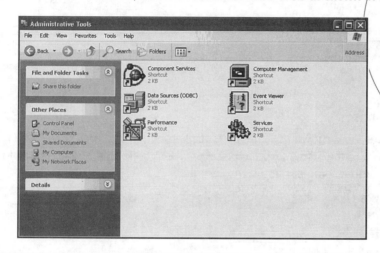

Figure 5.15

The Computer Management console allows you to perform a number of administrative procedures on your computer including monitoring network users as they access your computer's shared folders.

Double-click the Computer Management console to open it. This console allows you to see who is accessing your shared folders using any of three views under the Shared Folders view as shown in Figure 5.16.

The three options provided by the Computer Management console for monitoring network users are outlined here.

- Shares
- Sessions
- Open Files

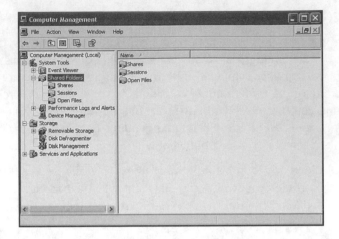

Figure 5.16

The Computer Management console provides three views for monitoring people who are accessing your shared drives and folders.

Open Shares

The Shares view, shown in Figure 5.17, displays currently shared drives and folders as well as the path to the resource, the type of network connection, the number of network connections, and a comment about the resource.

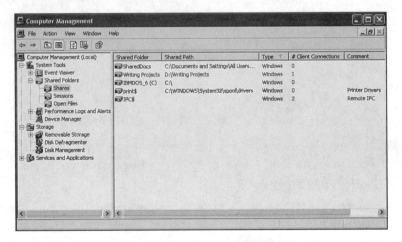

Figure 5.17

The Shares view displays all shared disk and folder resources as well as any network connections to them.

You can send a message to a network user from the Shares view by right-clicking Shares and then selecting All tasks followed by Send Console Message. This opens the Send Console Message dialog box, shown in Figure 5.18, where you can type a message and click Add to specify a recipient. Once you have typed your recipient list, just click Send and a message similar to the one shown in Figure 5.19 will appear on the recipient's display.

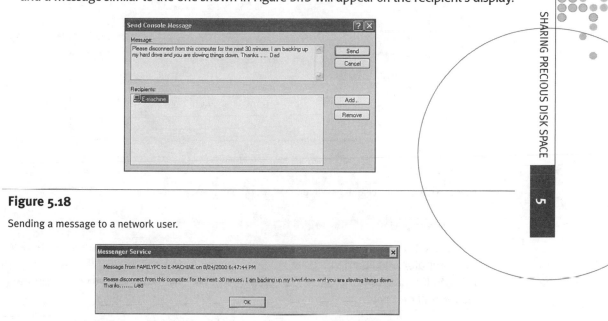

Figure 5.18

Sending a message to a network user.

Figure 5.19

A message received from another network user.

Active Sessions

The Sessions view, shown in Figure 5.20, displays active network sessions with the computer. This information includes

- The name of the network user
- The user's computer name
- The type of connection
- The number of open files
- The length of time that the connection has been established
- The amount of time that the connection has been idle
- Whether or not the Guest account is being used

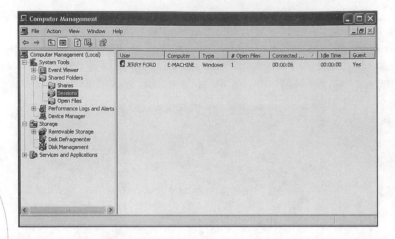

Figure 5.20

Viewing sessions on your computer with other network computers.

Terminating a Network Session

If you need to, you can forcibly disconnect a network session from the Session view on the Computer Management console. For example, if one of the kids was accessing a file that you did not want them to, you could disconnect his or her connection using the procedure outlined here.

1. Open the Computer Management console and select the Session view.
2. Right-click the session that you want to disconnect and select Close Session.
3. Click Yes when prompted for confirmation.

Closing All Network Sessions

If necessary you can close all network sessions with your computer at once rather than closing them one at a time. The procedure for doing so is outlined here.

1. Open the Computer Management Console and select the Session view.
2. Right-click the Sessions folder and select Disconnect All Sessions.
3. Click Yes when prompted for confirmation.

Open Files

The Open Files view, shown in Figure 5.21, displays a list of files on the computer that are currently being accessed by network users. In addition, the following information about each open file is displayed.

- The name and path of each opened file
- The name of the user accessing the file

- The type of network connection
- The number of files locked
- The type of permission granted to the user accessing the file

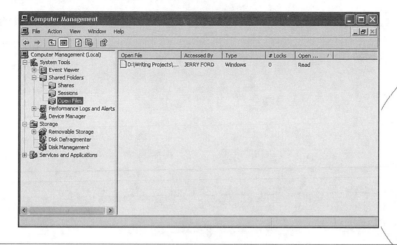

Figure 5.21

Viewing the files currently opened by network users.

Closing an Open File

Like network sessions with other computers, you can terminate a network connection to a particular file. The procedure for doing so is outlined here.

1. Open the Computer Management console and select the Open Files view.
2. Right-click the file that you want to close and select Close Open File.
3. Click Yes when prompted for confirmation.

If you want to terminate network access to all files on your computer, you can do so by following the steps outlined next.

1. Open the Computer Management console and select the Open Files view.
2. Right-click Open Files and select Disconnect All Open Files.
3. Click Yes when prompted for confirmation.

 To learn more about the Computer Management console check out Chapter 10, "Just When You Thought Your Work Was Done."

CHAPTER 6

MAXIMIZING YOUR PRINTER INVESTMENT

One of the best conveniences provided by home networks is the ability to share a single printer with every computer on the network. Not only will you save money by not having to purchase a printer for each computer but you'll be able to share it without having to get up and let somebody else use your computer. This chapter will show you how to install and then share a printer on your home network. The chapter also discusses how to use Windows XP's fax service as a way to send and receive faxes.

Here is what you'll learn:

- How to install a printer using Windows XP
- How to share your printer with your home network
- How to set up your other network computers to connect to a network printer
- How to manage your print jobs
- How to set up and use Windows XP's fax service

OVERVIEW OF WINDOWS XP PRINTING

Windows XP handles printing and faxing in much the same manner. Both are managed from the Printers and Faxes icons on the Windows XP Control Panel and both work by printing their output on your printer. In order to set up and use Windows XP's fax capabilities you need an old-fashioned modem that includes fax support, which most of them do. You also need a telephone line and a printer.

Windows operating systems have always included strong support for printing. Windows XP is no exception. Fax support, on the other hand, has come and gone. It was in Windows 95 but not in Windows 98 or Me and is back again. Once properly set up you'll find that it is easy to use and works a lot like Microsoft Outlook Express.

Another option for setting up shared printer access on your home network is to purchase an Internet gateway that provides built-in print server capability. For more information on Internet gateways and their ability to function as a print server check out Chapter 2, "Getting Your Hands Dirty: Assembling Your Network Hardware."

The Printer and Faxes Dialog Box

You can locate and manage your printer or fax from the Printers and Faxes dialog box shown in Figure 6.1.

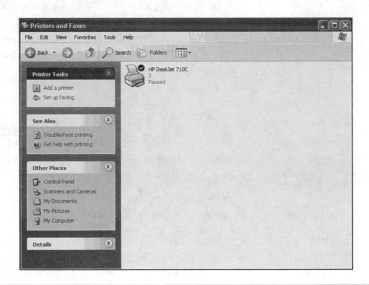

Figure 6.1

The Printers and Faxes dialog box is your focal point for print and fax management.

You can open the Printer and Faxes dialog box by clicking Start, Control Panel, Printers and Other Hardware, and then View Installed Printers or Fax Printers. You find an icon for every installed printer and fax as well as links to add a new printer or set up faxing.

Windows XP Print Features

Windows XP can support virtually any printer including parallel and USB printers. Windows XP comes equipped with the software drivers for hundreds of printers. When combined with its plug-and-play features, Windows XP is often able to automatically detect and install a new printer without any assistance from you.

Other significant Windows XP print features include

- Support for user-friendly printer names that can be up to 31 characters long
- Advanced plug-and-play support
- Support for standard parallel, bi-directions, and USB printers

Making Sure Plug-and-Play Printer Installation Works

In order for Windows XP to plug-and-play install a printer you must have the following hardware:

- A bi-directional printer
- An IEEE 1284 printer cable. Unlike regular parallel printer cables, this cable supports two-way communications between your printer and your computer. Without it Windows XP cannot gather the information it needs to automatically install your printer.

Printing Vocabulary

Before going too far into a discussion of Windows XP printing, let's make sure that we agree on the meaning of a few vocabulary words as shown here.

- **Printer**—The physical device that produces printed output.
- **Local Printer**—A printer attached directly to your computer, which has not been shared with the rest of the network.
- **Network Printer**—A printer that has been shared with all the computers on your network either by attaching it to a Windows XP computer and sharing it or by attaching it to a print server appliance.
- **Software Driver**—Software installed on Windows XP that gives it the ability to control a specific printer.
- **Spooling**—A process used by Windows XP to copy print jobs to disk as temporary files where they wait to be submitted to the printer.
- **Print Queue**—The location on your hard drive where spooled print jobs are stored and managed.

Understanding the Windows XP Print Process

Windows XP implements a device-independent print architecture. This means that you can submit a print job to any printer, regardless of type and model and Windows XP will format your print job as required in order to allow it to successfully print. Once you have set up your printer connections all that you have to do is select the printer to which you want to submit a print job and Windows XP takes care of the rest.

The actual steps involved in the Windows XP print process are summarized here.

1. A print job is submitted from a Windows application.

2. Windows XP checks to see which printer has been chosen to print the print job. If it's a local printer the print job is spooled to the printer queue on the local hard drive. If it's a network printer, the print job is sent to the print server that manages the printer where it is then spooled.

3. The print job waits its turn in the print queue. When all print jobs that arrived before this one have been printed, Windows submits the print job to the printer.

4. The printer prints the print job. When the printer has finished with the print job Windows XP deletes it from the print queue.

Windows XP stores all print jobs in the \Windows\System32\spool\printers folder as depicted in Figure 6.2.

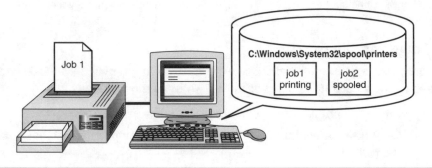

Figure 6.2

Windows XP spools all print jobs to hard disk and then prints them in a first-in first-out basis.

Each printer has its own print queue, which you can view to examine the status of print jobs sent to the printer. You can view a printer queue by double-clicking its icon in the Printers and Faxes dialog box. Figure 6.3 shows the print queue for a printer named HP DeskJet 710C. As you can see there are currently three jobs in the printer's queue. The first job is printing and the other two are spooled and waiting their turn.

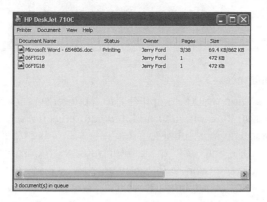

Figure 6.3

Viewing the jobs held in a printer's print queue.

Types of Network Printers

There are two types of printers that you will work with on your home network, local and network. A local printer is one that is attached directly to your computer and to which only you can submit print jobs. A network printer can be either of the following:

- A printer attached to a Windows XP computer that has been shared with the rest of the network, turning the Windows XP computer into a print server
- A printer attached directly to the network via a dedicated network appliance known as a print server appliance

Windows XP Printer Servers

The most common way to set up a network printer on a home network is just to have the computer that it's connected to share it as depicted in Figure 6.4. The computer where the printer is attached assumes the role of a network print server meaning that it will accept print jobs and spool them to its local hard drive and them submit them to its printer.

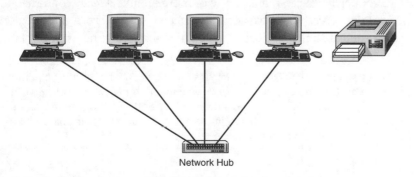

Network Hub

Figure 6.4

Any Windows XP system with a printer can be turned into a print server.

> **NOTE** Windows XP is not the only operating system capable of sharing a printer. Every Microsoft operating system since Windows 3.11 has this capability.

Printer Server Appliances

Anytime you turn a Windows XP computer into a printer server you are placing additional processing burdens on that computer and making things run a little slower for the person using that computer. The more print jobs that are submitted from other network computers the more memory and disk space that must be consumed on the print server. Fortunately, most home network print servers won't be getting hammered too much and the overall effect should be minimal. However, if you have a few extra bucks and want to get a little fancy with your home network you can always install a network print server appliance.

A print server appliance is a small device not much bigger than an external modem that connects directly to your network hub via a standard twisted-pair cable as depicted in Figure 6.5.

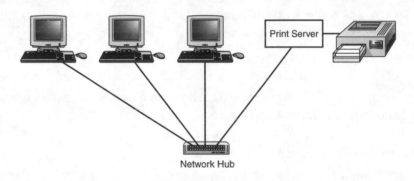

Figure 6.5

A printer connected directly to the network and managed by a print server appliance.

A print server appliance can manage one or more printers directly connected to it via parallel ports. Print server appliances come with their own storage and memory allowing them to accept and store print jobs as they arrive from other network computers.

 Because a print server appliance removes the requirement of locating a printer right beside a host computer you can now move your printer anywhere you want. This means that you can move your printer outside your home office or away from your desk if you want to cut down on the number of intrusions made by family members who want to use the printer while you are working.

INSTALLING A LOCAL PRINTER

If your printer is relatively new, then Windows XP Plug and Play should recognize it when you power it on and attach it to your computer. To see if this is the case, attach your printer, wait a few moments and then check out the Printers and Faxes folder by clicking on Start, Control Panel, Printers and Other Hardware, and then Printers and Faxes to see if an icon appears for your printer. If an icon does not appear, then Windows XP did not automatically detect and install your printer. You can, however, initiate a plug-and-play scan yourself or install the printer manually as described in the following sections.

Physical Installation

Windows XP, like other Windows operating systems before it is very flexible, especially when it comes to printer support. You do not even have to have a printer to install one, meaning that you can install all the software required to run a printer before installing the printer itself. For example, suppose you discover that your family is planning on giving you (or themselves!) a new color printer on your birthday. Windows XP allows you to manually install the printer's software driver in advance so that when the printer finally arrives all that you have to do is plug it in. Of course this actually works best if you are installing an older printer that Windows XP won't be able to plug-and-play install. After all, with plug-and-play installation what is the point of pre-installing a printer? Anyway, Windows XP will let you do it if you want to.

It's best to wait until your printer has been connected to your computer before you install its software. This way you can print a test page and verify that everything is working as it should.

Attaching a printer to your computer is a very straightforward process, which is outlined here.

1. Follow the instructions provided by the printer manufacturer to assemble your printer.
2. Attach its power cord and plug it into an outlet.
3. If this is a parallel printer, attach it to your computer's parallel port using a parallel printer cable; otherwise, use a USB cable to connect it to an open USB port on your computer.

If you computer is not running, turn it on and with any luck Windows XP will automatically detect and install your printer.

Initiating a Windows XP Plug-and-Play Printer Installation

Chances are pretty good that if you are installing a new printer, you won't have to do anything. Simply hook it up, power it on, and wait and see what Windows XP does. If all goes well, in a few moments you'll be ready to print, although you may be called upon to provide a CD or diskette containing the printer's software driver.

Sometimes Windows XP is unable to automatically detect when you have attached a new printer to your computer. If this happens, you can tell Windows XP to look for it and install it using the following procedure.

1. From the Windows XP Control Panel click Printers and Other Hardware. The Printers and Other Hardware dialog box appears.

2. Click Add a Printer. The Add Printer Wizard appears. Click Next.

3. By default the following two options are selected as shown in Figure 6.6:

   - Local Printer Attached to This Computer
   - Automatically Detect and Install My Plug and Play Printer

Click Next.

Figure 6.6

Tell the wizard to search for a new printer.

4. If a new printer is found, the Found New Hardware Wizard starts and a dialog box similar to the one shown in Figure 6.7 appears. By default the option to Install the Software Automatically is selected. Windows XP comes equipped with hundreds of printer software drivers and chances are pretty good that unless your printer is a brand-new design it will have the right driver. So leave the default option selected. If Windows XP cannot find the right software driver, it will ask you to provide it. Click Next.

5. Once The Found New Hardware Wizard finds the correct printer driver the dialog box shown in Figure 6.8 will appear. Select the driver that matches your printer and click Next.

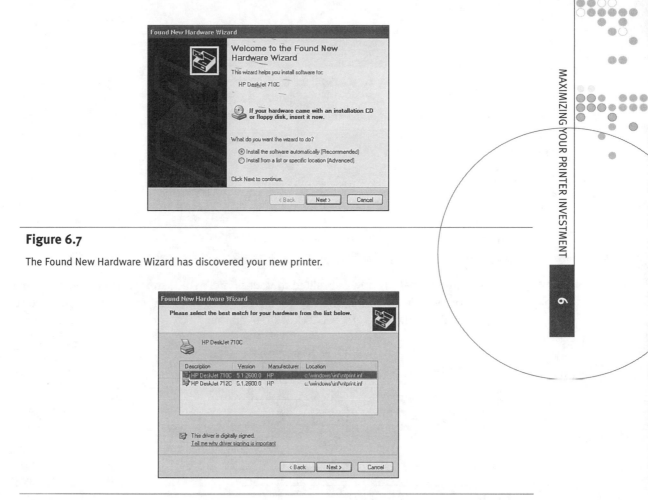

Figure 6.7

The Found New Hardware Wizard has discovered your new printer.

Figure 6.8

The Found New Hardware Wizard displays a list of printer drivers for you to choose from.

6. The Wizard begins copying all the software files required to install your printer. Then a new dialog box appears to let you know when it's done. Click Finish. The Add Printer Wizard should be visible now.

7. The Add Printer Wizard displays a dialog box, shown in Figure 6.9, asking if you want to submit a test print job to the printer. Printing a test job is the best way to verify that your printer has been correctly installed. Select Yes and then click Next.

8. Next the Add Printer Wizard displays a dialog box showing a summary of the information that it collected from you. Verify that the information is accurate and click Finish.

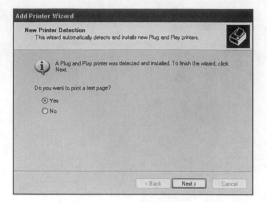

Figure 6.9

Always print a test page to make sure that your printer was properly installed.

    9. The test page is now submitted to your printer, which should begin printing. A dialog box similar to the one shown in Figure 6.10 will then appear asking if the test print job printed correctly. Click OK if everything looks good.

Figure 6.10

Tell Windows XP if the test page printed correctly.

    10. If there was a problem with the way the test page printed or if it did not print at all, you should click Troubleshoot when prompted. This will open the Windows XP Help and Support Center dialog box, which will then display the Printing Troubleshooter as shown in Figure 6.11.

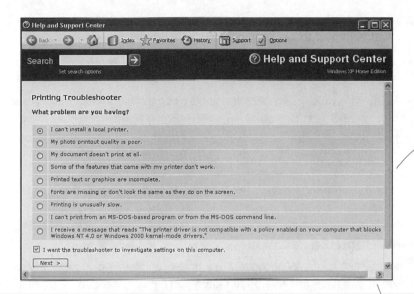

Figure 6.11

The Printing Troubleshooter will ask you a series of questions and help to diagnose most printing problems.

You should now see an icon representing your printer in the Printers and Faxes dialog box as shown in Figure 6.12. If this is the first printer to be installed on your computer, then it will be your default printer and a small black circle will be displayed just above it with a check mark.

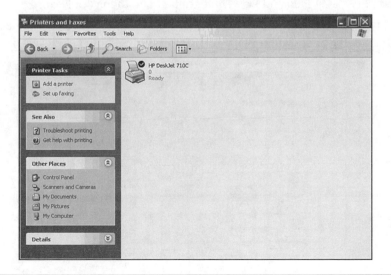

Figure 6.12

Examining the newly installed printer.

If all goes well, your printer should now be ready for use. If Windows XP did not automatically detect you printer, then double-check the following items:

- Make sure that the printer is powered on and that its printer cable is securely connected
- Verify that your printer is plug-and-play compatible by examining its documentation or visiting its manufacturer's Web site
- Double-check that you are using an IEEE 1284-compliant parallel cable
- Try running the Printing Troubleshooter

If none of these options work, then read on and learn how to perform a manual printer installation.

Manual Printer Installation

It's always best to let Windows XP try and use Plug and Play to install your printer. However, if you have an older printer, then you'll probably have to install it manually. The following procedure will step you through the process of manually installing your printer.

1. Select Start, Control Panel, and then click Printers and Other Hardware. The Printers and Other Hardware dialog box appears.
2. Click Add a Printer. The Add Printer Wizard appears.
3. Click Next.
4. Select Local Printer Attached to This Computer and clear the Automatically Detect and Install My Plug and Play Printer option and then click Next.
5. You are prompted to select the port where the printer has been connected. Usually this is LPT1 as shown in Figure 6.13. Select this entry and click Next.

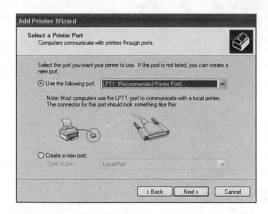

Figure 6.13

The first step in performing a manual printer install is to tell Windows XP where the printer has been attached.

Next you need to tell the wizard what kind of printer you have as shown in Figure 6.14.

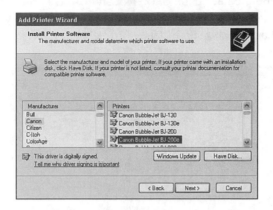

Figure 6.14

Windows XP needs to know your printer's model and manufacturer.

Select the manufacturer of your printer from the list in the Manufacturer column. A list of printers made by that manufacturer then appears in the printers column. Select your printer from the list and then click Next.

6. As Figure 6.15 shows, you are next prompted to provide a name for your printer. Keep the name of your printer under 31 characters and try to make it as descriptive as possible. If this is not the first printer that you have installed, then you'll also be prompted as to whether or not to make this printer your default printer. Click Next.

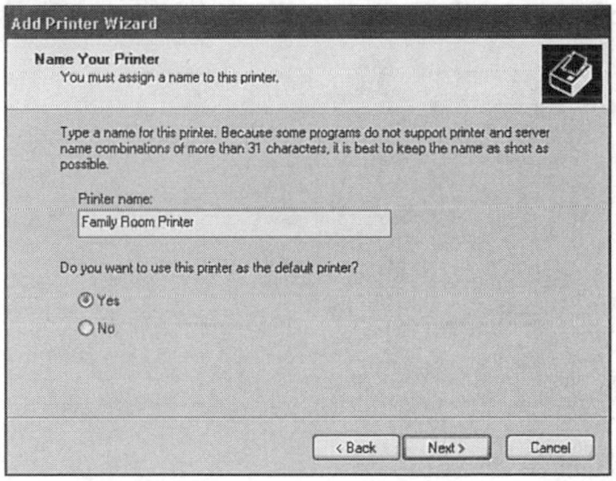

Figure 6.15

Give your printer a descriptive name that identifies its features or location.

7. Next you are prompted to share the printer over your network as shown in Figure 6.16. Leave the default option of Do Not Share This Printer in place to keep the printer all to yourself. To share it with the rest of your family select Share Name and type a name in the Share Name Text field. Click Next.

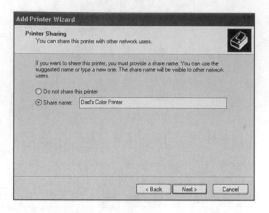

Figure 6.16

The Add Printer Wizard offers to set up your computer as a printer server.

8. If you choose to share your printer over your home network, you are next given a chance to provide information about the location of the printer and to add a brief description as shown in Figure 6.17. This information will be visible to everyone on your home network. Click Next.

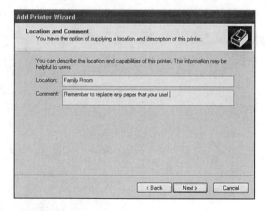

Figure 6.17

The Add Printer Wizard gives you a chance to provide network users with descriptive information about your printer.

9. Next you are asked if you want to test the setup of the printer by submitting a test page. Select Yes. This will provide you with immediate feedback regarding how well you did in setting up your printer.

10. The Add Printer Wizard displays a summary of the information that it has collected from you. Review this information and click Finish.

11. The Add Printer Wizard will then install the software files for your printer. If you elected to print a test page, it will then print. You'll see a dialog box appear asking how the page printed. If everything looks good, then click OK. Otherwise, click Troubleshoot. Follow the steps presented by the Printing Troubleshooter to identify and correct any problems.

Assuming that your test page looks good then you are all done. You should see a new icon in the Printers and Faxes dialog box identifying your printer. If this is your only printer or if you elected to make it your default printer, you'll see a small black circle with a check mark in it just above the printer's icon.

SHARING YOUR PRINTER WITH THE REST OF YOUR HOME NETWORK

You can share a local printer over your home network at any time. This will turn your computer into a print server and allow it to accept and manage print jobs submitted from any computer on your home network. The following procedure outlines the steps involved in sharing your printer.

1. Open the Printers and Faxes folder.

2. Right-click the printer that you want to share and select Sharing from the context menu that appears.

3. The printer's properties dialog box appears with the Sharing property sheet selected as shown in Figure 6.18.

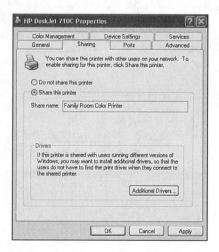

Figure 6.18

You can configure printer sharing from the Sharing property sheet on the printer's dialog box.

4. Select Share this printer and type a descriptive name in the Share Name field. This is the name that other family members will see when looking for the printer on the network.

5. If you are going to have computers on your home network running other operating systems than Windows XP, then you can instruct Windows XP to store printer drivers appropriate for each operating system so that your other computers can automatically download them as required. To do this click Additional Drivers. The Additional Drivers dialog box appears as shown in Figure 6.19.

Figure 6.19

You can go ahead and tell Windows XP to load software drivers used by other Microsoft operating systems and make them available to these operating systems when requested.

 If you are working on another computer on your home network, say a Windows 2000 system, and you decide to set up a connection to a Windows XP computer's shared printer, Windows 2000 will automatically download its own software driver if it's stored on the Windows XP computer. The same is true for Windows NT 4.0, XP, 95, 98, and Me systems.

6. Select the operating system for which you want to pre-load software drivers and click on OK.

7. A dialog box similar to the one shown in Figure 6.20 will appear asking you to select your printer from a list. Make your selection and click OK.

8. Click Close when returned to the printer's Properties dialog box.

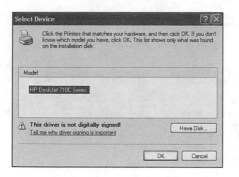

Figure 6.20

Select your printer model so that the proper printer software drivers will be loaded.

> If you gave your shared printer a name greater than eight characters in length, you'll see a pop-up dialog box appear warning that some MS-DOS systems will not be able to view and use it. Click Yes to leave the name as it is and finish the printer sharing process. Hopefully you are not running such an antiquated system on your home network. If you are, consider retiring this old dinosaur.

CONNECTING TO YOUR NETWORK PRINTER FROM OTHER COMPUTERS

Windows XP makes connecting to a network printer a breeze. In fact, if you wait a few minutes after sharing a printer, you may find that all the other Windows XP computers on your home network have discovered it and already installed it.

Figure 6.21 shows an example of a Windows XP computer on a network that has automatically discovered and installed a printer connected to a Windows XP print server. The Printer looks different from a locally installed printer. It shows a network cable connected to the bottom of the printer icon. In addition, the name assigned to the printer included the word *Auto* indicating that Windows XP automatically discovered and installed the printer itself.

Sometimes Windows XP may not recognize when a new network printer has been set up. When this occurs you can run the Add Printer Wizard and connect to it that way. This process is outlined in the following procedure.

Figure 6.21

Windows XP can automatically discover and connect to a shared network printer.

1. Open the Printers and Faxes dialog box and click Add a Printer. The Welcome screen of the Add Printer Wizard appears.

2. Click Next.

3. Select a network printer, or a printer attached to another computer and click Next as shown in Figure 6.22.

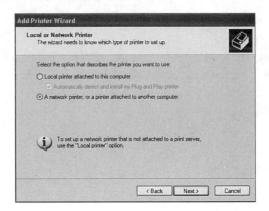

Figure 6.22

Tell the wizard that you will be installing a network printer.

4. You'll see the following options for locating the network printer:

- **Browse For a Printer**—Select this option and click Next to browse your network and look for the printer.
- **Connect to This Printer**—Select this option to provide the name of the printer using its Universal Naming Convention or UNC name. For example, if the printer is named BubbleJet and it is connected to a computer named Mikes-PC, then its UNC name would be \\Mikes-PC\BubbleJet.
- **Connect to a Printer or the Internet or on a Home or Office Network**—Use the printer's URL in the format of `http://printserver name/Printers/share name/.printer`.

If you know the share name of a printer, you can also access it using the format of `http://printserver/share name`. If you don't know the share name, you can type `http://printserver/printers` and view a list, all the available printers on the specified computer.

Complete your preferred option and click Next.

5. If this is not the first printer to be set up on your computer, you'll next be asked whether or not to make the printer your default printer. Select either Yes or No and click Next.

6. The Add Printer Wizard displays a summary of the information that it has collected from you. Make sure that this information is correct and click Finish.

7. An icon for the network printer will now appear in the Printers and Faxes dialog box.

Deleting a Printer

From time to time you may want to uninstall a printer. For example, perhaps after faithfully printing thousands of pages for you it finally breaks down. Or perhaps you want to move it to another computer on your home network. In either case you are going to want to delete it from its host computer using the following procedure.

If the printer that you are deleting is also a network printer, then after a short period the Windows XP computers on your home network should automatically realize that it has been removed and delete their connection as well. If this does not happen, then you'll need to use the following procedure to delete the network printer on any computer that was connected to it. In addition, you'll have to delete any reference to the printer from any non-Windows XP computer.

1. Open the Printers and Faxes dialog box and right-click the printer to be removed from your computer.

2. Select the Delete option from the context menu that appears.

3. You'll be asked to confirm your decision to delete the printer. Click Yes.

WINDOWS XP PRINT MANAGEMENT

Windows XP allows you to manage each printer individually from the Printers and Faxes dialog box. Print management includes a number of tasks including

- Pausing the print job
- Pausing all print jobs
- Canceling all print jobs in the printer's queue
- Canceling an individual print job
- Resuming a print job from the point where it was paused
- Restarting a paused print job from the beginning

Managing Your Printer's Queue

To manage a printer's print queue you must first display it. You can do this by double-clicking the printer's icon in the Printers and Faxes dialog box. Figure 6.23 displays an empty print queue.

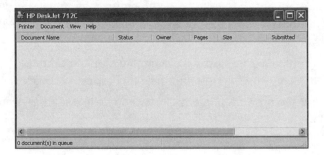

Figure 6.23

A print job sent to a printer will appear in its print queue and remain there until canceled or printed.

Each user has the ability to manage his or her own print jobs but not those of other users. However, users that have a user account with administrator privileges can manage all print jobs.

Working with Printer Level Controls

Windows XP supplies a number of commands that you can execute that affect the entire print queue and the printer itself. These commands are located on the Printer menu on the printer's dialog box. These commands include

- **Set as Default Printer**—Sets the printer as your default printer.
- **Printing Preferences**—Lets you specify things like paper orientation and print quality.
- **Pause Printing**—Pauses all activity in the print queue. Selecting this option again un-pauses all print queue activity.

- **Cancel All Documents**—Purges all print jobs from the print queue without printing them.
- **Sharing**—Opens the Sharing property sheet where you can turn printer sharing off and on.
- **Properties**—Opens the printer's properties dialog box allowing you to alter the printer's configuration.

Figure 6.24 shows a print queue with three print jobs in it. The first print job in the queue is currently printing and the other two jobs are waiting their turn. The following information is provided about each print job.

- **Document Name**—The name of the document being printed.
- **Status**—The status of each print job (for example, printing, spooling, paused).
- **Owner**—The name of the user who submitted the print job.
- **Pages**—The number of pages that make up the print job.
- **Size**—The total file size of the print job.
- **Submitted**—The time that the print job was submitted.
- **Port**—The port where the printer is attached.

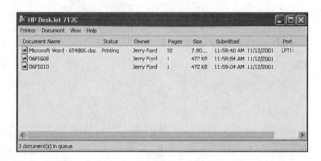

Figure 6.24

A Windows XP print queue with three print jobs.

Working with Document-Level Controls

You can work with individual print jobs in the print queue by selecting them and then clicking one of the following commands located under the Document menu.

- **Pause**—Pauses the selected print job without affecting other jobs in the print queue.
- **Resume**—Restarts a paused print job at the point where it was printing when the job was paused.
- **Restart**—Restarts a print job from the beginning.
- **Cancel**—Deletes a print job from the queue.
- **Properties**—Provides information about the print job including its owner, size, print layout, and print quality.

Changing the Order in Which Documents Will Print

By default Windows XP prints all print jobs in a first-in first-out basis. This order is represented by the location of print jobs in the print queue. The print job at the top of the queue is the first to be printed and the job at the bottom of the queue will be the last to be printed. However, you can change the order in which print jobs are printed if you need to. For example, suppose you have a really important business paper to print but when you open the printer's print queue you see that one of your children has just sent a dozen print jobs to the printer ahead of you. When this happens you can use the following process to override the order in which your job will print.

1. Open the print queue for the printer where you have submitted your print job.

2. Select your print job and click on the Properties option under the Document menu. The Document's Properties dialog box appears as shown in Figure 6.25.

Figure 6.25

Changing the order in which documents are printed.

3. All Windows XP print jobs are assigned a priority. By default this priority is 1. By changing the priority of a given print job to a higher priority you can cause it to print sooner. Use your cursor to move the slider bar in the Priority section to the right. The further to the right the bar is moved the higher the priority assigned to the print job.

Establishing Your Default Printer

If you have more than one printer set up in the Printers and Faxes dialog box, then one of the printers has been set up as your default printer. The default printer is the printer where your documents will print unless you specify otherwise.

You can tell which printer has been set up as your default printer by looking for a small black circle with a check mark in it just above the printer's icon. The following process shows you how to change your default printer.

1. Open the Printers and Faxes dialog box.
2. Right-click the icon for the printer that you want to set as your default printer.
3. Select the Set as Default printer option from the context menu that appears. The icon for the selected printer should now be changed to reflect its status as your default printer.

Advanced Printer Management Techniques

In the next few sections I am going to show you how to set up some advanced printer options on your home network. These options include

- **Controlling Printer Availability**—Lets you set times when other family members can use your shared printer over the network.
- **Setting Up a Printer Pool**—Lets you set up two or more printers as a single logical printer. When a print job is submitted it will be sent to the first available printer in the printer pool.
- **Establishing Printer Priorities**—Lets you set up different instances of the same printer and assign different priorities to each instance. Family members who submit print jobs to the printer with the higher priority will have their print jobs printed sooner.

Establishing Network Printer Availability

Windows XP allows you to install multiple logical instances of the same physical printer. This allows you to share one instance and not the other. This way you can set up a printer availability schedule for the shared instance of the printer, which provides only limited access to the printer while still having unlimited access yourself.

The following procedure shows you how to configure the shared instance of your printer that limits the rest of the family's access to the hours between 8:00 a.m. and 8:00 p.m.

1. Open the Printers and Faxes dialog box and install a second instance of your printer.
2. Share this second instance.
3. Right-click the new instance's icon and select Properties from the menu that appears. The Properties dialog box for that instance appears.
4. Select the Advanced property sheet as shown in Figure 6.26.

Figure 6.26

Configuring a network printer's available hours of operation.

5. By default the Always Available option is selected providing 24-hour access. Select the Available From option. This enables the two entry fields to the right of the option. Using the up and down arrows select 08:00 a.m. in the first entry field and 08:00 p.m. in the second entry field.

6. Click OK.

That's it. Now anyone in the family who submits print jobs to the printer before or after its available hours of operation will have to wait until 08:00 in the morning. If this printer happens to be located in your bedroom, you'll now have a quiet and uninterrupted night's sleep.

Establishing a Printer Pool

If you have two printers that are of the same model and type or that just happen to use the same printer driver then you can combine them into a printer pool. Printer pools are useful when you find that your family does a lot of printing and sometimes one printer seems to get backed up with work while the other one remains idle.

Once you have set up a printer pool Windows XP will send each print job to the next available printer. Unfortunately there is no way to tell which printer will actually be assigned to print a given document so it helps a lot if the two printers are located beside one another.

The following procedure outlines the steps required to set up a printer pool.

1. Open the Printers and Faxes dialog box and install both printers if you have not already done so.

2. Set up both printers as shared network printers.

3. Right-click either of the two printers and select Properties from the menu that appears. The Properties dialog box for that printer appears.

4. Select the Ports property sheet.

5. Select the Enable Printer Pooling option at the bottom of the property sheet.

6. Next use your mouse to select the printers that will make up the printer pool as shown in Figure 6.27.

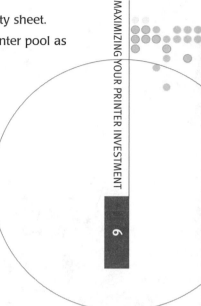

Figure 6.27

Configuring a network printer pool.

7. Click OK.

Controlling Printer Priority

If you want to ensure that the children's print jobs are always printed at a lower priority than your own, then you can do so by installing two logical instances of the same printer and assigning a different priority to each instance. Then set up a printer connection for the children that uses the instance of the printer that has the lower print priority.

The following procedure shows how you can set this up.

1. Open the Printers and Faxes dialog box and install a second logical instance of your printer.

2. Set up both instances as shared network printers.

3. Right-click the instance that you'll be using and select Properties from the menu that appears. The properties dialog box for that instance appears.

4. Select the Advanced property sheet.

5. By default the value assigned in the priority is set to 1. Change this setting to 99 as shown in Figure 6.28.

Figure 6.28

Changing the print priority assigned to a Windows XP printer.

INSTALLING THE WINDOWS XP FAX SERVICE

Windows XP treats faxing like a combination of printing and e-mail. First of all, when you install the Fax server Windows XP places an icon for your fax device in the Printers and Faxes dialog box. Then when you run the Windows Fax Console you can't help but realize just how much it is organized like Outlook Express.

Before you can use the Windows XP fax services you must perform the following actions.

- Install a dial-up modem that supports faxing
- Connect your modem to a telephone line
- Install the Fax Console

 Refer to Chapter 8, "Going Online," for information on installing a dial-up modem on Windows XP.

By default The Fax Console will automatically configure your fax modem, if it finds one, to send faxes. However, to set up your computer to receive faxes you are going to have to configure it yourself.

 Unfortunately you cannot share a fax device using Windows XP Home Edition. If you need to do this, consider installing Windows XP Professional on one of your home computers and using it to set up a shared a fax service.

The Fax Console

Windows XP does not install the Fax Console by default. You find it located on the Windows CD. You can install it using the following procedure.

1. Open the Windows XP Control panel and click Add or Remove Programs. The Add or Remove Programs dialog box appears.

2. Select Add/Remove Windows Components icon on the left side of the dialog box. The Windows Components Wizard appears.

3. Choose Fax Services from the list of component software and click Next.

4. Insert the Windows XP CD if prompted.

5. The wizard will take a few moments to copy all the files that make up the fax services to your hard drive. Click Finish when prompted.

6. Click Close when returned to the Add Remove Programs dialog box.

To run the Fax console click Start, All Programs, Accessories, Communications, Fax, and then Fax Console. The first time you load the Fax Console the Fax Configuration Wizard executes. Use the following procedure to configure your fax console.

1. Click Next when the Fax Configuration Wizard's Welcome screen appears.

2. You are prompted to supply a number of pieces of information, which will be used in creating a cover page for your faxes as shown in Figure 6.29. Supply your information and click Next.

Figure 6.29

Provide the Fax Configuration Wizard with the information that it needs to create your fax cover page.

3. Next you are prompted to select the device that will be used with the fax service (for example, your dial-up modem) as shown in Figure 6.30. Select the right device from the Please select the fax device drop-down list. By default the Enable Send option is selected. However, the Enable Receive option is not. To set up your fax

service to be able to receive faxes select Enable Receive and then choose either Manual Answer or the Automatically Answer option and configure the number of rings that the service should wait for before answering incoming calls. Click Next.

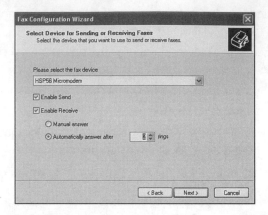

Figure 6.30

Configuring the fax server to send or receive faxes.

 techtv tip

If you have an extra phone line that you can dedicate to the fax service, select the Automatic Answer option. Otherwise, either select the Manual Answer option or set the number of rings for the automatic option high enough to give you a chance to answer the phone before your fax service kicks in.

4. Next you are prompted to type a Transmitting Subscriber Identification or TSID as shown in Figure 6.31. The TSID usually consists of your fax phone number and your name. Enter your TSID and click Next.

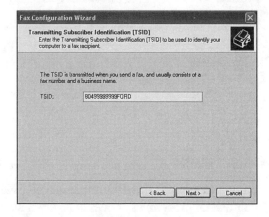

Figure 6.31

Enter your Transmitting Subscriber Identification Number.

5. This time you are prompted to type your Called Subscriber Identification or CSID information. The CSID also usually consists of your fax phone number and your name. Enter your TSID and click Next.

6. The next screen, shown in Figure 6.32, lets you specify what happens to incoming faxes. You can select any of the following options:

   - **Print It On**—Allows you to specify a printer on which your incoming fax will be immediately printed.

   - **Store a Copy in a Folder**—Lets you specify a folder where all incoming faxes will be stored.

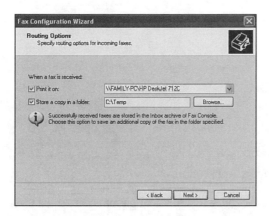

Figure 6.32

Tell the wizard what to do when an incoming fax is received.

Select whichever options you prefer and click Next.

7. The Fax Configuration Wizard next displays a summary of all the information that you have provided it. Verify that the information is correct and click Finish. The Fax Console now appears.

The Fax Console, shown in Figure 6.33, allows you to manage all your faxes. This Fax Console looks very much like Outlook Express. On the left side are folders for storing your faxes, which include

- **Incoming**—Stores a fax that is currently being received.
- **Inbox**—Stores copies of faxes that you have received.
- **Outbox**—Stores copies of faxes that you have scheduled to be sent.
- **Sent Items**—Stores copies of faxes that you have sent.

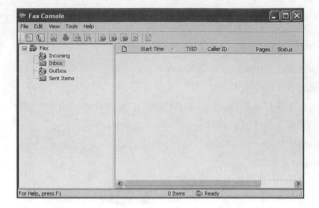

Figure 6.33

The Fax Console allows you to manage all your faxes.

Sending a Fax

You can send a fax using either of the following options.

- From the Fax Console
- From a Windows Application

Use the following procedure to send a single page fax from the Fax Console.

1. Open the Fax Console and select Send a Fax from the File menu.
2. The Send Fax Wizard appears. Click Next.
3. You are prompted to supply the name of the person to whom you are sending the fax and his or her fax number as shown in Figure 6.34. You also have the option of typing in multiple recipients.

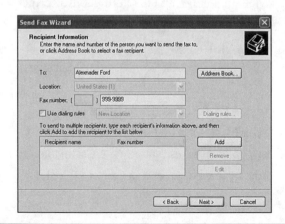

Figure 6.34

Provide the Send Fax Wizard with calling information.

4. The next dialog box, shown in Figure 6.35, lets you type a subject and a brief note. Click Next when you are done filling out the Subject line and Note fields.

Figure 6.35

Typing a fax subject and message.

5. You are then prompted as to how you want to send your fax as shown in Figure 6.36. To send the fax right away leave the default option of Now selected and click Next.

Figure 6.36

Telling the wizard to send your fax right away.

6. The Send Fax Wizard displays a summary of the information that is has collected from you. Click Finish. Your fax will now be sent.

To send a fax from an application, such as Microsoft Word, select Print from the File menu and then select your fax from the printer list. This will start the Send Fax Wizard, which will collect all the information that it needs to send your fax.

CHAPTER 7

BECOMING YOUR OWN NETWORK ADMINISTRATOR

Every network needs somebody to look after it and keep it running. This person is the network administrator. In this chapter you'll learn how to perform a number of important administrative tasks that will help you step up and prepare to perform this important role.

Here is what you'll learn:

- How to secure your wireless network
- How to set up user accounts for everyone in the family
- How to share a computer session without logging off
- About the Windows XP Security Event log
- How to establish disk quotas
- How to work securely
- How to work with event logs

ADMINISTERING YOUR 802.11X WIRELESS NETWORK

When first established, an 802.11x wireless network is relatively insecure. Its Internet gateway or access point can be administered by anybody who knows its default password. It is willing to allow any wireless client to connect to it and the network to which it is attached. In addition, all data is transmitted in the clear, meaning that no encryption or encoding scheme is employed to protect your data as it floats out over radio waves over which you have no control.

Fortunately wireless Internet gateways and access points provide you with ways to administer and secure your wireless home network. Administration of these devices is performed using the device's Web interface and an Internet browser. You can log in to these devices by opening your Internet browser, typing the IP address assigned to the device in the browser's URL field and pressing enter. You'll then be presented with some type of a login screen where you can type the device's default administrative account name and its password and press enter.

One of the first security measures that you will want to perform is to change the password assigned to the administrative account. This will prevent anyone else from making changes to the device's configuration. Another task that you'll want to perform right away is to type the MAC address of each of your computer network adapters into your wireless device's MAC table. You can then enable the restriction of unauthorized MAC addresses. This will prevent any computer whose MAC address has not been defined from communicating with your Internet gateway or access point. You may also be able to use MAC addresses to define which computers can access a wireless Internet gateway's shared Internet connection or print server.

In addition to the previous set of tasks, there are a number of other administrative tasks that you may also want to perform. These tasks include

- **Clone a MAC address**—If you already have an always-on high-speed Internet connection set up on one of your computers, then you will have already registered the MAC address of the network adapter installed in the computer with your ISP. Rather than contacting your ISP to unregister this MAC address and then register the MAC address of your Internet Gateway, you can simply clone the MAC address that you have already registered with your ISP onto your wireless gateway. This way your ISP will not be able to tell that you have switched your Internet connection from a PC to the Internet gateway.

- **Enable WEP security**—You can instruct your Internet gateway or access point to require that all data be transmitted in an encrypted format. You can choose between 64-bit or 128-bit shared key security. Some manufacturers of wireless devices have added support for 154-bit shared key security. Once enabled, all data that passes between your wireless devices will be encrypted so that only the intended recipient can decrypt or decode it.

- **Configure Virtual Service mapping**—You need to configure this option if you run an Internet service, such as a Web server, on one of your network computers. By default any unsolicited network traffic is automatically blocked by your Internet gateway. What this option does is allow you to define the TCP/IP ports that your Internet service uses and then associate them with a particular computer. This way if someone on the Internet tries, for example, to access your Web server, your Internet gateway will allow the request through and pass it on to the Web server for processing.

- **Set a timeout value for administrative connections**—Using this option you can define a period of time after which, if no activity has occurred during an administrative connection with the Internet gateway or access point, the session will be terminated. This way if you are in the process of configuring your Internet gateway or access point and you are interrupted and step away without closing your connection, it will automatically be closed after the amount of time, specified in the timeout interval, passes without any activity.

- **Enable remote administration**—By default a wireless Internet gateway can only be administered by a computer on the local network. However, you can use this feature to enable remote administration of your Internet gateway from over the Internet.

- **View the device's log**—Wireless Internet gateways and access points can be configured to maintain a log where they can record operational events as they occur. This feature allows you to review the device's log and make sure that everything is running smoothly.

- **Upgrade the device's firmware**—Wireless hardware vendors are constantly improving their products. This includes the software that runs on them. The software that runs on your Internet gateway or access point is known as firmware. Firmware updates usually contain problem fixes, performance enhancements, and security patches (which are designed to close security holes that have been discovered in the devices).

- **Backup configuration settings**—Once you have finished configuring your wireless Internet gateway or access point you should create a backup copy of your configuration settings. This way if something goes wrong, you'll be able to restore your configuration settings using this backup file rather than having to go back and perform the tedious chore of reconfiguring everything by hand.

OVERVIEW OF WINDOWS XP SECURITY ADMINISTRATION

Windows XP Home Edition provides greater security than Windows 98 and Me by providing an enforceable security model that requires anyone who wants to use a Windows XP computer to first log in and authenticate themselves using an assigned username and password. When set up this way you cannot simply click a Cancel button on the login dialog box, like you could on Windows 98 and Me systems and still have complete access to all the computer's resources.

NOTE

Although much more secure than Windows 98 and Me, Windows XP Home Edition is a great deal less secure than Windows XP Professional is. Windows XP Professional is capable of securing individual resources on a user-by-user or group-by-group basis at a very granular level. Windows XP Professional, however, costs a lot more than Windows XP Home Edition and is targeted at corporations where security is extremely important. Ease of use is usually a far more important consideration for the home user. Windows XP Home Edition, therefore, attempts to strike a balance between the home users need for ease of use and security.

Security for a home computer or network is often just a good lock on the front and back doors. Therefore, Windows XP Home Edition makes the implementation of username and passwords requirements for each logon session optional. However, it is strongly recommended that you assign each member of your family a username and password and require that they use it. This way you can:

- Prevent unauthorized access to any of your computers and the network
- Limit the amount of access granted to each family member
- Prevent small children from accidentally doing all sorts of damage to your computer and your files
- Review the Windows XP security log and discover who is using a computer and when
- Provide each member of your family with the ability to customize their desktops, preferences, and applications in a secure manner without interfering with each others' settings
- Use a technique called Fast User Switching that allows two or more people to share a computer without having to log off and close their open applications and files every time they want to take turns using the computer

Decentralized Administration

One of the features of a Windows home network is decentralized user account information. Each computer on a home network stores its own collection of user accounts in its own security database.

If you implement login and password requirements on each of your Windows XP computers, then you'll need to create a user account for each member of your family on each computer where you want to give them access, as depicted in Figure 7.1. This may sound like a lot of effort but you only have to do this once and if you are only going to have a handful of user accounts on a few computers, it should not take you very long at all to get it all set up.

For step-by-step instructions in creating new user accounts read "Account Management" on page xx (this chapter).

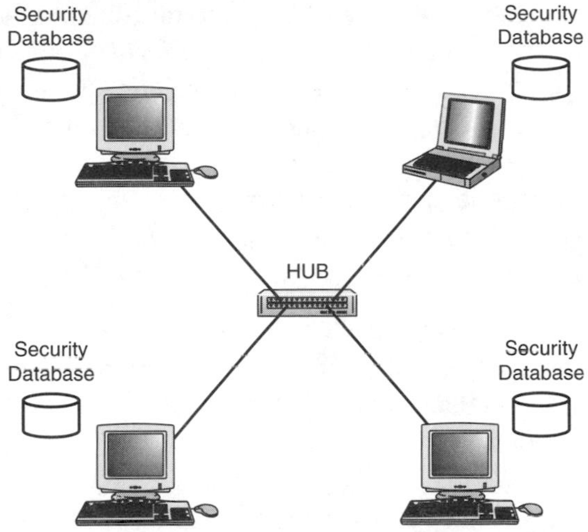

Figure 7.1

Each Windows XP computer maintains its own collection of user accounts.

Different Types of User Accounts

During the installation of Windows XP Home Edition a new user account known as the Owner account is created. This account has complete control over a computer and all its resources. In addition, Windows XP also creates a special Guest account that has very limited capabilities. The Guest account provides a means for allowing people who do not have a user account on the computer to still be able to access it and perform tasks such as accessing the Internet without being able to make changes to the computer or its configuration. By default Windows XP Home Edition disables the Guest account based on the assumption that you'll set up a user account for each user. However, you can enable it if you want to. You are also given a chance to create new administrative user accounts during the installation of the operating system.

Windows XP Home Edition automatically configures itself to require that each user identify themselves when accessing the computer. If you decide not to create additional user accounts during the installation of Windows XP Home Edition, the operating system will configure itself to automatically start up using the Owner account every time you turn on your computer. This means that whoever turns on the computer has the ability to perform any of the following actions:

- Make system configuration changes
- Delete or modify any file
- Edit the Windows registry database
- Create, modify, and delete user accounts
- Install and uninstall applications

When a computer is shared this way all users of the computer will also share the same configuration settings. This means that if one person changes the color scheme or background, then it will change for everyone. If two people in the family have strong feelings about the way that these settings or others like them should be set up, this can lead to a lot of bickering. The resolution to this dilemma is to assign everybody his or her own user account. This way when they log in to Windows XP Home Edition any changes that they make to the background, color scheme, desktop, and so on, will only affect themselves because Windows XP will store the changes in a profile unique to the individual.

If you choose not to create additional computer accounts when you first install Windows XP Home Edition, you can always create them later from the User Accounts dialog box, which will be covered in a little while. From this dialog box you'll be able to add, delete, and modify user accounts.

Assigning Different Levels of Access

If you decided to set up additional user accounts when you installed Windows XP Home Edition, then each of these accounts was assigned administrative level permissions. What this means is that each user that you assign one of these accounts to will have complete control over the computer where the account was created. This may be fine for mom and dad but may be more authority than you intended to provide to the rest of the family. If this is the case, you can go back and change the level of permission assigned to the accounts.

One advantage to waiting until after the installation of the operating system to create user accounts is that you'll have greater control over how the accounts are created. One difference is the ability to assign an account to a different group. Groups have different levels of permissions, which restrict what they can and cannot do. Windows XP user accounts automatically inherit all the permissions granted by the group to which they belong. Windows XP Home Edition allows you to assign a new user account to either of the following groups.

- **Computer Administrator**—Members of this group have complete control over a computer including the ability to modify system configuration, install new applications, and manage user accounts.
- **Limited**—Members of this group can perform most common operations such as running applications, editing files, and customizing their own configuration settings. However, user accounts that belong to this group cannot modify system settings and manage other user accounts. In addition, members of this group will not be able to install applications that require administrative permissions.

Technically the Guest account represents a third type of group account. However, there can only be one Guest account on a Windows XP computer. It can be disabled to prevent its use but it cannot be deleted. Therefore, it's not possible to create a new Guest account.

techtv tip

It's good practice that you assign a second user account to anyone whom you plan to give an administrative level account to. The second account should be assigned to the Limited group and should be used most of the time. This way a person is limited in the kind of damage that they might accidentally cause. For example, suppose a member of the family accidentally downloads a virus. The amount of damage that the virus can do is limited to the level of access that the account the person who downloaded has. Therefore, it is best to use an account with limited permission for most of your work.

USER ADMINISTRATION AND LOGON MANAGEMENT

To add security to your computer or home network you'll want to assign each user his or her own user account and password. This way, each member of the family can be uniquely identified. In addition, by assigning individual user accounts you can place limits on some of the things that individual members can do, especially your children.

Another important part of user administration is the configuration of the login process. This will determine how everyone logs in to the computer and therefore on to your home network. You'll need to think about this one a bit and decide whether you want to make things easy and fast or whether to make them a little more secure.

Working with User Accounts

You can add, delete, and modify user accounts on Windows XP at any time from the User Accounts dialog box, shown in Figure 7.2, as long as you have logged on using a user account that is a member of the Computer Administrator group.

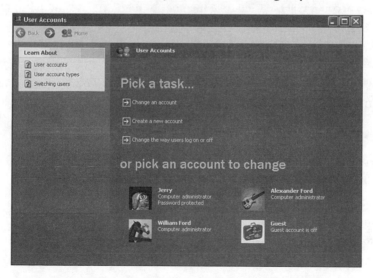

Figure 7.2

All user account administration is performed on Windows XP Home Edition from the User Accounts dialog box.

> **NOTE** If you have not yet set up any accounts, then Windows XP Home Edition will automatically log you on using the Owner account that is a member of the Computer Administrator group giving you all the permissions that you'll require to create new accounts.

The following procedure shows how to open the User Accounts dialog box.

1. Click Start and then Control Panel. The Windows XP Control Panel opens.

2. Click the User Accounts icon or link. The User Accounts dialog box appears.

The User Accounts dialog box is divided into two sections. The top section contains the following three links.

- **Change an Account**—Allows you to modify a number of user account settings including the account name, icon, and type.

- **Create a New Account**—Allows you to create a new account and assign it administrative or limited privileges.

- **Change the Way Users Log On or Off**—Allows you to enable or disable Fast User Switching and the Windows XP Welcome screen.

The bottom section displays a list of accounts defined on the computer. What you will see here the first time that you open the User Accounts dialog box depends on whether or not you created any new user accounts when you first installed Windows XP Home Edition. If you did not create any new accounts, you'll see icons for the Owner and Guest accounts. The Owner account will be listed as a member of the Computer Administrator Group and the Guest account will be listed as being off. If you created at least one user account during the install process, then you'll see each account that you define and the Guest account. The Owner account, even though it still exists, will not be visible.

Each user account is listed by username. The account's group membership is also displayed. In addition, any account with a password is listed as Password protected.

Account Management

You can create a new user account by clicking the Create a New Account option on the User Accounts dialog box and following the procedure outlined next.

1. Open the User Accounts dialog box and click the Create a New Account link. The screen shown in Figure 7.3 will appear.

2. Type a name in the Type a Name in the New Account field and click Next. (The name can be up to 20 characters long.) The screen shown in Figure 7.4 appears.

3. You can assign the new account to either of the following groups:
   - Computer administrator
   - Limited

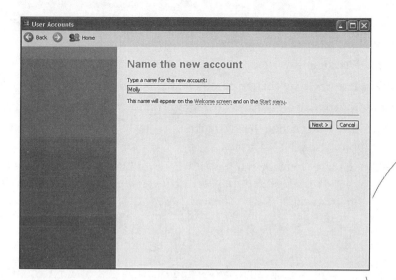

Figure 7.3

The first step in creating a new user account is to type a unique name for the account.

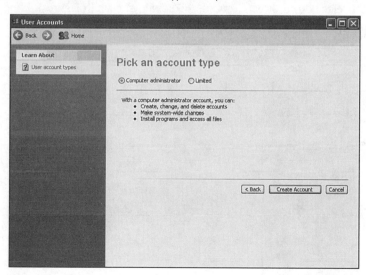

Figure 7.4

You can assign new accounts to either the Computer administrator or Limited groups.

Select the group to which you want to assign to the account and click Create Account. The main User Accounts dialog box reappears and you'll see the new account. A randomly assigned icon will also be assigned to the account.

Windows XP Home Edition allows you to modify a number of user account attributes on existing accounts. The attributes include

- **Name**—The name assigned to the user account.
- **Password**—You may change or remove the password associated with the account.
- **Icon**—You may select a different graphic icon to be associated with the account.
- **Type**—You may change the account group membership to either the Computer Administrator or Limited groups.
- **.NET Passport**—You may run the .NET Password Wizard to set up a .NET Passport. This enables Microsoft to track you whenever you visit its site or any Web site that uses the Microsoft Password Service.

The following procedure outlines the steps involved in Making Changes to an Existing User Account.

1. Open the User Accounts dialog box and click the Change an Account link.
2. A list of all user accounts (except for the Owner account) appears. Select the account that you want to modify and click Next.
3. If you selected the Guest account, the screen shown in Figure 7.5 appears. Click Turn On the Guest Account to enable it.

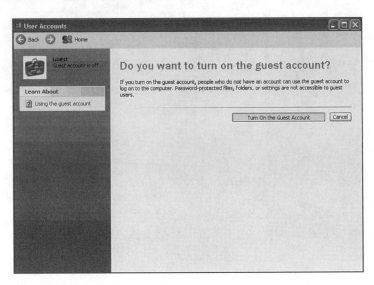

Figure 7.5

By default the Guest account is disabled but you can change this at any time.

The Guest account is different from all other accounts. If you select it again, the only options that you will see are the Change the picture and the Turn off the Guest account options.

4. If you selected any account other than the Guest account, a screen similar to the one shown in Figure 7.6 will appear.

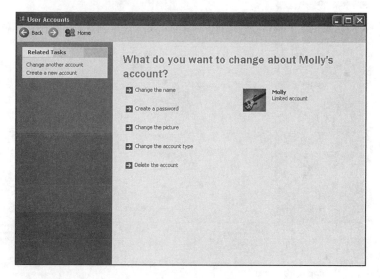

Figure 7.6

Changing the attributes of a typical user account.

5. Depending on the account that has been selected, any of the following options may be listed:
   - Change the Name
   - Create a Password
   - Change the Password
   - Remove the Password
   - Change the Picture
   - Change the Account Type
   - Delete the Account

6. If you selected the Change the Name option, then a screen similar to the one shown in Figure 7.7 appears. Type a new name for the user account in the field provided and then click Change Name.

7. If you selected the Create a Password option, then a screen similar to the one shown in Figure 7.8 appears. Type the new password twice in the fields provided. Alternatively, type a message that will remind the user of the password in case he or she forgets it and then click Change Password.

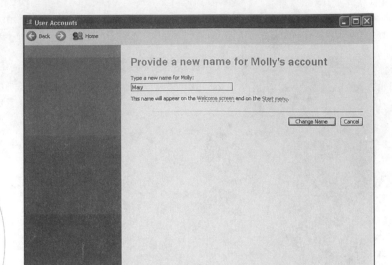

Figure 7.7

Changing a Windows XP computer's name.

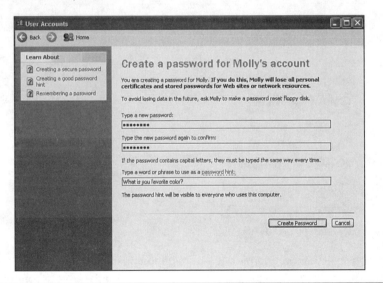

Figure 7.8

Assigning a password to a user account.

techtv tip

If you are going to go through the trouble of implementing passwords, there are a few good rules that you should follow. First of all make your passwords strong. A strong password is one that is at least eight characters long and contains a combination of lowercase and uppercase letters, numbers, and special characters. Also, never use common words or names that are easily guessed. Second, change your password from time to time. Changing your password once a month is an adequate interval to maintain security in most environments. This way if someone ever does guess your password, they won't be able to use it for long. Finally don't make them so difficult to remember that you end up deleting them.

8. If you select the Change the Password option, then a screen similar to the one shown in Figure 7.9 appears. Type the new password twice in the fields provided. Alternatively, type a message that will remind the user of the password in case he or she forgets and then click Change Password.

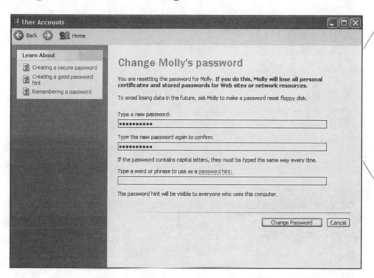

Figure 7.9

Changing the password assigned to a user account.

9. If you select the Remove the Password option, then a screen similar to the one shown in Figure 7.10 appears. Click Remove Password to delete the password assigned to the user account.

 If you are deleting your own password, then you will be prompted to type your password before you can delete it.

10. If you select the Change the Picture option, then a screen similar to the one shown in Figure 7.11 appears. Select a new icon from the list of available icons and click Change Picture. Alternatively click Browse for more pictures and specify a custom picture before clicking the Change Picture option.

Figure 7.10

Deleting a user account's password.

Figure 7.11

Changing the icon associated with a user account.

11. If you select the Change the Account Type option, then a screen similar to the one shown in Figure 7.12 appears. Select either Computer Administrator or Limited and click Change Account Type.

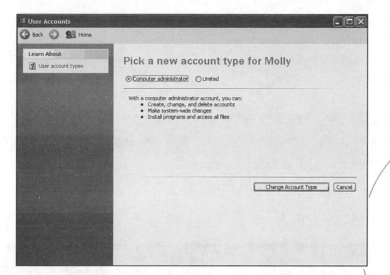

Figure 7.12

Changing an account's group membership.

12. If you select the Delete the Account option, then a screen similar to the one shown in Figure 7.13 appears. You have two options to choose from as outlined here:

- **Keep Files**—Tells Windows XP to save copies of the user's desktop files and any files in the user's My Documents folder before deleting the user account.

- **Delete Files**—Deletes the user account and any desktop files or files stored in the My Documents folder associated with the user account.

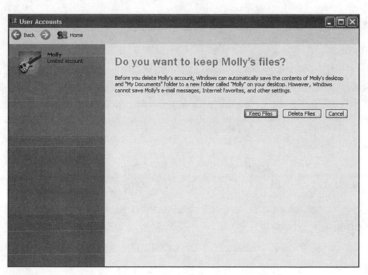

Figure 7.13

Deleting a user account.

You are then prompted to confirm the deletion of the user account by clicking Delete Account.

13. Close the User Accounts dialog box after you have finished making all your changes.

Setting Up the Windows XP Login Screen

Windows XP provided two different ways to control how to start a new session. They are

- The Windows XP Welcome Screen
- The Classic Windows Login Screen

By default the Windows XP Welcome Screen, shown in Figure 7.14, is enabled.

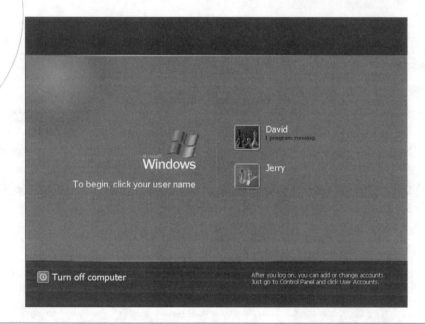

Figure 7.14

The Windows XP Welcome Screen.

However, if you like the more traditional Windows login screen, you can enable that option instead as outlined in the following procedure:

1. Click the User Accounts icon on the Windows XP Control Panel. The User Accounts dialog box appears.

2. Click Change the Way Users Log On or Off. The screen shown in Figure 7.15 appears.

3. To enable the Windows XP Welcome screen select the Use the Welcome Screen option and click Apply options. To use the classic Windows login dialog box clear the Use the Welcome Screen option and click Apply options.

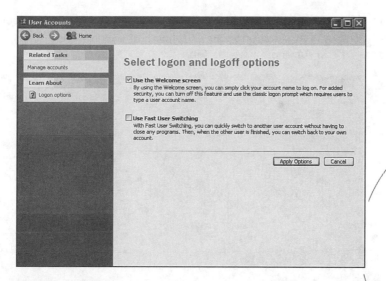

Figure 7.15

Setting up how users will log in to Windows XP.

If you choose to use the classic Windows login dialog box, then you'll have to type both your logon ID and password (if your account has one) in order to log on.

If you want to make your computer more secure, then make sure that every user account has a password and that the classic Windows login dialog box is being used. This will force every user of the computer to type both his or her username and password in order to access the computer. Unlike the Windows XP Welcome Screen, you won't be able to select your username using the classic option.

If you use the classic Windows logon dialog box, then you will also be able to log in using the Owner account. You cannot do this from the Windows XP Welcome screen because an icon for the Owner account is not listed there unless no other user accounts have been created.

Setting Up Fast User Switching

Windows XP introduces a new way to start a session with your computer, called Fast User Switching. Fast User Switching allows two or more people who share a computer to quickly jump between their sessions without having to log off. This way if you are using the computer and someone else needs it for just a minute, you don't have to shut down all your applications and save and close your files. Instead you can just allow that person to switch over to a new session, leaving all your programs and data running and stored safely in memory. When that user is done you simply switch back and keep going.

Fast User Switching is enabled by default when Windows XP Home Edition is installed. Figure 7.16, shows how Windows XP looks when Fast User Switching is enabled and waiting for someone to start up a new session.

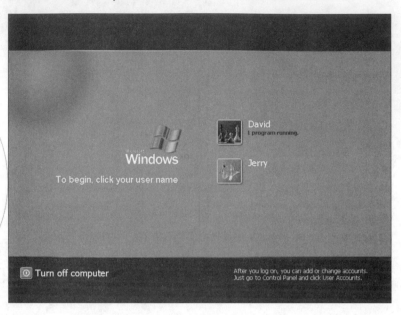

Figure 7.16

Fast User Switching makes sharing a computer with multiple family members a lot more convenient.

To check the status of Fast User Switching on your computer click the Change the Way Users Log Off option on the User Accounts dialog box. This opens the screen shown in Figure 7.17.

The Fast User Switching option controls whether or not Fast User Switching is enabled on your computer. When enabled, you'll see the Switch User option added to the Log Off Windows dialog box as shown in Figure 7.18.

ESTABLISHING QUOTAS

Anytime that you share a disk drive or folder on your computer with other users you open the drive up to the possibility of abuse. There is always the possibility that you will log on one day and find that your computer's hard drive is almost full.

A full disk drive can significantly slow your system down. Even worse, it can cause your computer to become inoperable. You might want to consider making the establishment of a disk quota a normal part of your user account management process. A disk quota is a preset limit placed on the amount of space that a user may use on a computer.

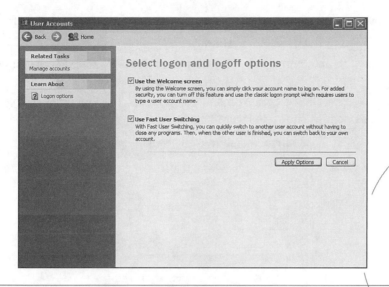

Figure 7.17

Managing Fast User Switching.

Figure 7.18

Fast User Switching lets you quickly share your computer.

By applying a disk quota to a disk drive you are able to limit the total amount of space that users are allowed to consume for personal storage thus protecting the integrity and security of your computer. Windows XP can only apply quotas to disk drives that have been formatted using NTFS. Therefore, you won't be able to apply quotas to your FAT32 partitions. NTFS is a more advanced file system with many benefits, not the least of which is a disk quota. Unless you have a specific reason to use FAT, it is strongly recommended that you use NTFS as the file system on all your disk drives.

In addition to disk quotas, the NTFS file system provides a number of services that FAT32 cannot. This includes the ability to apply advanced security permissions to protect files and folders. It also includes the ability to encrypt stored data and to create a searchable index of all the information stored on your local hard drive thus speeding up searches.

The following procedure explains how to enable a disk quota on an NTFS drive that affects all users.

1. Click Start and then left-click My Computer. The My Computer dialog box appears.

2. Right-click the disk drive to which you want to apply a disk quota and select Properties from the Context menu that appears. The Properties dialog box for the drive opens as shown in Figure 7.19.

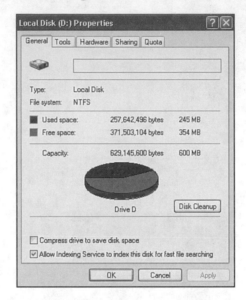

Figure 7.19

The Properties dialog box belonging to a local hard drive.

3. Select the Quota property sheet.

4. By default Windows XP does not enforce any disk quota settings. To enable disk quota management, select Enable quota management. This enables the rest of the fields on the property sheet as shown in Figure 7.20.

5. Select Deny Disk Space to Users Exceeding Quota Limit to prevent users from consuming more than their allotted amount of storage space. If you leave this option cleared, then users will still be able to store new files even after their quota has been exceeded.

6. The Do Not Limit Disk Usage option disabled quotas. Select the Limit Disk Space to option and type the amount of space that you want to limit each user to. Then select the appropriate unit of storage from the drop-down list.

7. To set a warning level type a value in the Set Warning Level to field and set its unit of storage from the provided drop-down list.

8. Enable the Log Event When Users Exceed Their Quota Limit option to tell Windows XP to create a log event when a user attempts to exceed his or her storage quota.

BECOMING YOUR OWN NETWORK ADMINISTRATOR

Figure 7.20

Enabling disk quotas.

9. Enable the Log Event When a User Exceeds Their Warning Level option to tell Windows XP to create a log entry when a user consumes more space than the value set in the warning field.

10. Click OK. A disk Quota prompt will appear stating that it may take several minutes for Windows XP to rescan the drive and complete the establishment of the quota value.

11. Click OK.

Some users may need more storage space than others. After setting up a disk quota for all the users on the computer you can go back and override the quota for specified individual user accounts using the following procedure.

The Built-in Administrators group is exempted from the disk quota setting.

1. Click the Quota Entries button on the Quota property sheet for the drive where the quota has been set up. The Quota Entries dialog box for the drive appears as shown in Figure 7.21.

2. A list of all user accounts on the computer will appear showing the amount of disk space that they are currently using, their current quota, and warning levels and the percent used. Select an account and then click the Properties option on the Quota menu. The Quota Setting For dialog box appears as shown in Figure 7.22.

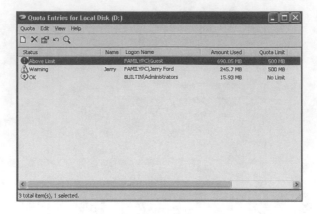

Figure 7.21

Overriding the disk quota for specific user accounts.

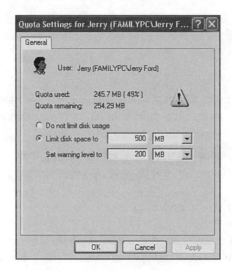

Figure 7.22

Changing a specific user account's quota.

3. Type a new quota limit in the Limit Disk Space to field. In addition you can alter the warning level as well.

4. Click OK.

WORKING SECURELY

There are a number of things that you and your family can do that will significantly add to the security of your home network. These tasks include

- Logging off whenever you are done working
- Shutting down your computer when it will not be used for long periods of time
- Setting up password protected screen savers

Logging Off When You Are Done

It's best to always log off whenever you are done working on your computer. Fast User Switching allows you to stay logged on while still allowing other family members to log on and use the computer. However, when you stay logged on this way you use up a portion of the computer's memory. Logging off frees up memory and improves the computer's performance.

Logging off does not mean that you have to shut down your computer. If others in the family share your computer, it can be very inconvenient to have to wait for it to power on and start up before you can begin working. Logging off, on the other hand, leaves the computer ready to go for the next person.

There are two convenient ways to log off of Windows XP. The easiest way is from the Start menu as outlined in the following procedure.

1. Click Start and select Log Off. The Log Off Windows dialog box appears.
2. Click Log Off to close all your open applications and files.
3. Your session ends and Windows XP displays Its Welcome screen.

Alternatively, you can log off using the Windows XP Task Manager as outlined here.

1. Press CTRL+ALT+DEL. The Windows Task Manager dialog box opens.
2. Click Shutdown and select the Log Off option.
3. Your session ends and Windows XP displays Its Welcome screen.

Shutting Down and Other Alternatives

If your computer is not going to be used for a while, then you should power it off. This protects the computer from possible damage that can occur during unexpected power outages. In addition, powering down the computer saves energy. Windows XP also provides the following energy saving options that allow you to temporarily place your computer in a near powered-off state.

- Stand By
- Hibernation

Windows XP Home Edition provides a number of options for shutting down or simulating a system shutdown. These options are available on the Windows XP Turn Off Computer dialog box.

You can set up your computer to go into Hibernation mode instead of Stand By. Hibernation works in much the same way as Stand By except that it first saves all your work to disk storage before placing the computer into a reduced power state. You can replace the Stand By option with a Hibernation option by opening the Windows XP Control Panel, clicking Performance and Maintenance and then selecting Power Options. This opens the Power Options Properties dialog box from which you can select the Hibernate property sheet and select the Enable Hibernation option.

To access Windows XP's Turn Off Computer dialog box, shown in Figure 7.23, click Start and select Turn Off Computer.

Figure 7.23

The Windows XP Turn Off Computer dialog box is accessed from the Start menu.

Table 7.1 outlines each of the options available on this dialog box.

TABLE 7.1—WINDOWS XP COMPUTER SHUTDOWN OPTIONS

Options	Description
Stand By	Places the computer in a reduced state of power consumption. Active programs and data are saved in memory and restored when you press a key or move the mouse.
Turn Off	Closes all active programs and files and prepares the computer to be powered off.
Restart	Closes all active programs and files and restarts the computer.
Cancel	Tells Windows XP to close the Turn Off Computer dialog box.

techtv tip

Think about saving all your files before placing your computer into Stand By mode. If a power interruption should occur before you return and resume working, you'll lose any unsaved work.

Password-Protected Screen Savers

There was a time that screen savers performed a very useful purpose because older monitors would burn in images that were left displayed too long. By starting up a screen saver to keep the screen active the monitor would be protected.

Over time monitor technology has improved and screen savers are no longer needed to protect monitors. However, they still retain a certain entertainment value. In addition, they can serve another useful purpose, strengthening Windows security.

Windows XP lets you set up a screen saver so that it automatically starts up after a pre-determined period of time. Then if you walk away from your computer and forget to come back, your screen saver will automatically start up. Windows XP also lets you configure your screen saver to require that you type in your password (if you have one) when you return in order to regain access to the computer. If you have little ones running around the house who love to play with the computer when mommy and daddy are not looking, then this feature can be a lifesaver.

The following procedure demonstrates how to set up a Windows XP screen saver and turn on password protection.

1. Right-click an open area of the Windows XP desktop and select Properties from the Context menu that appears. The Display Properties dialog box appears.

2. Click the Screen Saver property sheet as shown in Figure 7.24.

Figure 7.24

Setting up a Windows XP screen saver.

3. Select a screen saver from the drop-down list in the Screen saver section of the property sheet.

4. Use the up and down arrows to the right of the Wait field just below the drop-down list to specify the amount of time that Windows XP should wait for no user activity to occur before starting the screen saver.

5. Select the On Resume, Display Welcome Screen option to force Windows XP to prompt you to identify yourself and type your password.

6. Click OK.

The next time you leave your computer for longer than the amount of time that you applied to your screen saver, Windows XP will start your screen saver. When you later press a keyboard key or move your mouse Windows XP will display the Welcome screen and require you to identify yourself. Of course, if your user account does not have a password then the screen saver isn't of much help as far as security is concerned.

FORGETTING YOUR PASSWORD

With as many things as there are in life to keep track of, it's almost certain that somewhere along the line you or someone in your family is going to forget his or her password, especially if he or she is away from the computer for a while. A good way to help prevent this from happening is to supply Windows XP with a hint that it can use to remind you of your password should you forget.

To review your hint the next time that you log on to Windows XP click the blue question mark to the right of the password field that appears and Windows XP will display your hint as shown in Figure 7.25. Once you remember your password all that you have to do is type it in.

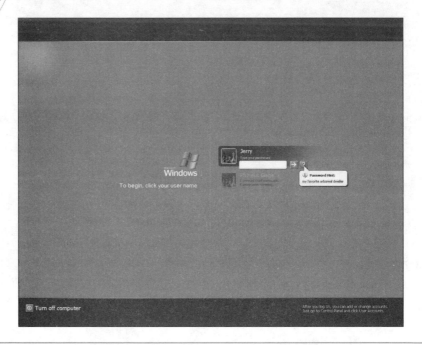

Figure 7.25

Using a hint to remember your Windows XP password.

WORKING WITH EVENTS LOGS

From time to time things happen on a computer that can be difficult to explain. Because a lot of things happen under the covers in Windows XP it's often difficult to figure out where problems lie. Windows XP Home Edition provides you with information by logging events into three different logs that you can view using a built-in utility known as the Event Viewer Console.

The three Windows XP event logs are

- **System log**—Stores records of events related to the operation of Windows XP. For example, the System log records information when a service fails to start or when a hardware component or its software driver produces an error.
- **Security log**—Stores events related to Windows XP security such as when users log on and log off the computer.
- **Application log**—Stores events that are generated by your application programs. The kinds of events recorded in this log depend on your applications.

Not all Windows applications record events in the Applications log. For example, if you are running an old 16-bit version of Microsoft Office, then you will never see any events from this application because it does not know how to generate a log event. Office 2000 on the other hand can record its event information to the Application log.

You can access the Windows XP Home Edition's Event Viewer Console using the following procedure.

1. Open the Windows XP Control Panel.
2. Click the Performance and Maintenance link.
3. Click Administrative Tools.
4. Double-click the Event Viewer icon. The Event Viewer Console opens as shown in Figure 7.26.

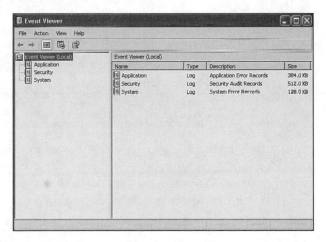

Figure 7.26

Opening the Windows XP Event Viewer Console.

The Event Viewer Console contains just three logs that are listed in a tree-like view. To view the contents of a particular log click it. Its contents will then appear in the right pane. Information about events is organized into columns. These columns include

- **Type**—The type of event that has occurred.
- **Date**—The date that the event occurred.
- **Time**—The time that the event occurred.
- **Source**—The component that caused the error.
- **Category**—The category, if any, associated with the event. Examples include Logon/Logoff and System Event.
- **Event**—The Windows XP event number that describes the event.
- **User**—The user that caused the event (if applicable).
- **Computer**—The computer where the event occurred.

Windows XP Home Edition classifies every event. It also identifies the event's classification by placing a graphic icon in the Type field of the event log. This allows you to quickly scan the log for certain types of events. For example, Table 7.2 outlines the types of events that you will find in the Application and System logs and Table 7.3 lists the types of events found in the Security log.

TABLE 7.2—APPLICATION AND SYSTEM EVENT TYPES

Type	Icon	Description
Information	White i	Non-critical events
Warning	Yellow !	Event that may indicate a possible problem
Error	Red X	A serious event that indicates a failure

TABLE 7.3—SECURITY EVENT TYPES

Type	Icon	Description
Success Audit	Key	Indicates a successful event such as a successful logon
Failure Audit	Lock	Indicates a failure event such as a failed login

From a security perspective, the log that you are going to want to keep an eye on is the Security log. Unlike Windows XP Professional, where you have granular control over the types of information recorded to the system logs, Windows XP Home Edition's security logging is pre-configured. Figure 7.27 demonstrates the contents of a typical Security log.

You can view the details of any particular event by double-clicking it. For example, the event displayed in Figure 7.28 shows the date and time that a user whose account name is Jerry Ford logged on the computer and that the logon was successful. Other types of information that you may find in the log include

- The date and time that individuals log on and off of the computer
- Information about failed logon attempts
- Information about activity regarding setting, changing, and deleting passwords
- Information about programs or services that attempt to register with the Windows XP
- Information about the changing of the system time
- Information regarding the management or activity of the Guest account
- Information about user account creation, modification, and deletion

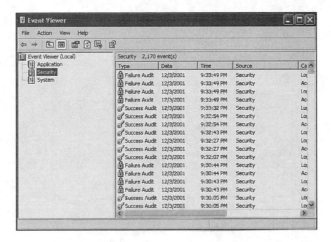

Figure 7.27

View security log events.

Figure 7.28

Examining a typical security log event.

CHAPTER 8

GOING ONLINE

Home networks allow everyone in your family to share printers and disk storage. They can also be used to share a connection to the Internet. By sharing a single Internet connection, everyone in the house is able to surf the World Wide Web (using a single Internet account) at the same time. This saves you the cost of paying for multiple Internet connections and modems. This chapter will discuss how to set up a shared Internet connection and how to keep your home network safe from intruders once it has been connected to the Internet.

Here is what you'll learn:

- How to work with cable and DSL connections
- How to establish a dial-up Internet connection
- How to install and configure Internet Connection Sharing
- How to set up an Internet gateway
- How to protect your home network with personal firewalls

HIGH-SPEED ALWAYS-ON CABLE AND DSL CONNECTIONS

Internet connectivity has become an essential component of modern life. For today's home user there is no better way to get connected than a high speed, always-on cable or DSL Internet connection. These connections usually provide connection speeds between 300–500Kbps and offer performance that is considerably better than traditional dial-up Internet access. Because cable and DSL provide an always-on connection, there is no waiting, just turn your computer on and you can start surfing.

Registering with a Cable or DSL ISP

Always-on high-speed Internet access can be delivered to your home by either your cable or telephone company. Cable companies have exclusive territories. Therefore, if your cable company does not provide cable Internet access in your area, then you are out of luck. Digital Subscriber Line or DSL access depends on whether or not your local telephone company offers the service, although, in some cases, you'll actually end up leasing your DSL access from a third-party ISP that has made arrangements with your local telephone company.

Finding a DSL provider requires a little work. One option that you have is to call your local telephone company and see if it provides the service and if it can recommend any local ISPs. Another option is to start calling local ISPs and see if any of them offer the service. Another option is to check out one of the following sites on the Internet, which provides a list of DSL ISPs.

- www.getconnected.com
- www.thelist.com

There are a number of different variations of DSL services. However, of these, one is designed specifically to fulfill the needs of home users and small businesses. This version of DSL is known as Asynchronous Digital Subscriber Line or ADSL and is the type of DSL service that ISPs provide to home users.

You can expect to pay somewhere between $30–50 per month for cable or DSL access and to receive unlimited Internet access, technical support, and a cable or DSL modem as part of the deal.

Both cable and DSL Internet connections require their own special kind of modem. Cable and DSL ISPs will lease you a modem as part of your monthly subscription fee for around $10 a month. This fee is sometimes built into their $30–50 monthly fee. If you sign up for a DSL connection, then you'll have to lease your modem because most of the systems in place that provide DSL service are designed to work with modems made by specific manufacturers and will differ depending on where you live. This makes it nearly impossible to swap one DSL modem for another.

NOTE Many ISPs will also allow you to purchase your modem from them rather than rent it for a monthly fee. To determine if this is a good option, you will need to consider the monthly rental fee and the time you are likely to use the service. If the rental fee is $10 per month and the purchase price is $150, the device will have paid for itself in 15 months. Just keep in mind that if you purchase a modem, it may only be useful with the particular service your ISP provides.

Cable subscribers often have the option of purchasing their own cable modem. A cable modem standard called DOCSIS was developed in 1998. It is slowly being implemented by most of the cable industry. A company named CableLabs tests and certifies modems to ensure that they comply with this standard. If your local cable company supports this standard, then you probably have the option of leasing or purchasing your own cable modem. Just make sure that if you decide to purchase one, that it has been labeled as CableLabs Certified.

Cable and DSL modems provide equivalent features. Their primary difference is that cable modems provide a connection for cable and DSL modems provide a connection to your telephone outlet. Both connect directly to either a computer or home network. To connect directly to a computer you just use an RJ-45 twisted-pair cable to connect the modem to your computer's Ethernet network adapter (which will be supplied by your ISP if you don't already have one). To connect to a home network just use the same cable to plug the modem into your network Internet gateway or hub. New modems are beginning to appear that provide the option of connecting to your computer using a USB connection. However, you'll need to stick with the Ethernet connection when connecting the modem directly to your home network.

 For more information about Ethernet and Ethernet network connections, refer to "Ethernet Hardware" in Chapter 2.

The Trouble with Always-on Internet Access

Cable and DSL ISPs provide always-on high-speed Internet access. *Always on* means that any time your computer is running you are connected to the Internet. This stands out in stark contrast to traditional dial-up access where your computer is connected to the Internet only when you start a dial-up session and ends when you either close the session or it times out.

The longer that you are connected to the Internet the greater your exposure. This exposure comes in the form of individuals, sometimes referred to as hackers, which search the Internet looking for computer systems to break into. Sometimes these people just want to have a little fun and will simply just poke around your computer to see what they can do. Other times they may play a little joke on you by leaving you a funny message saying that they were there. However, other less scrupulous visitors may instead be looking for your Quicken or Microsoft money files. They may also try to remotely take over your computer

and use it and hundreds or even thousands of other computers that they have breached to launch a distributed denial-of-service attack on a Web site server in an effort to cripple it by bombarding it with more requests than it can handle.

Regardless of his or her intentions, you do not want anyone to be able to access your computer this way. The IP address that cable and DSL ISPs assigned to their customers tend to remain unchanged over long periods of time, meaning that the IP address assigned to your computer is likely to be the same month after month. This means that it is easy for an intruder that has targeted your computers to come back and visit again and again. This makes cable and DSL Internet connections a lot more vulnerable than dial-up connections, whose IP addresses change every time a new Internet session is established.

So while cable and DSL Internet access is fast and convenient, it is also vulnerable. Fortunately there are ways to combat this vulnerability and the best way is to use a personal firewall. Personal firewalls are software applications or hardware devices that are designed to keep intruders out of your computer without restricting your ability to surf the Internet.

If you are going to connect your home network to the Internet using a shared always-on high-speed Internet connection, then you absolutely must protect yourself with a personal firewall.

 The different types of personal firewalls and their capabilities are described later in this chapter in "Protecting Your Home Network with a Personal Firewall" on page 206.

INSTALLING YOUR HIGH-SPEED INTERNET CONNECTION

Setting up an always-on high-speed Internet connection is a lot like setting up a regular Ethernet network client connection. First you must install your cable or DSL modem using the installation instructions that came with it. Then you use a CAT-5 twisted-pair cable to connect your modem to one of your computers or to your Internet gateway.

Most cable and DSL ISPs only allow a single computer to use a connection. They do this by blocking all computers that try to connect from your home that you have not registered with them. One of the steps involved in setting up your connection is to call your ISP and register the MAC address of your cable or DSL modem and the network adapter used by your computer. This works fine for one computer and will also support shared Internet access if that computer is set up to share its Internet connection. A better way to share your Internet connection with all computers on a wireless home network is to connect the modem to your wireless Internet gateway and let it provide the shared access as depicted in Figure 8.1. Both ICS and an Internet gateway provide shared Internet access for your entire home network by routing all network traffic through themselves.

Figure 8.1

Sharing a single Internet connection with all the computers on your home network.

The first step in setting up shared Internet access using a cable of DSL connection is to set up your modem. To keep things simple for now, let's focus on the steps required to set up a connection between the modem and a single computer as depicted in Figure 8.2. Then, in "Setting Up Shared Internet Access," later in this chapter you'll see how to share the Internet connection using ICS as well as how to reconfigure it to work with an Internet gateway.

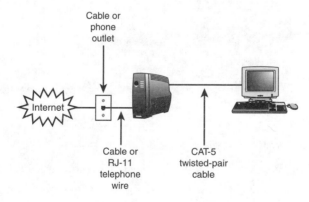

Figure 8.2

Setting up your cable or DSL modem to work with a single computer.

The process of setting up high-speed Internet access for a computer is outlined here.

- Install a network adapter in the computer.
- Connect the modem to the computer and to its cable or DSL connection and then attach its power supply.

- Run the Installation Wizard supplied with the modem.
- Call your ISP and register the MAC addresses of your cable modem and computer's network adapter.

To see how to install and configure a network adapter refer to Chapter 2, "Getting Your Hands Dirty: Assembling Your Network Hardware," and Chapter 3, "The Softer Side of Network Setup."

The process of running the modem's Installation Wizard or following its installation instructions will vary from modem to modem. By way of an example, let's examine the process used to set up a Toshiba PCX1100 cable modem.

1. Insert the PCX1100's CD into your CD-ROM drive. Its Installation Wizard automatically appears as shown in Figure 8.3.

Figure 8.3

Starting the modem's Installation Wizard.

2. The wizard provides a review of the installation process. Click Next.

3. You'll see a list of cable providers to choose from. Select your cable provider as shown in Figure 8.4.

4. The wizard performs a system qualification check to make sure that the computer has the appropriate hardware.

5. A series of dialog boxes will then be displayed that guide you through the process of connecting the modem to the computer. If you have not already connected the modem, then now would be the time to do so.

6. The next few dialog boxes will take you through the process of configuring the computer's TCP/IP settings and testing communications with the modem. Then you'll see a dialog box similar to the one shown in Figure 8.5.

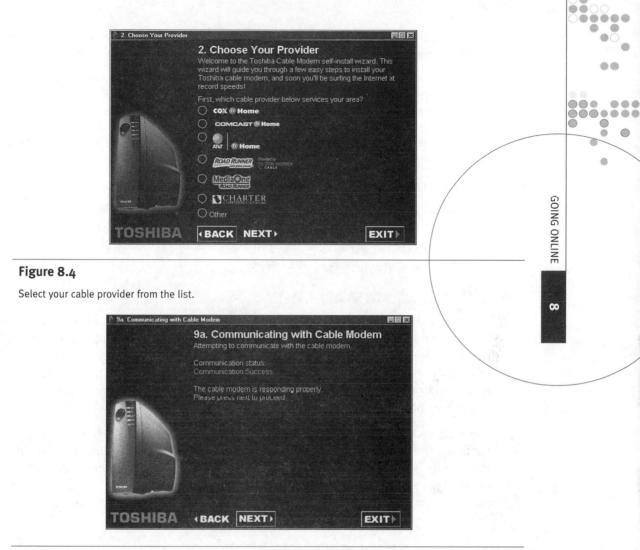

Figure 8.4

Select your cable provider from the list.

Figure 8.5

The wizard confirms that the computer is able to communicate with the cable modem.

7. The wizard will next display the cable modem's MAC address.

8. Finally, the wizard finishes the installation process. Reboot your computer when requested.

Just because you have signed up for always-on high-speed Internet access and set up your cable or DSL modem does not mean that you are ready to start surfing. You still have one more chore to complete.

You have to call your ISP and provide it with the MAC address of your modem. You'll also have to provide it with the MAC address of the computer's network adapter. Hopefully you

GOING ONLINE

8

took note of your cable modem's MAC address when you installed it. If you didn't then check on the bottom or back of the modem and it should be displayed there.

To determine the MAC address of your computer's network adapter use the IPCONFIG command. To do so open a Windows XP command prompt and type the following command.

```
IPCONFIG /ALL
```

You'll see a bunch of output scroll past. Scroll back up and look for a line of output similar to the following.

```
Physical Address. . . . . . : 00-00-00-00-00-00
```

Your network adapter's MAC address is listed as Physical Address and will appear as six pairs of numbers and characters separated by dashes. Now call your ISP and register your MAC addresses. Usually the registration process is instantaneous and you'll be able to start surfing by the time you hang up the phone.

DIAL-UP MODEM INSTALLATION

One of the most common ways to get connected to the Internet is a dial-up connection. A dial-up connection uses a modem and your phone line. Until the recent arrival of always-on high-speed Internet access, a dial-up connection was the only way a typical home user could get connected to the Internet. Unfortunately there are still plenty places today where cable and DSL Internet access is still not available, making dial-up Internet access the only viable option for many families.

A *dial-up modem* can be an internal network card or an external device connected to your computer via a serial or USB connection. The modem converts a computer's digital signals into analog signals through a process known as modulation and transmits them over telephone lines to another computer. A modem at the destination computer receives the signals and converts them back into their original digital format through a process known as demodulation.

The fastest dial-up modems available today are advertised as 56K modems. When 56K modems first appeared on the scene there were two competing standards, which were incompatible with one another. Over time a single standard, known as the V.90. standard emerged. Make sure that your modem is V.90-compatible.

A dial-up modem connects to a standard telephone jack using an RJ-11 telephone cable. These modems provide a second connection, which allows you to plug in a telephone. This way you can continue to use your telephone to make calls when you are not using your modem.

Before you can go online with a dial-up connection you must complete a few steps. These steps include

- Installing a dial-up modem
- Signing up with an ISP
- Setting up a dial-up connection

Modem Installation

Windows XP should automatically detect and install your dial-up modem after you have installed or connected it to your computer. Because Windows XP comes with a number of modem software drivers you may not even notice Windows XP installing it.

Use the following procedure to verify the installation of your modem.

1. Click Start and then Control Panel. The Windows XP Control Panel will appear.
2. Click Printers and Other Hardware.
3. Click Phone and Modem Options. The Phone and Modem Options dialog box will appear as shown in Figure 8.6.

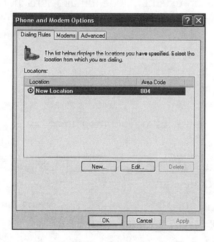

Figure 8.6

You can manage your dial-up modem from the Phone and Modem Options dialog box.

4. Click the Modems property sheet as shown in Figure 8.7.

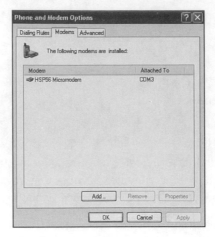

Figure 8.7

The Modems property sheet displays a list of all installed dial-up modems.

If your modem is not listed on the Modems property sheets then Windows XP did not plug-and-play install it. If it is an external modem make sure that it is powered on. If that did not work, then you can always install the modem by running the Add New Hardware Wizard.

 You can start the Add New Hardware Wizard by clicking the Add Hardware link on the Printers and Other Hardware dialog box.

You might want to run a quick test of your modem before proceeding. You can do so using the following procedure.

1. Open the Phone and Modem Options dialog box and select the Modems property sheet as described previously.

2. Select your modem and click Properties. This opens the Properties dialog box for that specific modem as shown in Figure 8.8.

3. Select the Diagnostics property sheet as shown in Figure 8.9.

4. Click Query modem. You'll see a pop-up message asking you to wait for a moment while Windows XP talks to the modem. The message will go away after a few moments and if all goes well, you should see a series of attention or AT commands and their responses listed in the middle of the property sheet. Otherwise you'll see an error.

Figure 8.8

Examining the properties of a specific modem.

Figure 8.9

Testing modem communications.

techtv tip

If you received an error when testing your modem, select the General property sheet and click Troubleshoot. This will open the Windows XP Help and Support Center, which will then display the Modem Troubleshooter.

Signing Up with an ISP

Once you are sure that your dial-up modem is operating properly you are ready to configure your computer to work with an Internet service provider or ISP. An *ISP* is a company that provides leased access to the Internet by charging you a monthly service fee. There are a few very large ISPs such an AOL and CompuServe to which you can sign up. Microsoft also has its own MSN Explorer Internet service. In addition, you'll probably be able to find a number of small local ISPs in your area that would love to sign you up with their Internet service.

 A dial-up connection uses a wide area connection network protocol known as the point-to-point protocol or PPP. Windows XP automatically configures your dial-up connections to use PPP.

You can configure dial-up connections using the New Connection Wizard as explained in the next section. The wizard will guide you through the process of creating a new Internet account or if you already have an Internet account it will help you connect to it instead.

Setting Up a Dial-up Connection

In order to establish a dial-up session to most ISPs you need to create a dial-up connection. All network connections are managed in the Network Connections view of the My Network folder as shown in Figure 8.10. You can access this view by opening the My Network Places and clicking on the View Network Connections link located in the Network Tasks section on the left side of the folder.

 The setup of an Internet account with a larger ISP such as AOL is done a bit differently. These large ISPs usually provide you with their own special setup programs. In order to setup an account with an ISP such as AOL all that you have to do is run the set up program provided on one of the AOL CDs that they are constantly giving away in the mail or at retail stores.

As Figure 8.10 shows, only one network connection has been set up on the computer. You can set up additional connections, including dial-up connections by clicking the Create a New Connection link in the Network Tasks section. The first step in preparing to set up a dial-up connection is to set up a connection with an ISP. The following procedure outlines the steps involved in setting up a new Internet account.

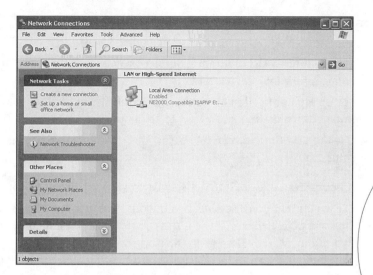

Figure 8.10

Viewing your computer's network connections.

1. Open the My Network Places folder and click View Network Connections.
2. Click Create a new connection. The New Connection Wizard appears.
3. Click Next. The New Connection Wizard displays the following list of options as shown in Figure 8.11.

   - **Connect to the Internet**—Connects your computer to the Internet.
   - **Connect to the Network at My Workplace**—Helps you set up a Virtual Private Network or VPN connection.
   - **Set Up a Home or Small Office Network**—Helps you to set up a home network.
   - **Set Up an Advanced Connection**—Lets you set up your computer to accept or receive a direct connection with other computers.

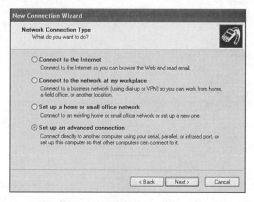

Figure 8.11

The New Connection Wizard is used to create different types of network connections.

4. Select Connect to the Internet and click Next.

5. You are presented with several options as outlined here.

- **Choose From a List of Internet Service Providers (ISPs)**—Select this option to create a new Internet account.

- **Set Up My Connection Manually**—Select this option if you already have an Internet account and know how to set it up.

- **Use the CD I Got From an ISP**—Select this option if your ISP has given you a setup CD.

Select Choose from a list of Internet service providers (ISPs) and click Next.

6. The next screen that you'll see has two options. The first one allows you to sign up with Microsoft MSN Explorer service. The second option will help you sign up with a number of other large ISPs. Obviously being the developer of the operating system has its advantages, not the least of which is being able to push your products and services over those of the competition. Select whichever options you prefer and click Finish.

If you selected not to use MSN Explorer as your ISP, you'll next be presented with the Online Services folder as shown in Figure 8.12. Here you'll find several icons including yet another opportunity to sign up for Microsoft's MSN Explorer. (Guess which one Microsoft wants you to select.)

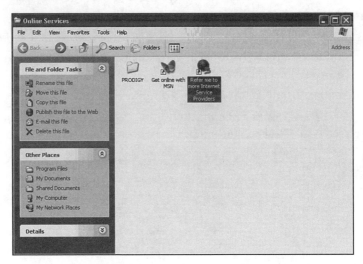

Figure 8.12

Finding an ISP.

Click any of the icons in this folder to set up a new Internet account. If you click the Prodigy folder, you see Web pages that you can click to learn more about this Internet service provider. If you click the Get Online with MSN icon, you'll start the MSN signup process. If you click the Refer Me to More Internet Service Providers icon, you'll start the Internet Connection Wizard, which will step you through the process of signing up with a number of other ISPs. Select whichever of these options is best for you and then follow the instructions presented to establish your new Internet account.

NOTE

If you choose the Refer Me to more Internet Service Providers option, the Internet Connection Wizard will attempt to dial a toll-free telephone number and connect to Microsoft's referral service. The list of ISPs that you'll be presented with will include most of the major ISPs. However, it will not include many excellent local ISPs that may reside in your area. To make this connection your computer will have to have a modem. If Windows XP has not installed your modem, you'll be prompted to do so before the Internet Connection Wizard can continue.

If you already have an ISP, then you can use the following procedure to configure Windows XP to use it.

1. Open the My Network Places folder and click View Network Connections.
2. Click Create a New Connection. The New Connection Wizard appears. Click Next.
3. Select Connect to the Internet and click Next.
4. Select Set Up My Connection Manually and click Next.
5. Select Connect Using a Dial-Up Modem and click Next.
6. Type your ISP's name in the ISP Name field and click Next.
7. Type the phone number that you use to connect to your ISP in the Phone number field and click Next.
8. Next you'll have to type the username assigned to you by your ISP as well as your account password as shown in Figure 8.13. You have three other options to choose from. The first option allows you to set up your computer to automatically use this account along with the username and password that you just supplied when connecting to the Internet. The second option lets you make this connection the default Internet connection. The last option allows you to turn off and on Windows XP's Internet Connection Firewall.

   Make your selections and click Next.

NOTE

The Internet Connection Firewall or ICF is Windows XP's built-in personal firewall. It protects your computer from hacker attacks while you are connected to the Internet. More information on ICF is presented in "The Internet Connection Firewall" on page 207 later in this chapter.

9. The wizard displays a summary of the information that it has collected. Verify that everything looks correct and click Finish.

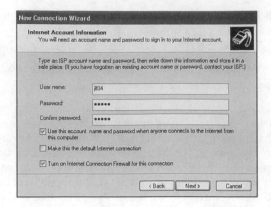

Figure 8.13

Manually setting up your Internet account.

A new icon representing the dial-up connect has been added to the Network Connections folder as shown in Figure 8.14.

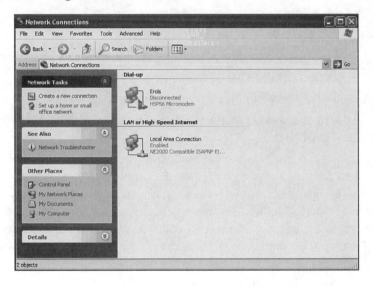

Figure 8.14

The new dial-up connection is displayed in the Network Connections folder.

Double-click the connection's icon to open it as shown in Figure 8.15.

You have the option of configuring the connection to work for everyone that shares your computer or just for yourself. Click on Dial to establish an Internet connection. You'll see a small dialog box appear showing the status of connection while it is being dialed and authenticated with your ISP. Once connected the dialog box will disappear. You can then open up your Internet applications such as Internet Explorer and begin accessing the

Internet. A small dial-up connection icon will appear in the system tray area on the right side of the Windows XP taskbar. You can use it to disconnect from the Internet when you are done working. Simply right-click the icon and select Disconnect from the context menu that appears.

Figure 8.15

Opening your dial-up connection.

SETTING UP SHARED INTERNET ACCESS

By now you should have set up one of your computers to connect to the Internet using either an always-on high-speed cable or DSL connection or a dial-up connection. It is time to look at what's required to share that connection with the rest of your home network. You have three options.

- **Third-party proxy software**—Client/server software where one computer on the home network runs proxy software and the rest run client software. The proxy receives requests for Internet resources from the clients and retrieves them on behalf of the clients.

- **Microsoft's Internet Connection Sharing service or ICS**—A built-in Windows XP service which allows a computer with an Internet connection to share it with the rest of the network. You can use the Windows XP Network Connection Wizard to set up the ICS server as well as each ICS client computer.

- **An Internet Gateway appliance**—A small hardware appliance that connects a computer or home network to a shared Internet connection. You can use the Windows XP Network Connection Wizard to set up each computer to use an Internet gateway.

Third-party proxy applications involve the installation of server and client software on your network computers. There are a number of third-party proxy programs, each of which operates a little differently. A discussion of these programs is beyond the scope of this book. Instead the latter two options are covered here.

NOTE Examples of third-party proxy software include Wingate from www.wingate.com and winproxy from www.winproxy.com.

Internet Connection Sharing

Internet Connection Sharing or *ICS* is a built-in Windows XP service that allows you to set up the computer that has an Internet connection as an ICS server. The ICS server then shares that connection with the rest of the network. The ICS server provides a number of network services, including

- **Network Address Translation or NAT**—Computers on the Internet have public IP addresses. Computers on home networks, on the other hand, use private IP addresses meaning that they are not visible on the Internet. NAT allows the ICS server to accept Internet requests from computers with private IP addresses on the home network and reissue them to servers on the Internet using its public IP address. When a response is returned the ICS server receives it and forwards it back to the requesting home network computer. This way the only computer that is visible to the Internet is the ICS server. The ICS server has two IP addresses, a private one for the home network and a public one assigned by your ISP.

- **DHCP**—This allows the ICS server to dynamically assign TCP/IP IP addresses and other TCP/IP settings to computers on your home network. This ensures that all the computers on your home network are properly configured and can communicate with the ICS server.

- **DNS Name Resolution**—This service allows the ICS server to provide name resolution for computers on your home network. Name resolution is the process of identifying the IP address of a network computer when provided with the computer name.

The nice thing about ICS is that it is free. You set up the ICS service on a computer with an Internet connection. One drawback of ICS is that this computer must be on any time that someone on the home network wants to connect to the Internet. Another drawback is that ICS consumes CPU and memory resources on the computer where it runs. However, ICS works well and provides a reliable means of sharing a single Internet connection with a home network.

In addition to providing you with a solution for setting up shared Internet access, Windows XP also provides you with a number of software applications that are specially designed to help you be productive and have fun on the Internet. These applications include

- **Internet Explorer**—Microsoft's Internet browser, which allows you to surf and explore the World Wide Web.
- **Outlook Express**—Microsoft's e-mail client, which allows you to send and receive electronic messages to any other Internet e-mail account.
- **Windows Messenger**—Microsoft's equivalent to AOL's Instant Messenger and Yahoo!'s Messenger utilities. It allows you to send instant messages and audio and video to other Windows Messenger users.

The sharing of a high-speed cable or DSL Internet connection is very similar to the sharing of a dial-up connection except that the two network connections on the ICS computer are both regular network connections as depicted in Figure 8.16. One network connection is to an access point and the other is to a cable or DSL modem.

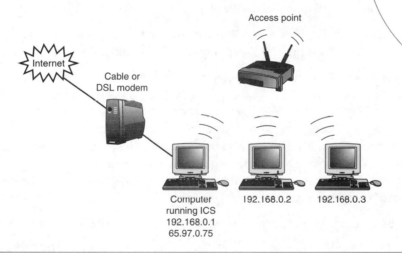

Figure 8.16

Sharing a high-speed cable or DSL Internet connection.

An ICS computer that shares its high-speed Internet connection will have two regular network connections. ICS can share always on high-speed Internet and dial-up connections. If you use it to share a dial-up connection, as depicted in Figure 8.17, then the computer configured as the ICS server will also have two network connections. This first connection is a dial-up connection with the Internet. The second connection is to your home network.

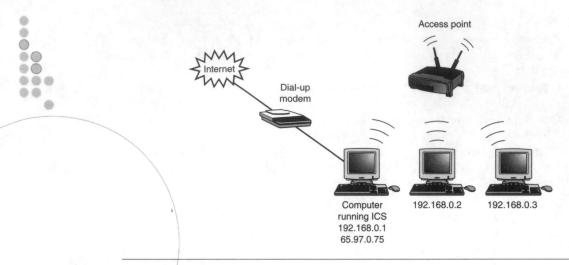

Access point

Internet

Dial-up
modem

Computer
running ICS
192.168.0.1
65.97.0.75

192.168.0.2

192.168.0.3

Figure 8.17

Sharing a dial-up connection to the Internet using ICS.

As you can see in Figure 8.16 and Figure 8.17 the ICS server has two IP addresses because it is connected to two networks, your home network and the Internet.

By default each Windows XP computer on a home network automatically configures itself with an IP address on a 169.254.0.0 network with a subnet mask of 255.255.0.0. However, as soon as you set up your ICS server and configure the rest of your network computers as ICS clients Windows XP reconfigures all your computers to run on a 192.168.0.0 network. This happens because ICS also provides a DHCP service, which immediately begins assigning TCP/IP configuration settings to all your home network computers. The ICS server always assigns itself an IP address of 192.168.0.1. These TCP/IP settings assigned to ICS client computers include

- Each computer's IP address, which will be between 192.168.0.2 and 192.168.0.254

- A subnet mask of 255.255.255.0

- A default gateway address of 192.168.0.1

NOTE
The default gateway is just another name for the computer or Internet gateway that is providing shared Internet access on your home network.

You can configure your ICS server and clients using the Network Setup Wizard. The following procedure outlines the steps required to set up an ICS server.

1. Click Start, All Programs, Accessories, Communications, and then Network Setup Wizard.

2. The Network Setup Wizard's Welcome dialog box appears. Click Next.

3. Next the wizard displays an overview of the steps involved in setting up a network. Click Next.

4. The dialog box shown in Figure 8.18 appears. Select the This computer Connects Directly to the Internet option and click Next.

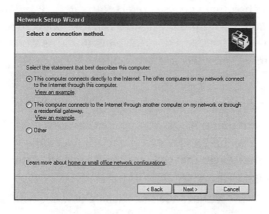

Figure 8.18

Setting up your ICS server.

5. You are then presented with a list of network connections that have been set up on the computer as shown in Figure 8.19. Select the connection that lets your computer communicate with the Internet and click Next.

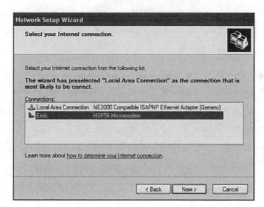

Figure 8.19

Select the Internet connection.

6. The next dialog box lets you change the name assigned to your computer as well as its description. Leave these settings as they are and click Next.

7. The next dialog box lets you change the workgroup that your computer has been assigned to. Leave this setting as it is and click Next.

8. Next the wizard will display a dialog box that lists all the information that it has collected from you. As you look through this information you'll see that the wizard is automatically enabling Windows XP's Internet Connection Firewall. Verify that everything looks correct and click Next.

9. The last dialog box that you'll see offers to create a disk that you can use to run the Network Setup Wizard on your non-Windows XP computers. Select this option if necessary. Otherwise select Just Finish the Wizard; I Don't Need to Run the Wizard on Other Computers and click Finish.

Once you have set up one of your network computers as an ICS server you can configure the rest of your computers as ICS clients using the following procedure.

1. Click Start, All Programs, Accessories, Communications, and then Network Setup Wizard. If this is a non-Windows XP computer, insert the disk that you made when setting up the ICS server that contains the Network Connection Wizard and click on Start, Run, and type **A:SETUP**.

2. The Network Setup Wizard's Welcome dialog box appears. Click Next.

3. Next the wizard displays an overview of the steps involved in setting up a network. Click Next.

4. The next dialog box presents options for creating an ICS server and client. Select This Computer Connects to the Internet Through Another Computer on My Network or Through a Residential Gateway and click Next.

5. The next dialog box lets you change the name assigned to your computer as well as its description. Leave these settings as they are and click Next.

6. The next dialog box lets you change the workgroup that your computer has been assigned to. Leave this setting as it is and click Next.

7. Next the wizard will display a dialog box that lists all the information that it has collected from you. Verify that everything looks correct and click Next.

8. The last dialog box that you'll see offers to create a disk that you can use to run the Network Setup Wizard on non-Windows XP computers. Select this option if necessary. Otherwise select Just Finish the Wizard; I Don't Need to Run the Wizard on Other Computers and click Finish.

Once your ICS server is set up and you have configured all your ICS clients everyone in the family should be able to start surfing the Internet.

Internet Gateways

ICS provides a good way for setting up shared access to the Internet. However, it does have some drawbacks for the computer that runs the ICS services.

- The ICS computer must be kept running in order to service other network computers.

- The computer acting as the ICS server must dedicate CPU and memory resources to the ICS service.

- Response time for the owner of the ICS computer may be affected when it is being heavily used.

Another way to provide shared Internet access to your home network is to purchase an Internet Gateway. ICS and Internet gateways are mutually exclusive technologies meaning that they cannot co-exist. So you must disable ICS before installing an Internet gateway. As soon as it is operational the Internet gateway will reconfigure your home network by reassigning a new range of IP addresses to all network computers.

The nice thing about using an Internet gateway appliance is that you don't have to leave your computer running all the time or worry about having your hard drive crash or frying your motherboard as a result of being left on during a storm.

Other names for Internet Gateways appliances include Ethernet cable/DSL routers and residential gateways.

Internet gateways provide all the features found in ICS including

- NAT
- DHCP
- DNS name resolution

In addition Internet gateways offer a number of services not provided by ICS including

- **A Network hub**—Most Internet gateways include a number of Ethernet ports allowing it to replace your network hub.
- **A Built-in firewall**—Internet gateways also provide built-in personal firewalls to keep your computer or home network protected.
- **Event logs**—Internet gateways can be configured to create logs and record information about its activity including information about hacker attacks.
- **Caching**—Some Internet gateways are able to place copies of recently accessed Web pages into their memory and to load the Web page from cache when they are requested again thus speeding up access time.

There are a number of different Internet gateway appliances available today made by companies such as Linksys, NetGear, and D-Link. Although they will vary in the way that their web interface is designed, each of these devices provides the same basic set of features.

Figure 8.20 depicts a typical home network that uses an Internet Gateway to provide shared access to its always-on high-speed Internet connection.

More information about how to set up an Internet gateway can be found in "Setting Up a Wireless Network" in Chapter 2.

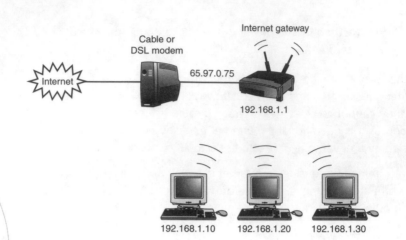

Figure 8.20

Sharing an Internet connection using a wireless Internet gateway.

As you can see the Internet Gateway has been assigned two different IP addresses. The first IP address is a public address assigned by your ISP. In this example, the IP address is 65.97.0.75. The second IP address is a private address that the Internet Gateway has assigned to itself. The IP address is 192.168.1.1. Because the Internet gateway is also a DHCP server it will manage the assignment of all TCP/IP configuration settings for all the computers on your home network as soon as it begins operating. This reconfiguration of network IP addresses will be completely transparent to you.

PROTECTING YOUR HOME NETWORK WITH A PERSONAL FIREWALL

Now that you have everything that you need to know to get your home network connected up to the Internet let's examine the steps involved in protecting it from intruders using personal firewalls. Three types of personal firewalls will be considered as listed here.

- Windows XP's Internet Connection Firewall
- Third-party software-based personal firewalls
- Personal firewall features built into Internet gateways

Each of these options and their advantages and disadvantages is discussed in the sections that follow.

The Internet Connection Firewall is only available on Windows XP operating systems and will not be an available option if you are using older Microsoft operating systems.

The Internet Connection Firewall

Windows XP's Internet Connection Firewall or ICF is automatically installed on a computer when you set it up to run ICS. This way it can begin protecting your home network from Internet hacker attacks right from the start. ICF is a good basic personal firewall and it will block all unsolicited Internet communications. However, it has a number of limitations. For example, ICF does not provide any alerts or notifications of intruder activity. Therefore, you may want to disable it and install a more industrial strength personal firewall

It's not a good idea to try to run ICF and another software-based personal firewall at the same time. Although you might be able to get away with it you won't get a lot of benefit from it and you might actually create some problems. Because Installing ICS also means installing ICF you should go back and disable ICF before installing another software-based personal firewall. You can do so using the following procedure.

1. Click Start and then right-click My Network Places and select Properties from the context menu that appears.

2. A list of network connections is displayed. Select your Internet connection and click the Change Settings of this Connection option in the Network Tasks section on the left side of the dialog box.

3. The properties dialog box for the Internet connection will appear. Select the Advanced property sheet as shown in Figure 8.21.

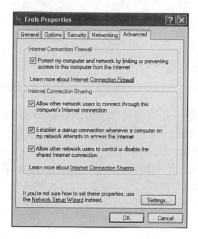

Figure 8.21

Disabling the Internet Connection Firewall.

4. There are four settings that you can configure on this property sheet as listed here.

   • **Protect My Computer and Network by Limiting or Preventing Access to this Computer from the Internet**—This option determines whether or not ICF runs.

- **Allow Other Network Users to Connect Through This Computer's Internet Connection**—This option determines whether or not the computer will operate as an ICS server.

- **Establish a Dial-Up Connection Whenever a Computer on My Network Attempts to Access the Internet**—This option allows Windows XP to automatically initiate a dial-up connection to the Internet on behalf of a network user if a connection is not already established on the ICS server.

- **Allow Other Network Users to Control or Disable the Shared Internet Connection**—This option allows you to control whether or not network users can manage the ICS service.

  Clear the option in the Internet Connection Firewall section and click OK.

techtv tip

As a shortcut you can configure an ICS server from the Internet connection's properties dialog box and bypass the Network Setup Wizard by right-clicking the icon that represents the connection and selecting properties.

Working with Third-Party Software-Based Personal Firewalls

Windows XP's Internet Connection Firewall is a good firewall and it does what it is supposed to do very well. However, it lacks a number of features found in more established personal firewalls. ICF's missing features include

- No protection against Trojan Horse, worms, and similar programs
- No alerting
- No logging
- No way to customize security policies or adjust the firewalls security settings

Because of these and other missing features you may want to disable Windows XP's ICF and install a more industrial strength personal firewall. There are a number of good personal firewalls currently available including the McAfee Firewall, ZoneAlarm, and BlackICE Defender. By way of an example, this section will examine the operation of the ZoneAlarm personal firewall. ZoneAlarm provides a complete range of personal firewall features and is free for personal use.

ZoneAlarm can protect your dial-up, DSL, and cable connections from attack when your computer is connected to the Internet and unlike many other software-based personal firewalls, ZoneAlarm has built-in features specifically designed to accommodate operation on a network. ZoneAlarm is also designed to coexist with and protect local area networks making it a great choice for any home network.

Installing Your Personal Firewall

The first step in installing ZoneAlarm is to close any open programs. You should also disable ICF as described earlier in this chapter. Once these two prerequisites are completed you can install ZoneAlarm as outlined here.

NOTE You can download a free copy of ZoneAlarm from www.zonelabs.com. At the time that this book was written the current version of ZoneAlarm was version 2.6.

1. Download ZoneAlarm and then double-click its setup icon.
2. The ZoneAlarm Installation Welcome dialog box appears. Click Next.
3. The Product Information dialog box appears. Click Next.
4. Type your name and e-mail address in the space provided. Optionally select the entries to register ZoneAlarm and to receive update notifications. Click Next.
5. Click Accept when presented with ZoneAlarm's license agreement.
6. Click Next to accept the default installation directory.
7. The install process next asks you if you'd like to configure ZoneAlarm to mark your default Internet browser as a trusted application that is permitted to communicate with the Internet. Click Yes, Please Give These Components Permission to Access the Internet and then click Next.
8. The Ready to Install! dialog box appears. Click Next.
9. The User survey dialog box appears. Fill out the survey and click Finish.
10. The installation of ZoneAlarm is completed. A pop-up dialog box appears asking if you'd like to start ZoneAlarm. Click Yes.

Working with ZoneAlarm

The first time ZoneAlarm is started you'll see the ZoneAlarm Getting Started dialog box, which tells you a little about ZoneAlarm and how it works. The next thing that you will see is the ZoneAlarm Tips dialog box. If you want, you can disable this dialog box from appearing in the future by clicking the Don't Show this Message Again option at the bottom of the dialog box.

The ZoneAlarm dialog box, shown in Figure 8.22, allows you to configure the personal firewall and its security settings.

Figure 8.22

The ZoneAlarm dialog box.

The ZoneAlarm dialog box is divided into five sections. Each section has an icon and a link. The five icons are outlined here:

- **Graphs**—Four bar graphics showing current upload and download traffic and traffic over time.

- **Padlock**—You can click this icon to toggle applications access to the Internet on and off (except for exempted applications).
- **Stop**—Allows you to block all incoming and outgoing Internet traffic.
- **Applications**—Displays an icon representing all active Internet applications.
- **ZoneAlarm Logo**—Provides a link to the ZoneLabs Web site.

Under the icons are the five links that are described following:

- **Alerts**—Opens the Alerts panel where you can view and configure log and alert settings.
- **Lock**—Lets you set up the firewall to block all Internet traffic after a specified period of inactivity.
- **Security**—Lets you apply different security settings for a local area network connection and an Internet connection.
- **Programs**—Lets you control which Internet applications on your computer can communicate with the Internet.
- **Configure**—Lets you set up ZoneAlarm to start when your computer starts.

Configuring Home Network and Internet Security

There are two types of security settings that you are going to want to configure in ZoneAlarm. One is the security setting that is applied to network and Internet zones. You do this on the Security panel, which you can open by clicking the Security button as shown in Figure 8.23.

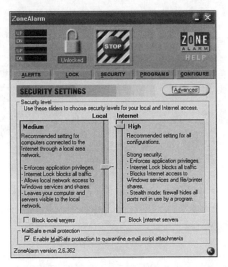

Figure 8.23

Configuring the security settings for your computer's network and Internet connection.

Home network security is configured on the left side of the panel by moving a slider bar up and down to adjust security settings. The following three settings are available:

- **Low**—Allows your computer to be seen on your home network and also allows file and print sharing. If the Lock icon is clicked, this option blocks all application traffic.
- **Medium**—Allows your computer to be seen on your home network and also allows file and print sharing. If the Lock icon is clicked, then this option blocks all network to and from the computer. This is the default security setting.
- **High**—This option prevents the computer from being seen on your home network and inhibits file and printer sharing.

Internet security is configured on the right side of the panel by moving a slider bar up and down. The following three settings are available:

- **Low**—This option lets your computer be seen on the Internet and allows file and printer sharing of local resources over the Internet.
- **Medium**—This option blocks NetBIOS services while still allowing file and printer sharing of local resources over the Internet.
- **High**—This option makes your computer invisible when connected to the Internet and blocks file and printer sharing over the Internet. This is the default security setting.

Defining Trusted Applications

If you click the Programs button, you'll open a panel from which you can configure which Internet applications on your computer are and are not permitted to communicate with the Internet as shown in Figure 8.24.

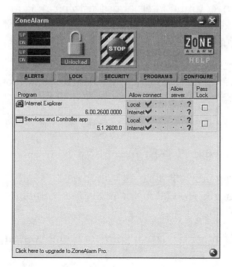

Figure 8.24

Configuring application access.

The first time that you start any Internet application ZoneAlarm steps in and temporarily blocks its Internet access asking you how it should handle the applications. You can view the status of all the Internet applications that you have defined to ZoneAlarm from this panel. You can also change their status. Unless you configure it otherwise ZoneAlarm communicates with you by displaying alerts and recording your responses. For example, Figure 8.25 shows a typical ZoneAlarm alert that you'll see the first time that you run an application that tries to communicate over your Internet connection.

Figure 8.25

By responding to its alerts you can tell ZoneAlarm which applications you want to allow or prevent from communicating with the Internet.

When you see an alert such as the one shown in Figure 8.25 you can click Yes to allow the application to connect to the Internet or No to block it. Managing applications in this manner is important because it helps prevent Trojan Horse and worm programs that may have infiltrated your computer from opening secret connections back to the Internet.

 To learn more about working with the ZoneAlarm and other software-based personal firewalls check out the *Absolute Beginner's Guide to Personal Firewalls* published by Que (ISBN # 0-7897-2654-4).

Internet Gateway Firewall Features

Software-based personal firewalls such as Windows XP's Internet Connection Firewall and ZoneAlarm provide strong protection for individual computers. However, they do have some drawbacks, including

- Software firewalls must be run on your computer consuming memory and CPU resources.
- As software programs it is always possible that a clever virus program may be able to disable or turn off your software firewall.

- Software firewalls are unable to ward off impending attacks until they have reached the computer.

A hardware firewall overcomes each of these obstacles and provides protection for all the computers on your home network. A hardware-based personal firewall is a small network appliance that operates in-between your cable or DSL modem and your computers. Personal hardware firewalls are implemented as a component of Internet Gateways. These devices provide a number of additional features, including

- **Hub**—Lets you use the device as a network hub for connecting all your computers into a home network.
- **Router**—Controls the flow of network traffic between your home network and the Internet.
- **Switch**—Creates temporary dedicated connections between computers on your home network in order to speed throughput of your games and multimedia content.
- **NAT (Network Address Translation)**—Allows the device to send and receive requests to the Internet on behalf of network computers.
- **DHCP Server**—Lets the device handle the automatic assignments of TCP/IP configuration settings to all the computers on the home network.

All these features combine to allow these devices to help you create a home network, provide it with Internet connection sharing, and protect it with a personal hardware firewall. Because these devices are self-contained they place no processing demands on the computer or network that they service. They also simplify network setup.

techtv tip

Consider using an Internet gateway and its personal firewall features to protect your home network as well as a software-based personal firewall on each of your computers. When configured this way your hardware and software-based personal firewalls will not interfere with one another and will provide your home network with two layers of defense.

TESTING YOUR HOME NETWORK'S VULNERABILITY TO HACKER ATTACK

The security of a home network is only as strong as its least secure computer. Fortunately your home network resides safely within your home and its access is limited to the members of your family and your close friends. This makes for a pretty safe environment. However, the serenity and security of a nice little home network can easily be blown completely away any time it or one of its computers connects to the Internet.

Your home network is even more vulnerable if you have set up an always-on high-speed shared Internet connection. Unlike a dial-up connection, which is active only when someone in the house is actually using it, a cable or DSL connection is on 24×7. Therefore, there

is a far greater chance that someone with ill intent on the Internet will find and attempt to hack into your computer or home network.

The best way to protect yourself, your home network, and the data that you store on it is to set up a personal firewall. In fact, the best of all solutions is to set up an Internet gateway appliance and use it to provide shared Internet access to your home network along with a personal software firewall on each of your network computers.

Additional information on Internet gateways can be found in Chapter 2, "Getting Your Hands Dirty: Assembling Your Network Hardware."

However, just because you have a personal firewall watching over your home network does not necessarily mean that all is well. For example, a cleverly written virus program might sneak onto one of your network computers and silently disable all your software-based personal firewalls. Or you may have configured security settings on your personal firewalls that are too weak, allowing more than you realize to get through.

To verify that your home network is as secure as you can make it from Internet attack you need to test it. This does not mean finding a hacker and asking him or her to try and break in. That would be like asking a pit bull to try and jump your fence just to see if it can keep him out. Instead you can test your defenses using any number of free Internet security scans.

One of the better free Internet security scans is provided by the grc.com Web site. Using the scanning tools provided at this Web site you can test your home network's defenses and receive immediate feedback that is written in plain English.

Running a Security Scan

The following procedure outlines the steps involved in running the free Shields Up!! security scan found at grc.com.

1. Start up your Internet browser, type **grc.com** in the URL field, and press Enter.
2. Wait a few moments for the site to completely load and then click the Shields UP!! link. The Shields UP!! Web page will appear as shown in Figure 8.26.
3. Click the Test My Shields button to initiate an Internet scan of your computer.
4. Within a few moments you'll see the results of the scan as demonstrated in Figure 8.27.

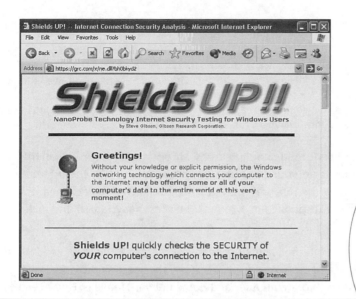

Figure 8.26

The Shields Up Web page provides links for running two different scans.

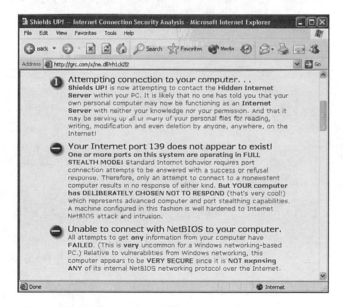

Figure 8.27

A sample of the type of results that you may see when you run the Internet scan.

As the results in Figure 8.27 indicate, the scan was not able to learn anything about the computer.

NOTE If you run the Internet scan with and without your personal firewall turned on, you'll probably notice that it runs much faster when the firewall is not on. This is because when it is on, your personal firewall is thwarting the scan's attempts to examine your computer, thus making it run longer.

In addition to performing and Internet scan, you can also run a scan that attempts to probe the TCP/IP ports on your computer. Communications over the Internet depend on TCP/IP ports. By hiding them a port scan, a personal firewall makes them invisible for all intensive purposes. Except of course, to the Web sites that you visit and initiate communications with.

These two free Internet scans use many of the same tricks and techniques to try to scan your computer that hackers use. Therefore, these scans provide a pretty good indication as to how secure your computer and home network really is. However, things change over time. Hackers develop new tools and viruses get cleverer over time. To truly remain secure when connected to the Internet you must keep your personal firewall updated and check your defenses regularly. Otherwise you may fool yourself into thinking that your home network is a lot safer than it really is.

CHAPTER 9

REMOTE ACCESS: DON'T LEAVE HOME WITHOUT IT

Home networks are great because they allow you to access your files from any computer in your house. But what happens when you find yourself away from home and still needing access to your data? Windows XP provides two solutions to this dilemma. It enables you to remotely connect to your home network using a dial-up modem or an Internet connection. This chapter discusses how to set up and use remote access. In addition, it looks at the remote access capabilities of wireless networking.

Here is what you'll learn:

- How to set up and secure a dial-up server
- How to create a dial-up client connection
- How to configure a Windows XP VPN server
- How to establish a VPN connection over the Internet
- How to secure your remote connection

UNDERSTANDING REMOTE ACCESS

A home network is really just a local area network set up inside your house. Using features built into Windows you can create a remote connection to your home network from anywhere that you have either a modem or Internet connection. These types of remote connections provide you with the ability to access your home network and the data that is stored on it from just about anywhere that you can find a phone line or Internet connection, irrespective of how far away you may actually be.

In addition, if your home network is built using a wireless Internet gateway or if you have expanded your home network using a wireless access point, you may find that you can connect to your home network from several hundred feet away using a wireless connection.

Remote Wireless Networking

A local area network is commonly defined as a computer network located within a single building or portion of a building. Likewise a home network has traditionally been defined as operating within the confines of a home. However, with the advent of wireless networking this definition has begun to break down because wireless networks can broadcast their signals well past the perimeter of your front and back yards.

With 802.11x wireless networking, it is possible to maintain a wireless network connection hundreds of feet from your house. Technically speaking, this is still a local connection. However, for all practical purposes, you are working remotely. For example, if you live in a downtown apartment, this means that you may be able to meet with an associate at a café across the street or around the corner. Using a laptop, you'd still be able to access the data stored on your home network or even use its shared Internet connection. Likewise, if you live across from a park, you may be able to take both your laptop and your children out to play.

However, the farther that you roam from your home network the slower your wireless connection is going to be. 8092.11x-based networks implement an automatic fallback scheme that reduces the transmission speed between a wireless network client and a wireless Internet gateway or access point as the signal strength between the two devices declines. Signal strength often declines because of interference generated by other electrical devices operating in the same radio frequency range. Signal strength also declines as the distance between the two devices increases. For example, while an 802.11b wireless is capable of 11Mbps transmission speeds, its connection may fall back to 5.5Mbps, 2Mbps, or 1Mbps as the strength of the radio signal degrades. Moving large files, such as those associated with audio and video, is impractical at lower speeds. However, smaller files and even a shared high-speed Internet connection will usually work just fine.

NOTE   Remember that an always-on high-speed cable or DSL Internet connection will usually provide for transmissions speeds between 300–500Kbps, which can easily be accommodated by even a 1Mbps wireless connection.

Dial-up and Internet Remote Access

Windows XP Home Edition provides you with two ways to connect to your home network remotely. These remote access options are

- A dial-up connection
- A virtual private network or VPN connection

A dial-up connection is established between a dial-up server and a dial-up client over modems attached to each computer. So if you have switched your home network over to an always-on high-speed cable or DSL connection, you may still be able to get some use out of your old dial-up modems.

A dial-up server is a computer that has been set up to accept an incoming connection request from another computer over a telephone line connection. Therefore, a dial-up client is a computer set up to dial into a dial-up server.

A dial-up connection is essentially the same as any other network connection. The main difference is that your network data is routed through a modem instead of a network adapter. By connecting to the dial-up server, you not only gain access to any shared resources that have been defined on that computer but you also get access to your entire home network. However, because you are using a 56K or slower connection, things are going to be a little slow.

A VPN connection is a different kind of beast. It is a connection established between two computers over the Internet as opposed to telephone lines. Therefore, a VPN connection can be established regardless of whether the computers use dial-up or high-speed Internet access (or both).

A remote connection gives you access to the shared resources on your network from anywhere in the world. It also lets you share your home network with family and friends who do not live with you. It is perfect for:

- Accessing files when you are on the road
- Submitting print jobs so that they will be ready when you return home
- Getting access to the Internet via your home network Internet Gateway or ICS (Internet Connection Sharing) server

Like any other Windows networking service, remote access places an additional burden on the computer set up as the dial-up server, especially if the connection will be used to transfer large files. If you expect light use of this feature, then you can select any computer with a modem. However, if you think it will be used heavily, then you may want to pick a computer with a little more memory and a faster CPU or even dedicate a computer to perform this duty.

9

To set up a remote connection both computers must be using a common protocol It's possible to set up a Windows XP remote network connection using any of the following protocols:

- TCP/IP
- IPX/SPX
- NetBEUI

However, as discussed in Chapter 3, TCP/IP is the protocol you should use when you set up your home network.

 For more information on these protocols see Chapter 3, "The Softer Side of Network Setup."

 Microsoft is breaking off its support for NetBEUI. However, it still works and can be found on the Windows XP CD in \VALUEADD\MSFT\NET\NEBEUI.

UNDERSTANDING HOW DIAL-UP ACCESS WORKS

There are a number of steps involved in setting up remote dial-up access to your network. These steps include

- Install a modem on the computer designated as the dial-up server
- Install a modem on the computer designated as the dial-up client
- Use the New Connection Wizard to set up the dial-up server
- Use the New Connection Wizard to set up the dial-up client
- Create duplicate user accounts on both the dial-up server and client

Once properly configured a connection between a dial-up server and a dial-up client works as depicted in Figure 9.1

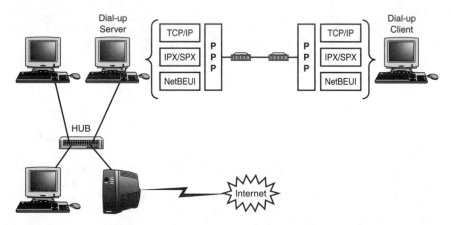

Figure 9.1

An overview of a Windows XP dial-up connection.

As Figure 9.1 shows, dial-up connections use a protocol known as the *point-to-point protocol* or *PPP* to transport data over the dial-up connection using one or more standard networking protocols. A dial-up connection is a WAN connection and PPP is a WAN protocol designed to support the transmission of multiple protocols including TCP/IP, IPX/SPX, and NetBEUI.

A computer running Windows XP Home Edition can only run one dial-up remote connection at a time. If you think that you'll ever have two people who need to remotely connect to your network at the same time, then either one person will have to wait or you'll need to install a second phone line and set up another computer as a dial-up server. Windows XP Home Edition only allows a dial-up server to support one remote dial-up connection at a time so even if you have a computer with two modems and two phone lines you'll only be able to set up a single remote connection.

Windows XP lets you set up a dial-up connection using any of the following types of connections:

- Telephone
- ISDN
- X.25

This book will show you how to set up remote access using a standard telephone connection. ISDN and X.25 are less commonly used technologies for home networking. ISDN is a special type of communications connection set up by your telephone company to provide up to 128K network connections. X.25 is an older WAN technology that provides 64K network connections over poor quality communication lines and is seldom found anymore.

For you to remotely connect to a dial-up server and your home network you must have a user account set up on the dial-up server that matches the one that you'll be using on the remote computer. Otherwise, Windows XP won't let you in unless you are not using password protection for your user accounts. It is extremely important to use password-protected accounts before setting up a dial-up or VPN connection in order to prevent an outsider from breaking into your network. Once a dial-up connection is established, you'll have whatever access your user account on the dial-up server provides you with.

It is strongly recommended that you use passwords for user accounts. It's also a good idea to delete user accounts that are no longer in use. The User Accounts dialog box, accessed through the Control Panel, is used to add and delete user accounts and to manage account passwords. Look to Chapter 7, "Becoming Your Own Network Administrator," for more on the use of the User Accounts dialog box.

Windows XP Home Edition's dial-up server can work in conjunction with dial-up clients from other Windows operating systems including

- Windows 95 (requires Microsoft Plus for Windows 95)
- Windows 98 and Windows 98 2nd Edition
- Windows NT 4
- Windows 2000

SETTING UP A DIAL-UP SERVER

The New Connection Wizard can be used to set up your dial-up server. The steps involved and the selections that you'll have to make are explained in the following procedure. Please note that I am assuming that you already have installed a dial-up modem on the computer.

1. Click Start, All Programs, Accessories, Communications, and then Select New Connection Wizard.

2. The New Connection Wizard opens. Click Next.

3. Select Set Up an Advanced Connection as shown in Figure 9.2. Click Next.

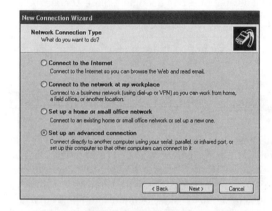

Figure 9.2

Setting up a dial-up server is considered to be an advanced option.

4. Select Accept Incoming Connections as shown in Figure 9.3. This will allow the computer to answer its modem when an incoming connection request is detected. Click Next.

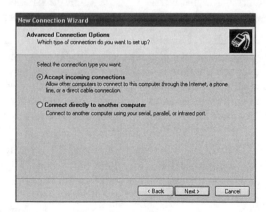

Figure 9.3

An incoming connection is a connection request from a dial-up client.

5. Select the dial-up modem that should be used to support the connection as demonstrated in Figure 9.4 and then click Next.

Figure 9.4

Choose the modem that will be used to establish the remote connection.

6. The dialog box shown in Figure 9.5 appears. It does not matter which of the available options you select. Neither applies to a dial-up connection. Click Next.

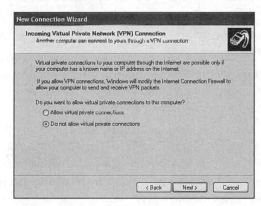

Figure 9.5

VPN connection options do not apply to dial-up connections.

7. A list of user accounts that are defined on the computer appears as shown in Figure 9.6. Select the user accounts belonging to the individuals that will need remote access. You can create a new user account by clicking Add and supplying a User name, full name, and password. This creates a new user account on the computer. Similarly you can remove an account by clicking Remove.

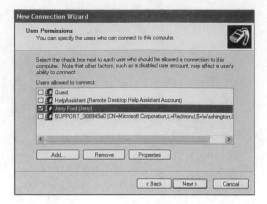

Figure 9.6

You can select who will and will not be able to connect to the dial-up server remotely.

8. You can apply a little extra security on an account-by-account basis by selecting a user account and clicking the Properties button when selecting the user accounts that are to be permitted to remotely connect to the dial-up. This opens a properties dialog box for the selected user as shown in Figure 9.7. From this dialog box you can select the Callback property sheet and select from any of the following options:

- **Do Not Allow Callback**—This option allows the selected user to connect to the dial-up server.

- **Allow the Caller to Set the Callback Number**—This option forces the user to provide a telephone number which the dial-up server will then use to hang up the connection and then call the dial-up client.

- **Always Use the Following Callback Number**—This option allows you to type a specific phone number, which the dial-up client computer must use when remotely connecting. Again the dial-up server will hang up when the dial-up client first attempts to connect and then call the dial-up client back at the specified phone number.

After applying the appropriate options for each user account click Next.

9. Select the network software components that you want to use over the dial-up connection as shown in Figure 9.8.

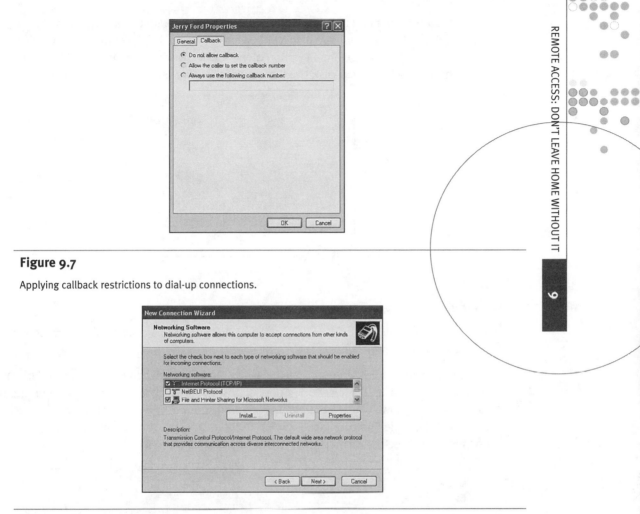

Figure 9.7

Applying callback restrictions to dial-up connections.

Figure 9.8

You can limit the networking software components that can be used over the dial-up connection.

10. Select each protocol that you are going to support over the dial-up connection and click Properties. This opens the Properties dialog box for incoming connections using that protocol. For example, the Incoming TCP/IP Properties dialog box is shown in Figure 9.9. From this dialog box you can enable access to your home network by leaving the default option of Allow Callers to Access My Local Area Network selected. Clearing this option restricts the dial-up client to the shared resources of the dial-up server. For the dial-up client to each use TCP/IP to communicate with the dial-up server or your home network, it will have to have an IP address for your local area network. The default option is to dynamically assign one to the dial-up client. Optionally, you can specify a limited range of IP

addresses that can be assigned or allow the dial-up client to assign its own IP address. Unless you have a special reason for doing so I recommend leaving the default address assignment option alone. Click OK when you have finished with this dialog box. Then click Next to continue setting up your dial-up server.

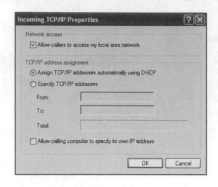

Figure 9.9

Configuring protocol properties for dial-up connections.

The New Connection Wizard announces that it is ready to set up your dial-up server to accept incoming connections. Click Finish.

Once you have configured your dial-up server, an icon representing your incoming connection is placed in the Network Connections folder as demonstrated in Figure 9.10. Windows XP is now set up to answer any incoming connection request from dial-up clients over the telephone line connected to your modem. You can look at the Incoming connections icon and see if a connection is in use and who is using it.

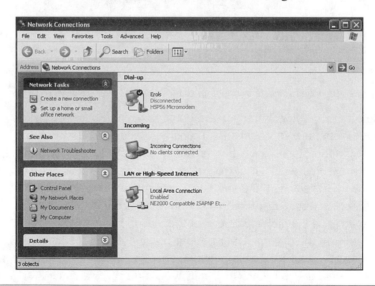

Figure 9.10

You can monitor incoming dial-up connections from the Network Connections dialog box.

NOTE If you right-click the Incoming Connections icon and select Properties from the context menu that appears, you can configure a number of attributes for the connection including which modem it uses, which users can use the connection, and which network software components can operate over the connection.

 NOTE Windows XP only allows you to define one incoming connection. If you attempt to run the New Connection Wizard again and create another incoming connection, you'll only end up replacing your existing connection.

SETTING UP A DIAL-UP CLIENT

Once you have configured your dial-up server you can configure your dial-up client. You can have any number of dial-up connections. For example, you may have a dial-up connection set up on your laptop for an Internet ISP as well as to your home network. The following procedure outlines the steps involved in setting up a dial-up client.

1. Click Start, All Programs, Accessories, Communications, and then Select New Connection Wizard.

2. The Network Connection Wizard opens. Click Next.

3. Select Connect to the network at my workplace as shown in Figure 9.11 and then click Next.

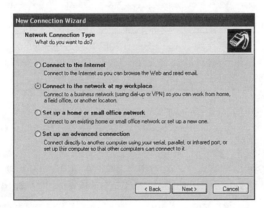

Figure 9.11

Starting the setup of your dial-up client connection.

4. Select Dial-up connection as shown in Figure 9.12 and click Next.

5. Type a name that describes your connection in the Company Name field as shown in Figure 9.13 and then click Next.

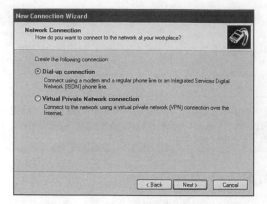

Figure 9.12

Select the dial-up connection option.

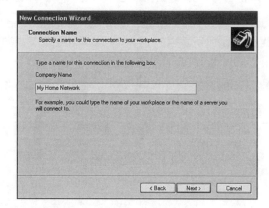

Figure 9.13

Naming your dial-up connection.

6. Type the phone number used by the modem that has been set up on your dial-up server in the Phone number field as demonstrated in Figure 9.14 and click Next.

7. The New Connection Wizard announces that it is ready to set up your dial-up client connection. Click Finish.

Figure 9.14

Supply the phone number of the dial-up server.

An icon representing the dial-up connection is placed in the Network Connections folder. Double-click this icon to initiate a connection with your dial-up server. This will open a connection dialog box where you specify the username and password of an account that exists on the dial-up server and then click Dial to make the connection.

You can also select the Save this username and password for the following users option. This enables the following options:

- **Me Only**—Only allows the person who set up the connection to use it.
- **Anyone Who Uses This Computer**—Makes the connection available to anyone who uses the computer.

Once a connection is established with the dial-up server you can use the My Network Places folder to access the shared resources on the dial-up server. If the dial-up server's incoming connection has been configured to allow access to your home network, then you can connect to any shared network resource as well.

Once a dial-up connection is established between the dial-up server and dial-up client an icon representing the connection is displayed in the system tray of each computer. You can double-click it to open the dialog box where you can view the connection's status. You can also terminate the dial-up connection from either computer by clicking Disconnect.

Think twice before forcibly disconnecting a dial-up session from the dial-up server. If the person at the dial-up client is working on a file and has not saved his or her changes, then his or her unsaved work will be lost.

If you find that you are creating some pretty big long-distance phone bills because of your dial-up connection, you may want to seriously consider using a VPN connection instead as discussed in the next section.

UNDERSTANDING VIRTUAL PRIVATE NETWORKING

A virtual private network or VPN operates in much the same manner as a remote dial-up connection in that it lets a remote computer connect to another computer and access shared resources. Because it operates over the Internet instead of over a dedicated telephone line connection you may use either a dial-up or high-speed connection to set a VPN up. Of course, using a high-speed connection will provide a VPN session with significantly better performance than a dial-up connection.

> Your VPN server must have its own connection to the Internet. Therefore, it can also be your ICS server. It cannot, however, be a computer located behind an Internet gateway appliance or an ICS client. If this is a feature that you plan on using, then you may want to consider using ICS instead of an Internet gateway appliance when setting up shared Internet access for your home network.

A VPN connection is a secure connection because its communications are encrypted such that only the sending and receiving computers can decrypt its communications.

A VPN session is established between two computers. If the VPN Server has been configured to allow it, the person working at the VPN client can access both the VPN server's and the home network's shared resources. A Windows XP Home Edition computer can support just one VPN connection at a time. A VPN connection is configured using the New Connection Wizard.

SETTING UP A VPN SERVER CONNECTION

A VPN server is established by defining an incoming connection that supports a VPN connection. Because a Windows XP computer can only support one VPN connection, the same connection is used to define both a dial-up and a VPN connection. If you already have an Incoming connection set up as described earlier in this chapter, then you can configure it to support an incoming VPN connection request using the following procedure.

1. Click Start, right-click My Network Places and select properties from the context menu that appears.

2. The Network Connections folder appears. Right-click the Incoming Connections icon and select Properties from the context menu that appears.

3. The Incoming Connection Properties dialog box appears as shown in Figure 9.15. Select the Allow Others to Make Private Connections to My Computer by Tunneling Through the Internet or Other Network option and click OK.

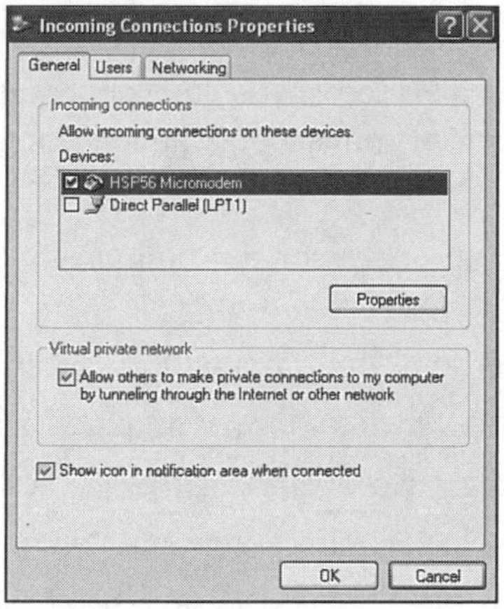

Figure 9.15

Configuring an Incoming Connection to support VPN access.

If you do not already have an Incoming Connection set up, then you can use the following procedure to create one for your VPN session from scratch.

1. Click Start, All Programs, Accessories, Communications, and then Select New Connection Wizard.

2. The Network Connection Wizard opens. Click Next.

3. Select Set Up an Advanced Connection and click Next.

4. Select Accept Incoming Connections and click Next.

5. The next dialog box displays a list of connection devices and asks you to select one. However, these devices do not apply when setting up a VPN connection so you may clear each option and click Next.

6. Select Allow Virtual Private Connections and click Next.

7. A list of user accounts that are defined on the computer appears. Select the User Accounts Belong to the Individuals that Will Need Remote Access to the Computer and click Next.

8. Select the network software components that you want to use over the dial-up connection and click Next.

9. The New Connection Wizard announces that it is ready to set up the Incoming Connection. Click Finish.

SETTING UP A VPN CLIENT CONNECTION

Once you have set up your VPN server you can connect to it from any Internet connection in the world using a VPN client connection. The following procedure outlines how to configure a VPN client.

1. Click Start, All Programs, Accessories, Communications, and then Select New Connection Wizard.

2. The Network Connection Wizard opens. Click Next.

3. Select Connect to the Network at My Workplace and click Next.

4. Select Virtual Private Network Connection and click Next.

5. Type a name for the VPN connection in the Company Name field and click Next.

6. The next dialog box asks how you want to establish the connection as shown in Figure 9.16. If your computer is directly connected to the Internet with an always-on high-speed connection, select Do Not Dial the Initial Connection. If you are using a dial-up connection, then select Automatically Dial this Initial Connection and then select the appropriate dial-up connection from the drop-down list. Make your selection and click Next.

Figure 9.16

Determining how your VPN connection is established.

7. Type the host name of the VPN server or its IP address in the Host name or IP address field as shown in Figure 9.17. Because this VPN connection is to your home network you'll need to type the IP address assigned to your VPN server by your ISP. Click Next.

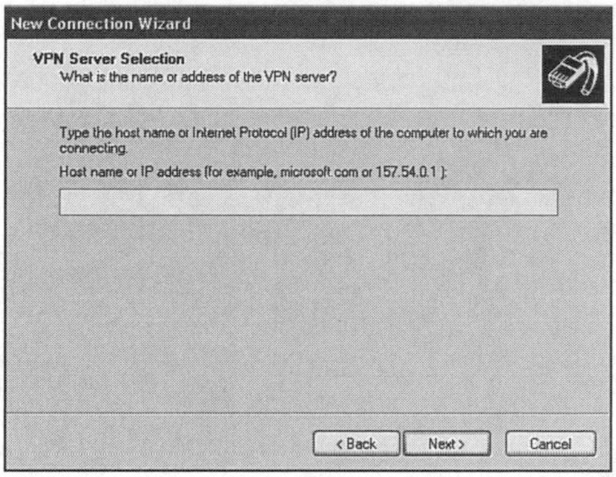

Figure 9.17

You must provide the IP address of your VPN Server.

If the computer that you set up as a VPN server uses a dial-up connection to the Internet, then its IP address will change every time it connects. This makes a dial-up connection a poor choice. However, if the connection to the Internet uses an always-on high-speed connection, then chances are that the IP address will remain constant over time. You can use the IPCONFIG /ALL command to determine a Windows XP computer's IP address.

8. The New Connection Wizard announces that it is ready to create the VPN client connection. Click Finish.

You'll find an icon for the VPN client connection in the Virtual Private Network section of the Network Connections folder as demonstrated in Figure 9.18.

To initiate a VPN connection over the Internet double-click its icon. What happens next depends on how you defined the client connection. If you have an always-on high-speed Internet connection, then you are prompted for a username and password that will be recognized by the VPN server as shown in Figure 9.19.

If you set up the VPN connection to use a dial-up connection and the dial-up connection is already active, then you'll be prompted to supply a valid username and password. However, if the dial-up connection is not active, you'll see a prompt asking for permission to start it first. Click Yes to start the dial-up Internet connection. Once the connection is established you then are prompted to supply a username and password for the VPN connection. Once your VPN connection is established you can use the My Network Places folder to access shared resources on the VPN server. In addition, if the VPN server has been configured to permit it, you'll be able to access shared resources on your home network as well.

Figure 9.18

The Network Connections folder displays all your network connections.

Figure 9.19

Initiating a VPN connection.

CHAPTER 10

JUST WHEN YOU THOUGHT YOUR WORK WAS DONE

At this point you have all the ingredients required to build a home network, wireless or otherwise, and connect it to the Internet. You've also learned how to share network resources such as disk drives and printers. However, to keep your home network up and running in a healthy state there are a number of tasks that you need to learn how to perform. This chapter also provides instruction on basic network troubleshooting in order to help prepare you to deal with network problems when they arise.

Here is what you'll learn:

- How to perform administrative tasks using the Computer Management console

- How to use the Task Manager utility to examine system status and control applications

- How to repair TCP/IP communication problems

- How to troubleshoot and fix common network problems

BASIC SYSTEM AND NETWORK ADMINISTRATION

By now you should have your own home network up and running. Everyone in the family should have their own user account. Your printers, folders, and even your Internet connection should be shared. In addition, you have set up personal firewall protection to guard against Internet intruders and have double-checked the lock on your front door.

If you have done all this work, then you are probably feeling pretty good and you should be. Setting up a home network is a nifty thing to do. However, your work is not done. From time to time every home network needs a little administrative tweaking to keep it running well. In addition, every network experiences problems from time to time. As the person who set up your home network you are its main administrator and will need to be prepared to handle these problems (or opportunities depending on how you look at them). The purpose of this chapter is to show you how to use various Windows XP utilities and programs to perform a number of administrative tasks. In addition, this chapter will give you an overview on how to deal with a number of common network problems that sometimes creep up.

The Microsoft Management Console

Windows XP provides an administrative framework known as the Microsoft Management Console or MMC. Using the MMC you can create management consoles that allow you to perform a number of administrative procedures and troubleshooting tasks. As a framework the MMC itself does nothing. However, by *adding snap-ins*, individual utilities that perform a specific task, you can create custom consoles that can perform a variety of things.

You can create a new MMC console using the following procedure.

1. Click Start, Select Run, type **MMC**, and click OK. An empty console opens as shown in Figure 10.1.

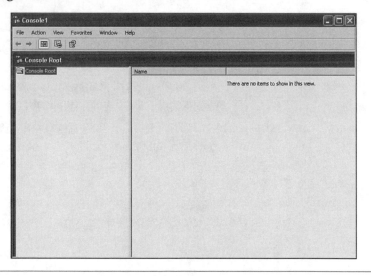

Figure 10.1

The MMC provides a framework for building administrative consoles.

2. To make your new console useful you need to add one or more snap-ins. You can do this by clicking File and then selecting Add/Remove Snap-in. This opens the Add/Remove Snap-in dialog box shown in Figure 10.2.

Figure 10.2

Adding snap-ins to your MMC console.

3. Click Add. This opens the Add Standalone Snap-in dialog box as shown in Figure 10.3.

Figure 10.3

Selecting an available snap-in.

4. You can add as many snap-ins as you want to your console by selecting them and clicking Add. You'll be prompted to configure each snap-in that you add as shown in Figure 10.4. You can choose from the following options.

- **Local Computer**—Sets the snap-in up to manage the local computer.
- **Another Computer**—Sets the snap-in up to manage the specified network computer.

- **Allow the Selected Computer to be Changed when Launching from the Command Line**—Allows you to change the selected computer when you open the console.

Make your selections and click Finish.

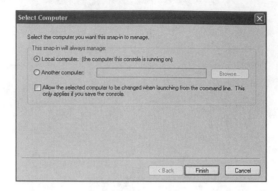

Figure 10.4

Configuring a snap-in for local or remote access.

5. Once you have finished adding snaps-ins click Close. Then click OK to close the Add/Remove Snap-in dialog box.

6. You are returned to your MMC console. At this point you can begin using your new console. You can also save it for later use by clicking File, selecting Save, typing a name for the console, and clicking Save. Your new console will be saved by default in your Administrative Tools folder, which you can open by clicking Start, All Programs, and the Administrative Tools.

> If Administrative Tools does not appear in the All Programs menu, you can adjust this with a few simple clicks. Right-click the Start button, choose Properties, click Customize, select the Advanced tab, and scroll down to System Administrative Tools in the Start menu items section. There you will see three options for the display of Administrative Tools.

The Computer Management Console

Although the ability to create your own MMC console is helpful to network and system administrators, it is usually overkill for home networking. Instead, Microsoft has made things easy for you by predefining a console that should accommodate most of your administrative needs. This console is the Computer Management Console, shown in Figure 10.5.

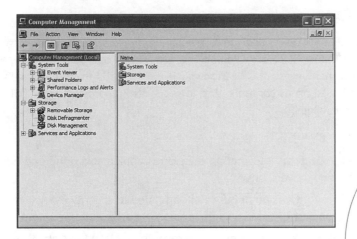

Figure 10.5

The Computer Management Console contains a pre-configured collection of snap-ins that should cover most of your administrative needs.

You can open the Computer Management Console by right-clicking My Computer and selecting Manage from the context menu that appears. The Computer Management Console is organized into a tree-like view with three main branches as follows:

- **System Tools**—Contains snap-ins that allow you to manage event logs, shared folders, performance logs, and hardware devices.
- **Storage**—Contains snap-ins that allow you to manage disk drives.
- **Services and Applications**—Contains snap-ins that allow you to manage computer services and the Windows XP Index Service.

 You'll need to log on with an account that has administrative-level privileges in order to use the Computer Management Console.

System Tools

The Systems Tools branch of the Computer Management Console contains four snap-ins, which provides the following administrative capabilities.

- **Event Viewer**—Provides access to system, security, and application logs where Windows XP records information, warning, error, and audit events.
- **Shared Folders**—Provides three different views for managing shared resources including By shares, Active sessions, and By open files.
- **Performance Logs and Alerts**—Lets you view performance logs and alerts.
- **Device Manager**—Lets you view and manage the computer's hardware devices.

Event Viewer

Windows XP displays critical error messages directly on the screen when they occur. However, Windows XP Home Edition is a very stable operating system so you won't usually see too many messages. Windows XP also records these messages to one of three event logs based on its contents. Windows XP also records a number of less critical information in these logs.

These event logs are

- **System**—Contains information related to problems with the operating system, hardware, and software drivers.
- **Security**—Contains audit information related to security events such as when people log on and off.
- **Application**—Contains information recorded by Windows applications.

The event logs are one of the first places that you'll need to check when one of your computers experiences a problem. Often, you'll find that Windows has not only recorded a record of the problem but also has identified a solution for it as well or at least has provided you with enough information to begin troubleshooting.

Windows XP automatically manages its event logs. Except for an occasional review of the logs, you should not have to do much with them. However, if you are experiencing a lot of problems with a particular computer or if you simply like tinkering and seeing how things work, you may want to learn how to perform a few log management tasks.

The most basic task that you'll perform with event logs is viewing them, which you can do using the following procedure.

1. Open the Computer Management Console.
2. Select the Event Viewer snap-in as shown in Figure 10.6.
3. Select an event log. You'll see the type, date, time, source, and category of each event recorded in the log displayed on the right side of the Computer Management Console.
4. To view more information about a particular event, double-click it. A dialog box similar to the one shown in Figure 10.7 will appear. In addition to the information that was display in the main event log you'll also see a detailed description of the event and possibly a remedy.
5. Click the up or down arrows to view the previous or next alert in the event log. Click OK to return to the Computer Management Console.

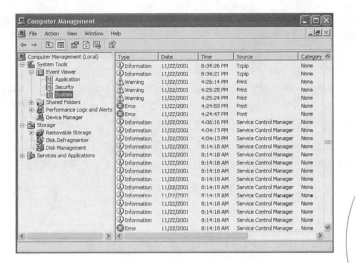

Figure 10.6

Examining Windows XP Event logs.

Figure 10.7

Viewing event details.

The next several procedures outline how to perform a number of event log management tasks, including

- Configuring event logs
- Clearing event logs
- Saving an event log
- Retrieving an event log

By default Windows XP Home Edition configures all three event logs to hold up to 512K of information and to overwrite older events when the logs become full to make room for new events. This ensures that the event logs are always available and that events are always recorded. For most home computers these settings are just fine. However, you may come across a problem somewhere down the line that requires a lot of research. Therefore you may want to increase the size of your log files or prevent them from overwriting old events until you have had a chance to examine them.

Each Windows XP event log is individually configured. The following procedure explains how to configure your log file settings.

1. Open the Computer Management console.

2. Select the Event Viewer snap-in.

3. Select an Event log and then select the Properties option on the Action menu. The Properties dialog box for the select event log will appear.

4. To change the size of the event log type value in the Maximum log size field.

5. Next select from one of the options that tells Windows XP what to do when the log file fills up:

   - **Overwrite Events as Needed**—This is the default option, which tells Windows XP to overwrite older events as needed when the log fills up.

   - **Overwrite Event Older Than—Days**—This option prevents Windows XP from overwriting events less than the stated number of days old. If the log fills up and there are no events older than this specified value, Windows XP stops recording new events until enough time passes to allow it to overwrite older events.

   - **Do Not Overwrite Events (Clear Log Manually)**—This option tells Windows XP to add events to the log as long as there is room. If the log fills up, Windows XP will not be able to record new events.

6. Click on OK.

If you elect to change the default event-log configuration settings, then you'll need to start manually performing the following log management tasks.

Think twice before you decide to get into the business of managing Event logs manually. It is easy to forget about them and if you let them fill up and a new problem occurs, you won't be able to turn to your Event logs for help.

If you have an Event log that has filled up and you want to clear it out and you are sure that you won't need to review it later, you can use the following procedure to clear its contents.

You will not see a message warning you when Windows XP's Event logs are full. You can tell when an Event log is full by opening it and examining the date and time of its last recorded event. If you've been using the computer regularly and it has been a while since a new event was recorded, then the log is probably full.

1. Open the Computer Management Console.
2. Select the Event Viewer snap-in.
3. Select an Event log and select the Clear All Events option on the Action menu.
4. Click No when Windows XP asks you if you want to save the log.

It's a good idea to keep copies of your log files around for a while, just in case. The following procedure shows you how to do so.

1. Open the Computer Management Console.
2. Select the Event Viewer snap-in.
3. Select an Event log and select the Save Log File As option on the Action menu.
4. Type a name for the file and click Save.

By storing copies of your Event logs you can create a valuable archive of information. The following procedure explains how to retrieve a saved log file.

1. Open the Computer Management Console.
2. Select the Event Viewer snap-in.
3. Select an Event log and select the Open Log File option on the Action menu. The Open dialog box opens.
4. Locate and select a previously saved event log and then click on Open.

Shared Folders

The Shared Folders snap-in provides tools for monitoring and managing shared disks and folders as demonstrated in Figure 10.8. It provides a view of all shared drives and folders, including hidden resources with names that end with the $ character.

 More information on hidden resources is available in "Examining Hidden Shares" in Chapter 5.

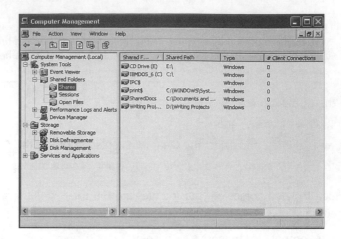

Figure 10.8

Monitoring and administering network shared sessions and open files.

The Shared Folders snap-in provides three separate views, which are outlined here:

- **Shares**—Displays a listing of all the shared resources that are available on the computer.
- **Sessions**—Displays information about all network users that are currently connected to the computer.
- **Opens Files**—Displays information about all files currently opened on the computer.

You can use the Shared Folders snap-in to perform a number of administrative tasks, including

- Sending messages to network computers
- Monitoring who is connected to your computer from over the network
- Closing network connections
- Monitoring network users as they access your files
- Closing open files

 Detailed coverage of the Shared Folders snap-in can be found in Chapter 5, "Sharing Precious Disk Space."

Performance Logs and Alerts

The Performance Logs and Alerts snap-in, shown in Figure 10.9, allows you to monitor and log detailed information about system performance. Windows XP views a computer as a collection of objects and spends a portion of its time collecting information about each object. The various measurements available for each object are known as counters. For example, one type of Windows object is PhysicalDisk. Windows XP provides a number of counters that describe the performance of the PhysicalDisk object. For example, one such counter is %Disk time, which is the percentage of time that a selected disk drive is busy processing read/write requests. Other objects that you can monitor include

- Server
- Print Queue
- Network Interface

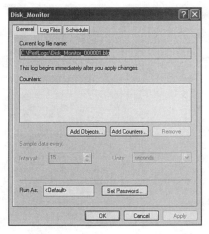

Figure 10.9

The Performance Logs and Alerts snap-in.

This snap-in can be used to monitor the previous objects using dozens of different measurements and can provide you with all kinds of information. However, unless you are trying to track down a specific performance problem, such as what process might be eating up too much CPU time or consuming too much disk time, you probably will never need to use this snap-in. Still, here's a quick overview of how to create a log that allows you to monitor and record specific objects and their counters.

The Performance Logs and Alerts snap-in manages three resources as listed here.

- **Counter Logs**—Records statistics about system performance at predefined intervals.
- **Trace Logs**—Records information based on the occurrence of a particular event.
- **Alerts**—Sends a message or executes a problem when a predefined threshold is reached.

Except for one example Counter log, Windows XP Home Edition does not come with any pre-configured Counter Logs, Trace Logs, or Alerts. This is probably because Microsoft sees these logs as an advanced tool that the average home user will not use. However, you can use the steps outlined in the following procedure to create new logs.

1. Open the Computer Management Console.
2. Select the Performance Logs and Alerts snap-in.

3. Right-click Counter Logs and select New Log Settings. The New Log Settings dialog box appears.

4. Type a name for the new log file and click OK.

5. A new dialog box appears as shown in Figure 10.10, which allows you to select the objects that you want to monitor and to choose specific measurements or counters related to the objects.

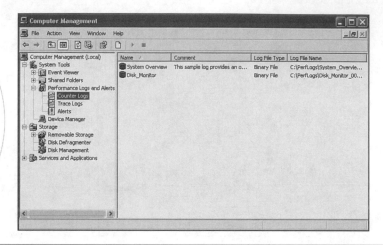

Figure 10.10

Creating a new counter log.

6. At the top of the General property sheet you'll see the location where Windows XP will store the log file. By default this is in C:\Perflogs. The Counters section in the middle of the General property sheet displays a list of objects and counters that you have selected for monitoring.

7. To add a new Object and all its counters to the list click Add Objects. The Add Objects dialog box appears. Select an object from the Performance object's list and click Add. Add as many objects as you want and then click Close.

8. Sometimes monitoring all an object's counters is overkill and you'll only want to monitor one or two specific counters. In this case click Add Counters and select an object from the Performance object drop-down list. Then select specific counters related to that object from the Select counters from list and click Add. You may add as many objects and counters as you want. Click Close when you are done.

9. You can configure the interval at which data about each counter is collected by selecting it from the Counters section and changing the value stored in the Interval field. The default is 15. You can also specify the units of time. The default is seconds but you can change it to minutes, hours, and days.

10. Optionally you can type the username of an account under which the log should run. If the user account has a password, then you'll also need to click Set Password and type the user account's password twice when prompted.

11. Once you have added all the objects and counters that you want to monitor in the log click OK. If this is the first time that you have used the Performance Logs and Alerts snap-in, then you'll see a prompt stating that the C:\Perflogs does not exist. Click Yes to create it.

NOTE The reason for specifying a user account under which the logs will run is to ensure that it can run even when you are not logged on to the computer.

Once you have created a new log you can stop and start it by right-clicking it and selecting Stop or Start. You can also right-click it and select Properties of modify it.

If you'd like to view a real-time graphical display of the data being recorded by the log, find the log in C:\Perflogs and double-click it. This will open the Performance dialog box similar to the one shown in Figure 10.11.

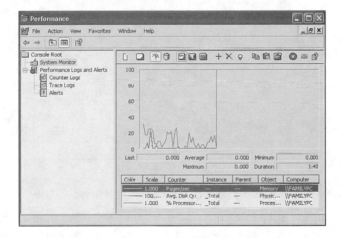

Figure 10.11

Viewing a graphical representation of data as it is recorded in a log file.

You can create a log file to monitor just about every aspect of Windows XP's operations. For example, you can create log files to monitor the activity of your network adapter. You can add new objects and counters and remove them from the Performance dialog box. You can also stop and start the collection of data and even change the view of the data to any of the following formats:

- **View Graph**—The Default display.
- **View Histogram**—Displays data in the form of a bar chart.
- **View Report**—Displays captured data in the form of a typed summary report.

The Performance Logs and Alerts snap-in and its accompanying Performance dialog box is an advanced tool and is complex enough to fill up an entire book. You can find a lot more information about it in the Windows XP Help and Support Center by clicking on Start and then selecting Help and Support.

Device Manager

The Device Manager snap-in allows you to view and modify the configuration of the hardware installed on your computer. When you open the Device Manager, as demonstrated in Figure 10.12, you see a listing of the hardware that Windows has installed and configured on the computer. Anytime a Windows XP computer has any devices that are in conflict with one another or that are not operating properly, the branches of the hardware tree under which they reside will be expanded to show the devices.

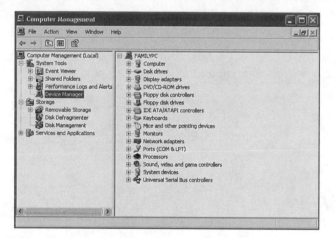

Figure 10.12

The Device Manager snap-in lets you view and configure hardware devices.

The Device Manager snap-in allows you to perform a number of tasks, including

- Viewing all the computer's installed hardware
- Locating hardware conflicts and problems
- Modifying hardware configuration settings
- Updating hardware device drivers
- Disabling and enabling hardware devices
- Uninstalling hardware devices
- Printing a device or computer hardware report

techtv tip

You can also open the Device Manager by clicking Start, right-clicking the My Computer icon, selecting properties from the context menu that appears, opening the Hardware property sheet, and clicking the Device Manager button.

You can sort the way that the Device Manager snap-in displays your computer's hardware by selecting one of the following options from the View menu.

- **Devices by Type**—Displays hardware devices by type. For example, all sound, video, and games controllers are grouped together. This is the default option.

- **Devices by Connection**—Displays hardware devices by their type of connection.

- **Resources by Type**—Displays allocated resources based on the type of hardware that uses them. Examples of resources include DMA, IO, IRG, and memory.

- **Resources by Connection**—Displays allocated resources based on connection type.

The View menu also contains the Show hidden devices option. This option allows you to toggle the display of hidden hardware devices. A hidden hardware device is a non-plug-and-play device or a device that has been removed from the computer without having its software driver uninstalled.

You can view the status of any hardware device using the following procedure.

1. Open the Device Manager snap-in and click a hardware category.

2. Right-click a hardware device and select Properties from the context menu that appears.

3. Examine the status of the device as listed in the Device status section on the General property sheet as demonstrated in Figure 10.13.

Figure 10.13

Examining the status of a hardware device.

4. Open the Resources property sheet and examine the Conflicting device list at the bottom of the property sheet.

Two types of hardware problems are common, software driver and resource conflicts. You can view information about a device's driver using the following procedure.

1. Open the Device Manager snap-in and click a hardware category.

2. Right-click a hardware device and select Properties from the context menu that appears.

3. Open the Driver property sheet. Information about the driver's provider, date, version, and signer is displayed as shown in Figure 10.14. In addition, you'll see four buttons that allow you to manage the device's software driver. These four driver management tasks include

Figure 10.14

Working with hardware drivers.

- **Driver Details**—Provides additional information about the driver.

- **Update Driver**—Allows you to replace the driver with a newer version. This option starts the Hardware Update Wizard, which steps you though the process of updating the device's driver.

- **Roll Back Driver**—Lets you reinstall the previous version of a driver in the event that the current driver causes a problem.

- **Uninstall**—Lets you remove the driver from your computer.

4. Click OK to close the property dialog box or click one of the previous buttons to manage the driver.

All hardware devices require computer resources in order to function. Examples of resources include DMA, IO, IRQ, and memory. Sometimes two hardware devices want the same hardware resources creating a conflict. Devices with conflicts or other hardware problems are graphically flagged in the Device Manager with yellow or red icons.

Most modern devices are capable of using alternate resources. Windows XP Plug and Play usually does a good job of finding a way to allocate adequate resources to hardware devices. However, there may be times when it is unable to do so. When this occurs check the documentation for the hardware devices in question. You may be able to resolve the situation by manually configuring the hardware resources for these devices as outlined by the following procedure.

1. Open the Device Manager snap-in and click a hardware category.

2. Right-click a hardware device and select Properties from the context menu that appears.

3. Open the Resources property sheet and clear the Use Automatic setting.

4. Select the hardware configuration that you want to change in the Settings based on the drop-down list.

5. Select the resource that you want to change in the Resource setting section.

6. Click the Change Setting button, type a new setting value when prompted and click OK.

7. Click OK to close the Properties dialog box.

techtv tip

Be verycareful when working with the Device Manager snap-in. Make sure that you do not try to assign a resource to a device that is already assigned to another device. If you incorrectly change the setting for a hardware device, you can render it inoperative. In addition you could even disable your entire computer.

If you are having problems with a hardware device and are unable to resolve the problem on your own, use the Device Manager snap-in to open the device's properties dialog box. Click the Troubleshoot button on the General property sheet. This will start the Windows XP Hardware Troubleshooter. Follow the instructions presented by the troubleshooter and see if this helps you to solve the problem.

Storage

The Storage branch in the Computer Management Console contains three snap-ins that provide tools for managing disk storage on your computer. These snap-ins include

- **Removable Storage**—This snap-in allows you to manage any removable storage device.

- **Disk Defragmenter**—This snap-in lets you defrag the data stored on your hard disk drive(s) in order to speed file retrieval.

- **Disk Management**—This snap-in lets you perform a number of tasks including assigning drive letters and creating and formatting disk partitions.

Although the storage-related snap-ins are useful for managing your disk drives, they are not necessarily closely tied to home networking, therefore, detailed coverage of these snap-ins will be left to other books.

Services and Applications

The Services and Applications branch of the Computer Management Console provides three snap-ins that allow you to manage the following Windows applications and services.

- **Services**—This snap-in allows you to view and manage Windows services. A service is a program that provides a particular operating system feature. For example, the Print Spooler service manages the Windows XP print queues.

- **WMI Control**—This snap-in lets you configure Windows Management Instrumentation or WMI. WMI provides a standard framework for accessing system information and managing system resources.

- **Indexing Service**—This snap-in allows you to manage the Windows Indexing service. This service examines the documents stored on your computers and builds a searchable index based on their content. This improves the ability of Windows XP to assist you in performing complex searches on your computer.

Although the Services and Applications related snap-ins are useful for managing various Windows applications and services, they are not necessarily closely tied to home networking. Therefore, detailed coverage of these tools will be left to other authors.

TROUBLESHOOTING WINDOWS XP HOME NETWORKS

From time to time every network has problems. Network problems can be software-related or hardware-related. Often it is difficult to tell where the problem lies or what is causing it.

Windows XP Home Edition provides you with an abundance of tools for gathering information and resolving computer and network problems. You've already read about some of the tools earlier in this book. These tools include

- Computer Management console snap-ins
- Windows XP commands such as PING and IPCONFIG
- The Windows XP Task Manager
- Software patches, fixes, and updates that are available on Microsoft Windows Update Sites and other vendor Web sites

In addition to these tools, it pays to have a good understanding of your network hardware and how to track down hardware problems. As a starting point, the following questions should be asked any time your computer or network has a problem.

- What error message, if any has appeared? Did you remember to check the Event logs?

- Have you or anyone in the family recently installed any new hardware or software? If something has changed you might try uninstalling it and see if that fixes the problem.

- What is the scope of the problem? Is one computer affected or does the problem affect all the computers on your home network? If every computer is affected, then you may have a hardware problem such a disabled network hub. If the problem is isolated to a single computer, then the problem could be hardware- or software-related. For example, the computer's network cable might have been disconnected from the hub or accidentally cut in two.

If your computer or home network is also connected to the Internet, then the problem could also be caused by a computer virus. To guard against these types of problem make sure that all your computers are running antivirus programs and that your network is protected by a personal firewall and remember to review the logs generated by these applications for possible warning messages.

Even if you take every possible precaution, bad things will still happen. Make sure that you have a good backup program and that you regularly back up your files and other important data. That way, even if your computers are stolen, you can always replace them and restore your data.

Gathering Information with the Task Manager

The Windows XP Task Manager utility provides a fast way to view the status of a number of critical performance measures. It is also one of the first places that you'll want to check when your computer or network seems to be running slow and you want to know why. You can open the Task Manager by right-clicking a free area on the Windows XP Taskbar and selecting Task Manager from the context menu that appears.

The Task Manager is organized into five property sheets, each of which supplies a different set of information regarding the operation and performance of your computer and network as explained here

- **Applications**—Displays information regarding the status of running applications and allows you to terminate them or start new applications.
- **Processes**—Displays information about the processes that are running and allows you to change their processing priority or terminate them.
- **Performance**—Displays a graphical view of the computer's CPU and memory performance.
- **Networking**—Displays a graphical view of network performance.
- **Users**—Displays a list of users with active sessions on the computer and allows you to send them messages and disconnect them.

Managing Applications

The Applications property sheet, shown in Figure 10.15, provides control over the applications currently running on a computer. Each application is listed along with its status, which can be either Running or Not Responding. Generally speaking a non-responding program is one that has stopped working and is refusing to accept further commands. You can forcefully terminate a hung program or even a running program by selecting it and clicking End Task. Windows XP will then ask for confirmation and then stop the application. You can use the Applications property sheet to manage your applications, including your network applications such as Internet Explorer and NetMeeting. You should use this option with caution because any of the application's unsaved work will be lost.

Figure 10.15

Managing active Windows XP applications.

You can jump to any application by selecting it and clicking Switch To. You can even start up a new application if you know its name by clicking New task and supplying its name.

Working with Processes

The Processes property sheet, shown in Figure 10.16, displays active Windows processes. Windows XP is a multiprocessing operating system, meaning that it can run more than one process at a time. While an application may run as a single process, it may also run as multiple processes. In addition, Windows XP runs a number of processes that are needed to support general operations. Each of these processes is visible on this property sheet.

By default Windows XP displays the following information for each process.

- **Image Name**—The name of a process.
- **User Name**—The name of the user who owns the process or started it.
- **CPU**—The percentage of time that a process has used the CPU since the last update interval.
- **Mem Usage**—The amount of memory currently assigned to the process.

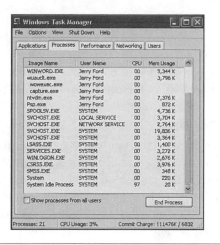

Figure 10.16

Managing active Windows XP processes.

By default, only the processes related to Windows XP and to your login session are displayed. However, you can select the Show processes from all users option at the bottom of the property sheet to view all processes. You can terminate any process by selecting it and clicking End Process. However, you should do so with great care because if you terminate the wrong process, the results can be unpredictable. For example, if you accidentally terminated an application that you were working with, you'd lose any unsaved work.

Monitoring Computer Performance

The top portion of the Performance property sheet, shown in Figure 10.17, provides a graphical depiction of the computer's CPU and memory usage. The bottom half of this property sheet provides more detailed statistics regarding the use of memory.

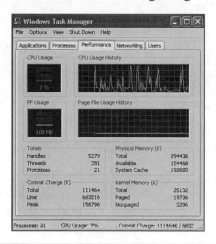

Figure 10.17

Viewing CPU and memory use.

You can use the Performance sheet to get a good look at how a computer is performing. If either CPU or memory is extremely high, you may have a runaway program. In this case you can terminate it using the Application's property sheet. You can use the information on this property sheet to get an idea of the impact that your network applications may have on the overall performance of the computer.

Analyzing Network Performance

The Networking property sheet, shown in Figure 10.18, provides you with a view of the data traffic on your home network. This property sheet graphically displays the percentage of your network's bandwidth consumed at any given point in time. Below the graphical representation of network traffic is a listing of each network adapter installed on the computer. Each adapter is listed by name. Also listed is the percentage of network utilization that the adapter is responsible for, its connection speed, and the current operational state.

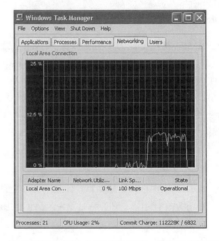

Figure 10.18

Examining the performance of your home network.

You can use the information displayed on the Networking property sheet to see how your network is operating. Under normal operating conditions a home network will use a very low percentage of the overall available bandwidth, typically between 5–20 percent. If you notice a slow-down in network response time, a quick look at this property sheet may provide a clue. For example, if you see that your network bandwidth is close to 100 percent, then something is flooding your network. For example, you might find that one of the kids is copying a massive file from one computer to another. On the other hand if no one in the family is moving lots of data around, then something may be wrong with one of the network adapters in your computers causing it to flood your network with useless data packets. You could track the offending computer's network adapter by examining the Network property sheet on each of the computers on your home network and look-ing for the one that has a network adapter whose network utilization percentage is maxed out.

If you have any non-Windows XP computers on your home network, you'll have to examine the transmission indicator lights on each of these computer's network adapters to find out which ones might be constantly transmitting.

You will not see the Networking property sheet on a Windows XP computer that does not have any network connections.

Keeping an Eye on Who Is Using Your Computer

The Users property sheet, shown in Figure 10.19, displays information about users who are currently logged on to the computer. This property sheet is only visible if Fast User Switching has been enabled.

Figure 10.19

Monitoring who is accessing the files on your computer.

At the bottom of the Users property sheet are three buttons, which provide the following functionality:

- **Disconnect**—Disconnects the user from the computer.
- **Logoff**—Logs the user off of the computer.
- **Send Message**—Displays a dialog box allowing you to send a message to the selected user.

Shutdown Options

The Task Manager also provides a number of options for shutting down your computer. You will find the options on the Shutdown menu. The exact set of options that you'll see depends on how you have configured your computer. They can include

- **Stand By**—Places the computer into a reduced power state while leaving the contents of memory active. When you return and click a key or move the mouse the system is restored to full power and is immediately ready to resume operation.

- **Hibernate**—Tells Windows XP to save any configuration settings or data stored in memory to the hard disk and then to turn off the computer. Upon restart, the system is restored to its previous state by retrieving the information that was stored on the hard disk.

- **Turn Off**—Tells Windows XP to prepare the computer to be turned off. This closes all open programs, stores unsaved configuration settings, and saves unsaved work before shutting down.

- **Restart**—Tells Windows XP to close all open programs, store unsaved configuration settings, and save any unsaved work before shutting down and restarting the computer.

- **Log Off**—Tells Windows XP to close any open programs associated with your log-in session and save any unsaved work or configuration settings before terminating your log-in session.

- **Lock Computer**—Places your log-in session in a secured state while leaving all your programs and files open. In order to begin using your session again you must retype your password.

- **Switch User**—This option allows two or more people to be logged in to the computer at the same time and to jump between user log-in sessions without requiring anyone to log off.

The Hibernate and Stand By options are available only if you have configured them on the Power Options dialog box, which you can find on the Windows XP Control Panel. You can learn more about these two options in Chapter 7, "Becoming Your Own Network Administrator."

Repairing TCP/IP Communications

Sometimes, though not often, a computer's TCP/IP configuration can become misconfigured. For example, you may think that you have a TCP/IP problem if one of the computers on your home network stops communicating with the other computers and you cannot find any other causes for the problem. There are a number of ways that you can try and deal with this situation.

The easiest way to try and repair a computer's TCP/IP configuration for a given network connection is to run the Windows XP repair process. You can view a network connection's current TCP/IP settings and attempt to repair them using the procedure outlined here.

1. Click Start and open My Network Places.

 NOTE
If My Network Places is not available in the Start Menu, you may need to enable it. To do this, right-click the Start button, select Properties, click the Customize button, select the Advanced tab, and scroll to the My Network Places checkbox in the Start menu items section. Check the box and click OK twice.

2. Click the View Network Connections link in the Network tasks section. The Network Connections dialog box opens.

3. Right-click the network connection and select Status. The dialog box shown in Figure 10.20 appears.

Figure 10.20

Gathering information about your network connection.

From this dialog box you'll see the following information:

- **Status**—The connection status will be either connected of disconnected.
- **Duration**—The length of time that the connection has been active.
- **Speed**—The speed of the network connection.
- **Bytes Sent**—The amount of data, in bytes, that the computer has sent over this connection.
- **Bytes Received**—The amount of data, in bytes, that the computer has received over this connection.

At the bottom of this General property sheet are the following two buttons.

- **Properties**—Displays the property dialog box for the network connection where you can modify its assigned protocols, clients, and services.
- **Disable**—Allows you to disable or terminate the network connection preventing any data from being sent or received over it.

4. Open the Support property sheet as shown in Figure 10.21.

Figure 10.21

Viewing the TCP/IP configuration settings assigned to your network connection.

The following information is displayed on this property sheet.

- Address Type
- IP Address
- Subnet Mask
- Default Gateway

You can click the Details button to open a Details dialog box like the one shown in Figure 10.22.

Figure 10.22

Viewing detailed information about the network connection.

Click Close to return to the Support property sheet.

5. Click Repair to tell Windows XP to attempt to repair the network connection's TCP/IP configuration settings.

6. A dialog box will appear telling you that the repair operation has completed. Click OK.

Windows XP does a number of things when you run the network repair process including re-registering with all available network services including DHCP and DNS. It also refreshes any stored data that it has about the network connection

If your network connection still does not work after running the repair process, double-check the status lights on your network adapter and make sure that they do not indicate an error with the adapter.

If you are troubleshooting an Internet connection, make sure that your dial-up, cable, or DSL modem is powered on and that its indicator lights show that it is working correctly. Try powering the modem on and off. If you still cannot connect to the Internet, call your ISP and see if it is experiencing any problems.

If this does not work, then another option is to rerun the Windows XP Network Setup Wizard. The wizard will step you through the process of reconfiguring your Internet connection, network adapters, computer name, workgroup, and file and printer sharing. You can run the wizard by clicking Start, All Programs, Accessories, Communications, and then Network Setup Wizard.

To learn more about working with the Network Setup Wizard check out Chapter 4, "Putting It All Together."

A third option for debugging TCP/IP problems is to try to manually diagnose and correct the problem using the information provided here.

First, open the Windows XP command prompt and type **IPCONFIG**. You should see output similar to that shown here.

```
C:\>ipconfig

Windows IP Configuration

Ethernet adapter Local Area Connection:

        Connection-specific DNS Suffix  . : va.mediaone.net
        IP Address. . . . . . . . . . . . : 192.168.1.101
        Subnet Mask . . . . . . . . . . . : 255.255.255.0
        Default Gateway . . . . . . . . . : 192.168.1.1
```

When examining the results of the IPCONFIG command, look for the following things.

- Is the assigned IP address correct? For example, for a Windows XP network that does not share an Internet connection all computers should have IP addresses for a 169.154.0.0 network. If ICS is used on the network, then all your network computers should have IP addresses for a 192.168.0.0 network. Or, if your network has an Internet Gateway, then the IP addresses should match the network set up by the gateway device, which in the case of the example shown previously is 192.168.1.0.

- Is the Subnet Mask set to 255.255.255.0? This is the subnet mask that is typically assigned on most home networks.

- Does the Default Gateway display the correct IP address? On a network with ICS the default gateway will be 192.168.0.1. The address of the default gateway on a network that uses an Internet Gateway will be the IP address that the Internet gateway assigns to itself, which in the case of the previous example is 192.168.1.1.

Fixing Addressing Problems

If you do not see the correct IP configuration settings, then you can tell Windows XP to release its current TCP/IP settings and request new ones by typing **IPCONFIG/RELEASE**. This tells Windows XP to release its current TCP/IP settings. Then type **IPCONFIG/RENEW**. This tells Windows XP to retrieve new settings. If the computer does not have shared Internet access, then Windows XP will assign itself new settings. If your network uses ICS or an Internet Gateway, the computer will request new TCP/IP settings from the DHCP service provided by whichever of these options has been installed.

Look Out for Duplicate IP Addresses

If you have chosen to manually configure the TCP/IP configuration settings on one of your network computers while letting the rest of the network get their configuration settings dynamically, you run the risk that at some point one of the other computers may be assigned a duplicate IP address. You can tell when a computer tries to start up with a duplicate IP address by examining the value of its subnet mask. If it is 0.0.0.0, then the computer has been assigned a duplicate IP address. To prevent this problem from occurring either set up all your computers to receive their TCP/IP configuration settings dynamically or make sure that the computer with the static IP settings is always started up before the rest of the computers on the network. You can also use the IPCONFIG/RELEASE and IPCONFIG/RENEW commands on the computer that has been set up to dynamically release its TCP/IP settings and to request a new configuration.

PINGing

When you have fixed any hardware problems that may exist and verified that your network connection has good TCP/IP configuration settings, you can test the computer's ability to communicate with another network computer using the PING command.

A PING command will tell you if your computer is able to find and talk to another computer on your home network. For example, to try and PING a computer with an IP address of 192.168.1.102 type:

```
PING 192.168.1.102
```

If the command is successful, you should see results similar to those shown here.

```
C:\>ping 192.168.1.102

Pinging 192.168.1.102 with 32 bytes of data:

Reply from 192.168.1.102: bytes=32 time=1ms TTL=128
Reply from 192.168.1.102: bytes=32 time<1ms TTL=128
Reply from 192.168.1.102: bytes=32 time<1ms TTL=128
Reply from 192.168.1.102: bytes=32 time<1ms TTL=128

Ping statistics for 192.168.1.102:
    Packets: Sent = 4, Received = 4, Lost = 0 (0% loss),
Approximate round trip times in milli-seconds:
    Minimum = 0ms, Maximum = 1ms, Average = 0ms
```

If the PING command fails, you will see output similar to that shown below.

```
C:\>ping 192.168.1.102

Pinging 192.168.1.102 with 32 bytes of data:

Request timed out.
Request timed out.
Request timed out.
Request timed out.

Ping statistics for 192.168.1.102:
    Packets: Sent = 4, Received = 0, Lost = 4 (100% loss)
```

If the PING command fails, investigate the following possibilities:

- Did you mistype the IP address in the PING command?
- Is the destination computer turned on?
- Does your network hub show that the connection for your computer and the destination computer is operational?
- Does the TCP/IP configuration on the destination computer look correct?
- If your network is using an Internet gateway, is it powered on and operational?

If you still cannot make the PING command work, try PINGing the computer's loopback IP address. The *loopback* address is a special, reserved IP address of 127.0.0.1 that every Windows computer can use to test whether TCP/IP is properly installed. To execute the PING command using the loopback address type:

```
PING 127.0.0.1
```

If the command is successful, then TCP/IP is properly installed and the problem is else-where. If the command fails, then there is something wrong with your TCP/IP installation. Uninstall and then reinstall TCP/IP and retry PINGing the loopback address.

 For help on working with and installing TCP/IP refer to Chapter 3, "The Softer Side of Network Setup."

Once the loopback test succeeds, try to PING the destination computer again. If it is suc-cessful, try PINGing your default gateway, if you have one.

Other Helpful TCP/IP Commands

Windows XP supports a number of TCP/IP commands, some of which can provide valu-able information when troubleshooting network problems. Here are two more TCP/IP commands that you may find helpful.

- Tracert—Traces the path used to establish communications with a target computer. This command is helpful on larger networks that use routers to connect different network segments and may also prove handy if your home network consists of more than one type of network technology such as Ethernet and phoneline or powerline.

- Netstat—This command displays TCP/IP network statistics and lists current TCP/IP network connections.

 More information about these commands is available in Appendix A, "Windows XP Networking Commands."

Troubleshooting Other Types of Network Problems

Hardware problems can be just as difficult to diagnose as software problems. Worse still, whereas software problems generally only affect a single network computer, a hardware problem can affect a single computer or the entire network.

One of the first things that you should do when investigating what you think may be a hardware problem is to determine the scope of the problem. In other words, does the prob-lem affect just one computer or is your entire network affected? If your entire network is affected, then look for problems with your:

- **Network hub**—Does it have power? Do its indicator lights show a problem? Try pressing the hub's reset button. If this does not work, try replacing the hub.

- **Internet Gateway**—Does it have power? Do any of its indictor lights show a prob-lem? Is it properly connected to your network hub? Also try pressing the Internet Gateways reset button.

- **ICS computer**—Is it powered on? Can it connect to the Internet? Have you checked its TCP/IP software configuration? You also might want to try restarting the computer. History has shown that restarting computers running Windows operating systems often fixes many mysterious problems.

If the problem is isolated to a single computer, then you may have a software problem, a wiring problem, or a faulty network adapter. Check each of the following possibilities.

- Does the computer have TCP/IP installed? What about the Client for Microsoft Network? Did you PING the computer's loopback address? Can you PING another computer or your default gateway?
- For powerline networks make sure that the power outlet where the computer is connected is operating by plugging a lamp into it.
- For phoneline networks make sure that the telephone outlet still works by hooking up a telephone and making sure that you still get a dial tone.
- For Ethernet-based networks visually inspect all your twisted-pair wiring for tears or other damage and make sure that your hub is powered on and working. Verify that the cable that connects the computer to the hub is properly connected to both the hub and your computer. You might also want to try replacing the cable.
- For wireless networks make sure that your access point has power and that its indicator lights do not show a problem.

Open the Windows XP Task Manager on one of your network computers and open the Networking property sheet. How busy is your network? If it is getting hammered even though nobody in the family is doing anything, then you may have a faulty network adapter installed in one of your computers that is flooding your network with useless data packets. Check the status lights on each of your computers' network adapters and if you find one that shows itself as constantly busy, disconnect it and see if your network begins working again. You could try disconnecting and reconnecting the network adapter and see if that fixes the problem. Otherwise just replace it with a new one.

Addressing 802.11x Wireless Issues

When setting up a wireless home network based on one of the 802.11x standards, it is recommended that you try and keep things consistent. There are a number of wireless vendors who make 802.11x-compatible hardware. These products should all be interoperable with their respective standard. In other words, one vendor's 802.11a wireless network adapter should be able to work with another vendor's Internet gateway or access point. However, things will be easier for you to work with if you stick with one vendor's hardware. This will eliminate any concern regarding possible compatibility issues and make working with your wireless hardware easier because you only have to learn how one vendor does things.

When purchasing your wireless hardware make sure that you do not accidentally try and mix incompatible 802.11x hardware. For example, unless you have a wireless Internet gateway or access point that supports both 802.11b and 802.11a wireless clients, don't try to use both. While similar, these two wireless standards operate on different radio frequencies, making them incompatible.

When you set up your home network take great care to make sure that you have correctly recorded the MAC address of each of your network adapters in your wireless Internet gateway or access point. Also make sure that if you have enabled or disabled encryption on this device, you have done the same thing for each of your network client computers. Otherwise things will not work.

Home networks are subject to interference from other electrical devices. If you find that once you have set up your wireless home network that things are running a little slower than you expected, look for possible sources of interference and try to eliminate them. If you can locate, but cannot eliminate the source of the interference, then move your Internet gateway or access point away from it. If the interference is located nearer to your network client computer, try repositioning the computer so that its wireless network adapter is facing toward your wireless Internet gateway or access point. If this does not help, try moving the computer away from the interference.

Also remember that network throughput depends on the number of active users and what they are doing. A wireless home network's true transmission speed may be 5-6Mbps or less. Further drops in transmission speeds can be caused by any of the previously mentioned environment factors, or by a combination of them, making the troubleshooting of a wireless network a little more challenging than its wired counterparts.

Fixing Wireless Internet Gateway and Access Point Problems

If you are experiencing a network problem that is affecting more than one computer on your wireless home network, then chances are the problem lies with your wireless Internet gateway or access point. If all your computers are able to communicate with one another but are unable to connect to the Internet, then the problem probably resides with your modem or its connection with the Internet, which is covered in the next section.

When you suspect that the problem resides within your wireless Internet gateway or access point start your problem resolution by checking the physical installation of the device. Make sure that its indicator lights do not indicate an error and that it has power.

Log on to your wireless Internet gateway or access point and double-check its configuration. If you cannot access its Web interface, double-check to make sure that you typed the right IP address. If you did, then try to PING it to see if you have any network connectivity with it. If the PING command fails, then try powering the unit off and back on. If this fails to resolve the problem or if you have forgotten its administrative account's password, then you can try resetting the device. This will reset all its default factory settings and should allow you to access the device again and reconfigure it.

For other types of unexplained or quirky problems, check the manufacturer's Web site to see if there is a firmware update that includes a fix for your problem. If there is, then log on to your wireless Internet gateway or access point and perform a firmware update.

If only one computer seems to be having a problem, then you can begin your troubleshooting process at that computer by looking around for sources of interference and either removing them or moving away from them. Also check your distance from your wireless Internet gateway or access point to make sure that you are not too far away.

Next check and make sure that your wireless PC card or USB network adapter is properly connected and that its indicator lights do not show any errors. If you see a problem, try removing and reattaching the network adapter. If you are using a USB network adapter, check your computer BIOS to make sure that its USB controller is enabled.

If everything looks good so far, check the Windows Device Manager utility and see if the network adapter has any resource conflicts. If it shows a conflict, then try uninstalling the network adapter's software driver and restarting the computer and see if Windows plug and play can reinstall it correctly.

If you do not have any discernable hardware problems, try checking the computer IP address assignment, subnet mask, and default gateway setting as discussed earlier in this chapter. If everything looks good, then go to your wireless Internet gateway or access point's Web interface and make sure that the computer's MAC address is registered and set to allow network access. If your IP configuration settings are incorrect, try repairing them and see if this corrects your problem.

 To review how to repair a network client's IP configuration settings refer to "Repairing TCP/IP Communications" earlier in this chapter.

Troubleshooting Shared Internet Access Problems

If you are experiencing a problem connecting to the Internet and only one computer is affected, then the problem most likely resides at that computer. Check its hardware, verify its IP configuration settings, and make sure its MAC address is properly recorded in your wireless Internet gateway. If the Internet communications problem is affecting your entire home network, then the problem probably lies at one of the following places:

- The connection between your wireless Internet gateway and your cable or DSL modem
- The connection between your cable or DSL modem and its telephone or cable connection.
- At your ISP

Make sure that the cable between your Internet gateway and always-on high-speed Internet connection is OK. Verify that your cable, DSL, or dial-up modem is powered on. Check to see if its indicator lights show any problems. Next check your cable or DSL

modem's telephone or cable connection. Try powering your modem off and on to see if this corrects the problem.

If you are using Windows Internet Connection Sharing feature instead of an Internet gateway, double-check its configuration. If you do not see any configuration problems, try restarting the computer that provides ICS. If this does not work, try reconfiguring ICS.

If after all this checking you still cannot determine what is going on, call you ISP and ask if it is experiencing any problems in your area.

SEEKING HELP

Windows XP has an excellent help system that also includes a number of troubleshooting and setup wizards that you can run to help diagnose common problems and configure networking features.

You can view a list of available troubleshooters and run them by opening the Windows XP Help and Support Center, clicking Index, and typing **troubleshooter** in the Type in the Keyword to Find field and then select the list of Troubleshooters options as shown in Figure 10.23.

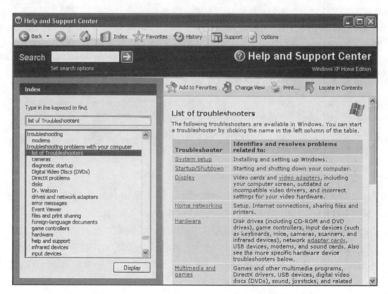

Figure 10.23

Locating Windows XP troubleshooters.

A list of troubleshooters that can assist you in diagnosing network-related problems includes

- Home Networking
- Hardware
- Drivers and Network Adapters

- Internet Connections Sharing
- Internet Explorer
- Outlook Express
- File and Print Sharing
- Printing

You can also view a list of available wizards and run them from the Windows XP Help and Support Center by clicking Index and typing `wizard`. Some wizards that you will find helpful include

- **The Add a Network Place Wizard**—Helps you set up connections to Web sites, FTP sites, and shared folders and drivers on a home network.
- **The Add Hardware Wizard**—Helps you to install new peripheral devices including modems and network adapters.
- **The Add Printer Wizard**—Steps you through the process of setting up a local or network computer.
- **The Network Setup Wizard**—Steps you through the setup of your home network by configuring your Internet connection, network adapters, computer name, workgroup, and file and printer sharing.

WINDOWS XP NETWORKING COMMANDS

Windows XP network configuration is easily performed from the Windows XP graphical user interface or GUI. Windows XP also provides a number of useful commands that allow you to work directly with Windows XP networking from the Windows command line. An experienced Windows XP user can save time by working directly from the command line to perform tasks that involve a number of mouse clicks and Windows menu selections.

In addition, these commands can also be used with Windows scripting languages to automate a number of administrative tasks. The purpose of the appendix is to provide you with a list of commands that you may find helpful when working on a Windows XP-based home network.

IPCONFIG

NOTE Some of these commands are designed to operate on both Windows workgroups and domains. However, because Windows XP Home Edition is not able to participate in a Windows domain-based network, references to domain components within these commands have been removed.

Displays or resets TCP/IP configuration settings.

Syntax:

ipconfig [/all | /renew [*adapter*] | /release [*adapter*]] [/fkushdns] [/displaydns]
[/registerdns] [/showclassid *adapter*] [/setclassid *adapter* [*classid*]]

Parameters:

/all	Displays a complete TCP/IP configuration listing. If omitted, then only the IP address, subnet mask, and default gateway settings for each network adapter are displayed.
/renew [*adapter*]	Renews DHCP configuration settings for the specified network adapter. If a specific network adapter is not specified, then DHCP settings are reset for all network adapters.
/release [*adapter*]	Releases the DHCP configuration settings for the specified adapter. If a specific network adapter is not specified, then all DHCP configuration settings are released for all network adapters.
/flushdns	Resets the computer's DNS cache removing all entries including old or invalid entries.
/displaydns	Displays all entries in the computers DNS cache.
/registerdns	Manually registers all the computer's DNS names.
/showclassid *adapter*	Displays the classid ID for the specified network adapter. Use * to display the class IDs for all adapters.
/setclassid *adapter* [*classID*]	Sets the classid for the specified network adapter.

NETSTAT

Displays TCP/IP statistical information and provides data about the status of current network connections.

Syntax:

netstat [-a] [-e] [-n] [-o] [-s] [-p *protocol*] [-r] [*interval*]

Parameters:

-a	Displays current network connections and listening ports.
-e	Displays Ethernet network statistics.
-n	Displays IP addresses and port numbers.
-o	Displays the process ID belonging to each established network connection.
-s	Displays per-protocol statistics (for example, IP, ICMP, TCP, and UDP).
-p *protocol*	Displays connections for the specified protocol (for example, TCP or UDP).
-r	Lists the entries in the routing table.
interval	Continually displays NETSTAT results at the specified interval.

PING

Tests the connection between two network computers.

Syntax:

ping [-t] [-a] [-n *cnt*] [-l *length*] [-f] [-i *ttl*] [-v *tos*] [-r *cnt*] [-s *cnt*] [{-j *hostlist* | -k *hostlist*}] [-w *timeout*] *destination*

Parameters:

-t	Sets the PING command to continue PINGing the target computer until interrupted.
-a	Instructs the PING command to try and resolve the destination IP addresses and to display its computer name.
-n *cnt*	Specifies the number of ECHO packets that the PING command will send to the target computer.
-l *length*	Specifies the amount of data that the ECHO packets will contain.
-f	Adds a Do not Fragment flag to the ECHO packet preventing gateways from fragmenting in route.
-i *ttl*	Specifies the TTL or Time to live value.
-v *tos*	Specifies the TOS or Type Of Service field to the value.
-r *cnt*	Records outgoing and incoming packet routes in the Record Route field.
-s *cnt*	Sets a timestamp for the number of hops set by the *cnt* parameter.
-j hostlist	Sets a loose route list of intermediate destinations to be used by the PING command.

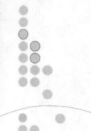

-k hostlist	Sets a strict route list of intermediate destinations to be used by the PING command.
-w *timeout*	Specifies the number of milliseconds to wait before timing.
destination	Specifies the destination computer that is to be pinged.

TRACERT

A diagnostic command that displays the route taken to reach a destination computer.

Syntax:

tracert [-d] [-h max_hops] [-j computer_list] [-w timeout] target_name

Parameters:

-d	Prevents the command from translating IP addresses to computer names when displaying results.
-h *max_hops*	Limits the number of hops when trying to reach the target computer.
-j *computer_list*	Provides a loose source route.
-w *timeout*	Specifies the number of milliseconds to wait before timing out when waiting for each reply.
Target_name	Specifies the name of the destination computer.

NET ACCOUNTS

Modifies the user accounts database and changes password and logon requirements for all user accounts.

Syntax:

net accounts [/forcelogoff:{*minutes* | no}] [/minpwlen:*length*] [/maxpwage:{*days* | unlimited}] [/minpwage:*days*] [/uniquepw:*number*]

Parameters:

None	Displays current password and logon settings.
/forcelogoff: {*minutes*	no}	Specifies (in minutes) the amount of time to wait for user activity before Windows XP terminates a user's session. The *no* option prevents a user from being forced off.
/minpwlen:*length*	Specifies a minimum number of characters for all user account passwords.
/maxpwage: {*days*	unlimited}	Specifies a maximum time limit (in days) that a user's password remains valid. The unlimited option specifies no maximum time.

| /minpwage:*days* | Specifies the minimum number of days that must pass before users can change their passwords. |
| /uniquepw:*number* | Instructs Windows XP to prevent a user from reusing a password for a specified *number* of password changes. |

NET CONFIG

Displays a list of started services that can be configured or changes the configuration settings for a service.

Syntax:

```
net config [service [options]]
```

Parameters:

None	Displays a list of services that can be configured.
service	Specifies a service to configure.
options	Sets configuration options specific to the specified services.

NET CONTINUE

Unpauses a previously suspended service.

Syntax:

```
net continue service
```

Parameters:

| *service* | Identifies the service to be continued. |

NET FILE

Lists all open shared files and optionally closes specified files.

Syntax:

```
net file [id [/close]]
```

Parameters:

None	Displays a list of the open files.
id	Specifies the identification number of a specific file.
/close	Closes an open file.

NET HELP

Displays a list of network commands or provides information regarding a specific command.

Syntax:

```
net command {/help | /?}
```

Parameters:

None	Displays a list of network commands for which help information is available.
command	Specifies a command for which to display information.
{/help | /?}	Displays the syntax of the specified command.

NET HELPMSG

Provides additional information regarding error messages.

Syntax:

```
net helpmsg msg#
```

Parameters:

msg#	The four-digit error message number to be displayed.

NET LOCALGROUP

Creates or changes localgroup membership or displays the membership of a localgroup.

Syntax:

```
net localgroup [groupname [/comment:"text"]]
net localgroup groupname {/add [/comment:"text"] | /delete}
net localgroup groupname name [ ...] {/add | /delete}
```

Parameters:

None	Displays the names of all local groups.
groupname	Identifies a specific local group name to add, delete, or change. If no other parameters are supplied, then the membership of the localgroup is displayed.
/comment:"text"	Assigns a comment message to the localgroup.
name [...]	A list of user or group names to be added to or deleted from the localgroup.
/add	Adds user or global group names to a localgroup.
/delete	Deletes user or group names from a localgroup.

NET NAME

Adds or removes an alias name or lists the names the computer can accept messages for as long as the messenger service is active.

Syntax:

```
net name [name [/add | /delete]]
```

Parameters:

None	Displays the list of names currently in use.
name	Identifies the name to receive messages.
/add	Adds a name to a computer.
/delete	Deletes a name from a computer.

NET PAUSE

Places an active service into an inactive or paused state.

Syntax:

```
net pause service_name
```

Parameters:

service_name	Specifies the name of the service to be paused.

NET PRINT

Displays or manipulates print jobs and print queues.

Syntax:

```
net print \\computer_name\share_name
```

```
net print [\\computer_name] job# [/hold | /release | /delete]
```

Parameters:

computer_name	Specifies the computer where the printer queue resides.
share_name	Identifies a specific print queue.
job#	Specifies unique job number assigned to each print job.
/hold	Holds the specified print job in the queue.
/release	Releases the specified print job in the print queue.
/delete	Deletes the specified print job from the print queue.

NET SEND

Sends a message to other network users or computers where the messenger service is active.

Syntax:

```
net send {name | * | /users} msg
```

Parameters:

name	Identifies the user or computer name to receive the message.
*	Sends the specified message to all computers in the sender's workgroup.
/users	Sends the message to all users currently connected to a computer.
msg	Specifies the message text.

NET SESSION

Displays a list of network sessions with other network computers and alternatively disconnects specified sessions.

Syntax:

```
net session [\\computer_name] [/delete]
```

Parameters:

None	Displays information about the computer's connected network sessions.
\\computer_name	Lists or disconnects the sessions for the specified computer.
/delete	Terminates a session with the specified computer. If \\computer_name is not used, then sessions are terminated.

NET SHARE

Creates and deletes shared resources or displays existing shared resources.

Syntax:

```
net share share_name

net share share_name=drive:path [/users:number | /unlimited] [/remark:"text"]

net share share_name [/users:number | unlimited] [/remark:"text"]

net share {share_name | drive:path} /delete
```

Parameters:

None	Displays information about the computer's shared resources.
share_name	Specifies the network name of a shared resource.
drive:path	Sets the path of the folder to be shared.
/users:*number*	Specifies the number of simultaneous network users who can access the shared resource.
/unlimited	Allows any number of network users to simultaneously access the shared resource.
/remark:"*text*"	Adds a comment to the shared resource.
/delete	Terminates the sharing of a resource.

NET START

Displays a list of started services or starts a specified service.

Syntax:

```
net start [service_name]
```

Parameters:

None	Displays a list of started services.
service_name	Specifies the name of the service to start.

NET STATISTICS

Displays statistics for the workstation or server service.

Syntax:

```
net statistics [workstation | server]
```

Parameters:

None	Displays a list of the started services that supply statistics.
workstation	Displays workstation service statistics.
server	Displays server service statistics.

NET STOP

Stops the specified Windows service.

Syntax:

```
net stop service_name
```

Parameters:

Service_name	Specifies the name of the service to be stopped.

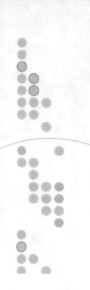

NET TIME

Synchronizes the computer's clock with the time as set on another computer or displays the time as set on a specified computer.

Syntax:

```
net time [\\computer_name] [/set]
```

Parameters:

\\computer_name	Specifies the name of the computer where time is to be displayed or set.
/set	Specifies the computers with which to synchronize the computer's clock.

NET USE

Establishes a mapping to a shared network drive or disconnects the mapping to that drive or displays information about connections.

Syntax:

```
net use [device_name | *] [\\computer_name\share_name] [password | *]]
[/user:user_name] [[/delete] | [/persistent:{yes | no}]]

net use device_name [/home[{password | *}] [/delete:{yes | no}]]

net use [/persistent:{yes | no}]
```

Parameters:

None	Displays a list of network connections.
device_name	Specifies a name for a new network drive or printer connection or sets the name of the network drive or printer to disconnect.
\\computer_name\ share_name	Specifies a particular computer and its shared resource.
password	Must be specified if the specified resource is protected by a password.
*	Displays a prompt that allows for the specification of a password.
/user	Allows you to specify a different user name when connecting to a network resource.
user_name	Specifies the user name to use when connecting to a network resource.
/delete	Terminates a connection to a network resource.

/home	Creates a connection to a user's home directory.
/persistent	Determines if a network connection should remain persistent across system restarts.
yes	Tells Windows XP to save all connections and restore them at login.
no	Tells Windows XP not to save the connections.

NET USER

Displays user account information or creates and modifies existing accounts.

Syntax:

```
net user [user_name [password | *] [options]]

net user user_name {password | *} /add [options]

net user user_name [/delete]
```

Parameters:

None	Displays a list of user accounts on the computer.
User_name	Sets the name of the user account to be added, modified, or deleted.
Password	Sets or modifies the password for the specified user account.
*	Tells the command shell to prompt you for the password.
/add	Creates a new user account.
/delete	Deletes a user account.
Options	Specifies any of the following:
/active:{no	yes}	Enables or disables the specified user account.
/comment:"text"	Adds comment about the user account.
/countrycode:nnn	Sets an operating system Country/Region code, which is used to implement the specified language's help files.
/expires: {date	never}	Sets an expiration date for the user account.
/fullname:"name"	Specifies user's full name.
/homedir:path	Sets the home directory path.
/passwordchg: {yes	no}	Determines if a user can change his or her password.
/passwordreq: {yes	no}	Determines if a user account must have a password.
/profilepath: [path]	Specifies the path to the user's logon profile.

/scriptpath:path	Specifies a user's logon script.
/times: {*times* | all}	Sets the times the user is permitted to use the computer.
/workstations: {*computer_name* [,...] | *}	Specifies a list of up to eight computers that the user can use to log on to the network.

NET VIEW

Displays a list of all network computers or the resources that are shared by a specific computer.

Syntax:

net view \\computer_name [/cache]

Parameters:

None	Displays a list of network computers.
computer_name	Specifies a computer whose shared resources are to be displayed.
/cache	Displays the entries listed in cache.

APPENDIX B

TCP/IP BASICS

TCP/IP is the protocol of the Internet. Most corporations around the world use it to run their networks. Since the release of Windows 98, Microsoft has made TCP/IP the default protocol for all Windows operating systems including Windows XP Home Edition.

You don't have to know very much, if anything, about TCP/IP to set up and happily run your own home network. However, some basic information about this protocol and how it operates will increase your understanding and provide you with invaluable insight, not to mention help you troubleshoot in the event that you have TCP/IP related problems on your home network.

TCP/IP'S BEGINNINGS

TCP/IP's roots can be traced back to the 1960s when the U.S. Department of Defense's *Advanced Research Projects Agency* or *ARPA* started investing in packet-switching technology. A packet-switching network is one that breaks data into small packets and routes them through multiple paths to their destination. Every data packet contains both a source and destination address and can travel independently over various network paths to its destination. The receiving computer collects each packet as it arrives and then reassembles them back into their original format.

The idea behind the ARPA's research was the development of a network that could survive a nuclear war. Packet switching technology suited this purpose well. In the event that a part of the network went down only the packets routed through that portion of the network would be lost. When the sending computer failed to receive the expected acknowledgement of receipt from the destination computer, it would resend the lost packets, which would then be transmitted over a different route.

The network that ARPA helped create was called *the Advanced Research Projects Agency Network* or *ARPAnet*. At first it was used to connect a small number of American universities. It operated using a protocol called the *Network Core Protocol* or *NCP*. Much of TCP/IP's basic design is based on NCP. In 1983 TCP/IP replaced NCP on the ARPAnet. The Department of Defense helped to further develop TCP/IP by requiring the University of California at Berkeley to implement it in its version of Unix, which the Department of Defense was also helping to fund. Because the Berkeley version of Unix was freely distributed to other universities, the use of TCP/IP rapidly spread to universities and colleges throughout the United States. By the mid-1990s the Internet was opened to the public and the use of TCP/IP quickly found its way into large corporations and government agencies around the world.

COMMUNICATING WITH TCP/IP

TCP/IP is a suite of protocols of which TCP and IP are just two member protocols. *Internet Protocol* or *IP* is a connectionless protocol meaning that its packets are sent out over a network such as the Internet without establishing a session between the sending and receiving computers. IP does not provide a guarantee for the delivery of packets nor does it control the order in which packets are received.

Transmission Control Protocol or *TCP*, on the other hand, is a connection-oriented protocol that establishes a logical connection between the sending and receiving computers that ensures the delivery of all data packets by requiring that the receiving computer acknowledge the receipt of all packets. Any lost packets are automatically retransmitted when the receiving computer fails to acknowledge their receipt. TCP uses IP as its transport mechanism.

The TCP/IP suite of protocols includes a number of other protocols including

- **UDP**—A protocol similar to TCP except that it does not guarantee the delivery of packets.

- **ARP**—Translates IP addresses to MAC addresses.
- **RARP**—Translates MAC addresses to IP addresses.
- **Telnet**—A remote access protocol that allows you to establish a remote text-based session with a network computer.
- **DHCP**—Supports the assignment of TCP/IP configuration settings to client computers from a DHCP server.
- **FTP**—Supports the transport of text and binary files over networks.
- **HTTP**—Supports the transfer of information between browsers and Web servers.
- **ICMP**—Handles protocol control and error messages.
- **SMTP**—Provides support for TCP/IP e-mail.
- **SNMP**—A network management protocol used by a number of network monitoring applications.

Microsoft's TCP/IP implementation has a number of features that make it an excellent protocol for home networks, including

- **Support for Internet**—TCP/IP is the language of the Internet making it the only protocol that you'll need for all your network communications.
- **Support for automatic configuration**—TCP/IP allows specialized servers known as DHCP servers to configure TCP/IP settings for client computers. In addition, it also supports APIPA, which allows computers running on a network without a DHCP server to assign their own TCP/IP configuration settings.
- **Routability**—While only a concern on larger networks, routing allows multiple networks to be connected into a single logical network with network traffic routed as necessary across network subnets.
- **Strong support for network utilities**—TCP/IP supports a number of utilities for troubleshooting network problems including PING, IPCONFIG, and NETSTAT.

For more information on PING, IPCONFIG, NETSTAT, and other networking commands, refer to Appendix A, "Windows XP Networking Commands."

UNDERSTANDING HOW IP ADDRESSING WORKS

At first glance the TCP/IP address scheme seems very complex. It can be difficult to understand and work with on larger networks where a network may actually consist of a number of separate subnetworks, each of which has its own set of IP addresses. Fortunately, when TCP/IP is implemented on small networks it's much easier to work with and understand.

TCP/IP Network Classifications

There are five different classifications of TCP/IP Internet addresses. However, only three of these are actually used. They are

- **Class A**—Defines ranges of IP addresses used by very large networks.
- **Class B**—Defines ranges of IP addresses used by medium- to large-sized networks,
- **Class C**—Defines ranges of IP addresses used on smaller networks.

Table B.1 outlines the basic features of each of these three network classifications.

TABLE B.1—TCP/IP NETWORK CLASSIFICATIONS		
Class	**No. Of Networks**	**# Of Host Per Network**
Class A	126	16,777,214
Class B	16,384	65,534
Class C	2,097,152	254

There are a total of 126 Class A networks. Each Class A network is capable of supporting over 16 million network connections. There are over 16,000 Class B networks, each of which can support more than 65,000 network connections. Finally, although there are more than 2 million Class C networks, none of them can support more than 254 network connections.

TCP/IP Configuration Settings

Every computer on a network that uses TCP/IP as its primary protocol requires a minimum of two pieces of information. They are

- **IP address**—The IP address assigned to the computer that uniquely identifies it on the network.
- **Subnet Mask**—A complementary TCP/IP setting that is used by the computer to determine which network the computer is connected to.

In addition, the following two TCP/IP configuration settings may need to be configured as well:

- **Default Gateway**—An optional IP address used to identify a computer or network device that has been set up to provide the network with shared Internet access.
- **DNS Server**—An optional IP address used to identify a computer on the network that has been set up to provide a name to IP address translation.

The Components of an IP Address

Every computer or network device on a TCP/IP-based network is identified by an IP address. This IP address must be unique, meaning that it cannot be assigned to any other computer or network device. Otherwise an IP address conflict occurs, which will inhibit one or both of the computers from being able to communicate on the network.

Every IP address is composed of two pieces of information that identify the network to which the computer is attached as well as its own individual address. These are known as the network ID and the host ID. Whereas each host ID must be unique on a particular network, all computers and network devices on the same network share a command Network ID.

Think of your TCP/IP address as working just like your street address. For example, every house on any given street has its own unique address while sharing the same street name. On a home network all your computers will reside on the same physical network and share the same network ID (for example, street address) while still having a unique host ID (for example, street number).

TCP/IP addresses are composed of 32 bits of 0s and 1s as shown in the following example.

`10101001.11111110.01101111.01100100`

The 32 bits are actually organized into four separate numbers, called octets, with a possible range of 00000000 to 11111111. As you can see, a 32-bit binary number is not very easy to work with. Fortunately, you don't have to. Instead, you can work with the decimal format of IP addresses. For example, the TCP/IP address shown here is the same as the previous example.

`169.254.111.100`

To see how I converted the TCP/IP address from 10101001.11111110.01101111.01100100 to 169.254.111.100 open the Windows calculator and switch it to scientific mode. Then select the binary setting and type **10101001** and click the Decimal option. You should see 169. Click Clear and try converting the rest of the octets until you have converted the full 32-bit IP address to decimal.

As I already mentioned, the first portion of any IP address identifies its network ID and the second portion identifies its host ID. You can use the information provided in Table B.2 to identify the network and host portion of an IP address.

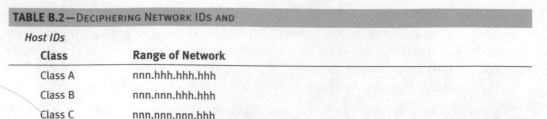

TABLE B.2—Deciphering Network IDs and

Host IDs

Class	Range of Network
Class A	nnn.hhh.hhh.hhh
Class B	nnn.nnn.hhh.hhh
Class C	nnn.nnn.nnn.hhh

On a Class A network the number stored in the first octet is the network ID. On a Class B network the network ID is composed of both the first and second octets. Similarly the network ID on a Class C network is made up of the first three octets in the IP address. The host ID portion of an IP address consists of all the values to the right of the network ID.

You can tell the TCP/IP classification of network by examining the first octet in an IP address. Table B.3 lists the possible values of the first octet in any IP address.

TABLE B.3—Identifying TCP/IP Network Classifications

Class	Range of Network
Class A	1–126
Class B	128–191
Class C	192–223

For example, an IP address of 169.254.111.100 is a Class B network (for example, the value of the first octet falls between 128 and 223). Using Table B.2 you can then tell that the network ID that this IP address belongs to is 169.254 and that its host ID is 111.100. The network on which this computer resides is 169.254.0.0.

Uncovering the Meaning of the Subnet Mask

The Subnet mask is a 32-bit that is used to identify the location of a computer. Every computer on a TCP/IP network must be assigned the same subnet mask. TCP/IP uses this information to determine the network ID and host ID of the computer. Each TCP/IP class has its own subnet mask. Table B.4 provides a list of subnet masks for each TCP/IP classification.

TABLE B.4—Class A, B, and C Subnet Masks

Class	Default Subnet Mask
Class A	255.0.0.0
Class B	255.255.0.0
Class C	255.255.255.0

For example, a subnet mask that would be assigned to a computer with an IP address of 169.254.111.100 would be 255.255.0.0 because this IP address belongs to a Class B network.

Default Gateways and DNS Servers

Although every computer on a TCP/IP network must have an IP address and a subnet mask, the Default gateway and DNS server's settings are optional and are only set if they apply to your network.

If you set up shared Internet access for all the computers on your network, then the computer or network device that provides the access is referred to as your network's default gateway. All the other computers on your home network will use the IP address assigned to the gateway to route their requests to the Internet. The computer or network device acting as the gateway will then collect each request and resubmit it on behalf of the network computer that submitted it. When a response comes back from the Internet the gateway will route it back to the network computer that originated the request.

Refer to Chapter 8, "Going Online," to learn more about setting up an Internet Gateway and establishing shared Internet access. Look to Chapter 2, "Getting Your Hands Dirty: Assembling Your Network Hardware," for more on wireless Internet gateway setup.

Another network service provided by a computer or device acting as an Internet gateway is DNS. *DNS* or *Domain Name Services* is a translation service to which each Windows XP computer on your home network registers its name and IP address. The DNS server gives this information to any network application or computer that requests it. For example, many network applications use DNS to determine the IP address of a network computer when the user only supplies it with the computer's hostname.

You are prompted to provide a Windows XP computer's hostname when Windows XP first installs a computer network adapter. You can change a computer's hostname at any time by running the Network Setup Wizard, which you'll find by clicking on Start, My Network Places and then selecting Set up a home or small office network in the upper-left corner of the My Network Places dialog box.

MANAGING TCP/IP ON A WINDOWS XP NETWORK

Windows XP, like all Microsoft operating systems since Windows 98, is designed to participate on a TCP/IP network without any manual configuration or setup on your part. Windows XP allows TCP/IP settings to be configured by any of the following means:

- **Automatic Private IP Addressing or APIPA**—This option allows a Windows XP computer to assign its own TCP/IP configuration settings.

- **Static or Manual Addressing**—This option allows you to manually assign a computer's TCP/IP configuration settings.

- **Dynamic Host Configuration Protocol or DHCP**—This option allows a central DHCP service to manage the assignment of TCP/IP configuration settings for all the computers on the network. DHCP is provided on a home network by either a hardware device known as an Internet Gateway or by Microsoft's Internet Connection Sharing service.

If you decide to manually configure the TCP/IP settings for each computer on your network, then you can set up your network to use any TCP/IP addresses that you want. Just remember that every computer's IP address must have the same network ID and a different host ID. Also you'll have to make sure that you provide the correct subnet mask for your network and configure your default gateway address if your network has one.

However, unless you just like making things harder on yourself, don't even consider using static addressing. First of all, you have to set down and work out the math to make sure that your subnet mask matches your network.

Otherwise nothing will work. You'll also have to be careful not to accidentally assign a duplicate IP address to any computers. Otherwise at least one of the two computers with the duplicate IP address is not going to be able to communicate. Finally there is the chance that you'll make a typo when supplying the IP address of your default gateway and mess up one of your computer's Internet connections. Given all the possible ways that things can go wrong, it's much better to let Windows XP do what it does best and let it manage your TCP/IP configuration.

TCP/IP Default Settings

If you choose to stay out of the business of manually managing your TCP/IP settings, then the manner in which your network IP addresses are assigned depends on how you have assembled your network.

Table B.5 outlines three possible network addresses and explains when they are assigned.

TABLE B.5—TCP/IP NETWORK ADDRESSES

Network Address	Service	Source of IP Configuration
169.254.0.0	APIPA	Windows XP TCP/IP
192.168.0.0	DHCP	ICS Internet Gateway
192.168.1.0	DHCP	Internet Gateway Device

As Table B.5 shows, if your home network does not have an Internet gateway, then each Windows XP computer will use APIPA to assign its own Class B IP address on a 169.254.0.0 network. If you have configured ICS to provide a shared Internet connection on one of your computers, then that computer will also double as a DHCP server and assign IP addresses to all network computers for a 192.168.0.0 network. If, on the other hand, you have installed an Internet Gateway device on your network then it will automatically configure itself as a DHCP server and assign IP configuration settings for whatever default IP network, it has been configured. In the case of the example in Table B.5 the Internet Gateway device automatically configures all network computers to run on a Class B network with a network address of 192.168.1.0.

Automatic Private IP Addressing or APIPA

Unless you change Windows XP's default settings, it will always look for a DHCP server on your network when starting up. If you have not installed ICS on one of your computers and are not running an Internet gateway appliance, then Windows XP will automatically configure its own TCP/IP settings using APIPA.

This will result in an IP address assignment for a 169.254.0.0 network. The possible range of IP addresses that your computer might assign itself is 169.254.0.1–169.254.0.254. The 169.254.0.0 network address has been reserved for home networking. This means that no network connected directly to the Internet is using this network address. Because this is a Class B network, a subnet mask of 255.255.0.0 will be assigned and there will be no default Gateway or DNS assignments. Figure B.1 depicts a typical home network consisting of four computers, all of which use APIPA.

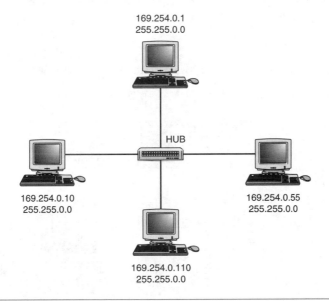

Figure B.1

A typical home network using APIPA.

Dynamic Host Configuration Protocol

If you have set up ICS on one of your network computers or have purchased and installed an Internet gateway appliance, then your network will have a DHCP server. Other than setting up and configuring the ICS server or Internet gateway, as described in Chapter 8, no additional network configuration is needed. Remember that by default all Windows XP computers are configured to look for a DHCP server on the network before defaulting to APIPA.

> **NOTE**
> Remember that Windows 98, Me, and 2000 also have the same default network behavior as Windows XP. First they look for a DHCP server and if they do not find one, they default to APIPA.

If you are using Windows XP's ICS services, then the computer providing the service will also double as a DHCP server and will assign TCP/IP configuration settings to all network computers for a 192.168.0.0 network. The IP address assigned to the ICS server will always be 192.168.0.1. This leaves IP addresses 192.168.0.2–192.168.0.254 as possible IP address assignments for the rest of the computers on your network. Because this is a Class C network the DHCP server will also assign a subnet mask of 255.255.255.0 to each computer. In addition, each computer will also be assigned a default gateway of 192.168.0.1 and a DNS entry of 192.168.0.1.

Figure B.2 depicts a typical home network consisting of four computers, one of which has been configured with the ICS service.

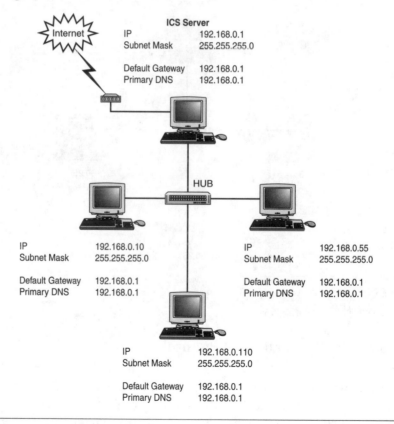

Figure B.2

A typical home network that includes a computer running the ICS service.

Windows 98 2nd Edition, Windows Me, and Windows 2000 also provide the ICS service.

Static IP Address Configuration

If you really want to manually configure static TCP/IP settings, this section will show you how. The important thing to remember is to assign all your computers IP addresses for the same network and to give them all the same subnet mask.

To configure TCP/IP settings for your local area network connection you must first open the connection's properties dialog box as outlined here:

1. Click Start and then right-click My Network Places and select Properties. The Network Connection dialog box appears.

2. Next, right-click Local Area Connection and choose Properties. The Local Area Connection Properties dialog box appears.

3. Select Internet Protocol (TCP/IP) and click Properties to open the Internet Protocol (TCP/IP) Properties.

4. Select the Use the Following IP Address option as shown in Figure B.3.

Figure B.3

Windows XP's TCP/IP settings are configured from the TCP/IP Properties dialog box for each network connection.

After selecting the Use the Following IP Address option you need to fill in the following settings:

- **IP address**—This is the IP address that you want to assign to the computer on your local area network.

- **Subnet mask**—Every IP address has an associated subnet mask setting that must be supplied in this field.

- **Default gateway**—If your network includes a shared Internet connection, type the IP address of the computer running ICS or the IP address of your Internet gateway.

Optionally, you can also fill in two more fields that set the IP address of DNS servers. If you are running ICS on one of your network computers, then its IP address, which will be 192.168.0.1, will be the IP address of your DNS server. If you are sharing an Internet connection via an Internet Gateway, then its IP address will be also be the IP address of your DNS server. The following DNS settings are available on the Internet Protocol (TCP/IP) Properties dialog box:

- **Preferred DNS server**—This is the network's primary DNS server.
- **Alternate DNS server**—If the network has an additional secondary DNS server, it can be specified here.

Unless your home network has two different shared Internet connections and you are running with two DNS servers, you will not have an alternate DNS server. For example, you might set up your network using an Internet gateway that provides shared access to the Internet via a cable modem. If guaranteed Internet access is important to you, you might have a second computer with a dial-up connection to the Internet standing by, ready to provide Internet access in the event your cable company experiences a problem. When a problem with your cable connection occurs, you could then power up the standby computer, log it on to the Internet, and reboot the rest of the computers on your home network. Assuming that all your computers are set up to access a dynamic IP address configuration, they'll get their new TCP/IP setting from the standby ICS server.

A P P E N D I X **C**

A TOUR OF TECHTV

TechTV is the only 24-hour cable television network dedicated to showcasing the impact technology has on our everyday lives and the world at large. By creating and delivering entertaining and insightful programming regarding today's and tomorrow's technology news, events, products, and people, TechTV enables viewers to stay current and connected with all things related to technology.

Offering more than a cable television channel, TechTV delivers a fully integrated Web site. TechTV.com enhances the TV viewing experience with compelling companion content and interactivity.

TechTV is owned by Vulcan Inc.

AUDIENCE

TechTV appeals to people who are excited by and curious about the many aspects of technology. By using technology as the backdrop, TechTV entertains, amazes and provides it viewers with insight into how technology enriches our lifestyles and the world around us.

WEB SITE

TechTV.com allows viewers to participate in programming, provide feedback, interact with hosts, send video emails, and further explore the latest tech content featured on the television cable network. In addition, TechTV.com has one of the Web's most extensive technology-specific video-on-demand (VOD) features, offering users immediate access to more than 5,000 videos as well as expanded tech content of more than 2,000 in-depth articles.

INTERNATIONAL

TechTV is the world's largest producer and distributor of television programming about technology. TechTV delivers a 24-hour international version via satellite that reaches all of Asia, the Pacific and the Middle East. TechTV Canada is a "must carry" digital channel that launched in September 2001.

NETWORK PROGRAM GUIDE

Big Thinkers

βιg 𝒯h÷ιnKeRſ

www.techtv.com/bigthinkers

Explore the future of technology through insightful and down-to-earth interviews with the industry's most influential thinkers and innovators of our time.

Call For Help

www.techtv.com/callforhelp

Host Chris Pirillo translates technical jargon into plain English, provides computing tips, answers live viewer questions and interviews guests who help demystify technology. It's interactive, informative and above all, fun.

CyberCrime

www.techtv.com/cybercrime

Hosts Alex Wellen and Jennifer London take an inside look at fraud, hacking, viruses, identity theft and invasions of privacy, to keep users secure and aware of the potential dangers on the Internet.

Extended Play

www.techtv.com/extendedplay

Host Adam Sessler provides comprehensive reviews of the hottest new games on the market, previews of games in development and tips on how to score the biggest thrills and avoid the worst spills in gaming.

Eye Drops

www.techtv.com/eyedrops

Breathtaking, beautiful, compelling, insightful, and sometimes even a little scary, but always entertaining, *Eye Drops* has something for everyone. *Eye Drops* showcases today's best computer generated animated short subjects.

Fresh Gear

`www.techtv.com/freshgear`

Host Sumi Das takes an in-depth look at the coolest new products out there from color PDAs to ultra-light notebooks, digital cameras to PVRs, virtual operating rooms to wearable computers. Catch reviews of the latest products, get advice on what to buy and what to bypass, and explore the technologies of tomorrow.

Future Fighting Machines

`www.techtv.com/futurefightingmachines`

Future Fighting Machines takes a look at the latest in military hardware and gadgets, from electromagnetic energy weapons, to high-tech soldiers' uniforms with built-in mine detectors, to flying spying micro-robots.

Max Headroom

`www.techtv.com/maxheadroom`

In a cyberpunk future where television is the fabric that binds society, Max Headroom is a computer-generated TV host at Network 23.

The Screen Savers

www.techtv.com/screensaver

TechTV's daily live variety show hosted by Leo Laporte and Patrick Norton features guest interviews and celebrities, remote field pieces, product advice and demos, and software reviews.

The Tech Of...

THE TECH OF:

www.techtv.com/thetechof

From the food we eat, to the sports we play, to buildings where we work, technology has a profound impact on the way we live. *The Tech Of…* is an engaging series that goes behind the scenes of modern life and shows you the technology that makes things tick.

Tech Live

www.techtv.com/news

Tech Live focuses on the technology world's most important people, companies, products and issues and how they affect consumers, investors and the industry through interviews, product reviews, advice and technology analysis.

Technogames

www.techtv.com/technogames

Homemade machines, robots and electronic devices face off in a high-tech international competition from London's Millennium Dome. Innovation and technical excellence are tested as robots compete at cycling, swimming, high jump, rope climb, solar-powered marathon and shot put.

TechTV's Titans of Tech

www.techtv.com/titansoftech

Through insightful interviews and in-depth profiles, *Titans of Tech* offer viewers an informed look at where the new economy is headed. These specials profile technology's most important movers and shakers — the CEOs, entrepreneurs and visionaries driving today's tech economy.

Tomorrow's World

www.techtv.com/tomorrowsworld

The BBC's *Tomorrow's World* takes a look at the latest innovation and discovery in medicine, space, entertainment, sports, transportation and law enforcement. Featuring reports from every corner of the globe, *Tomorrow's World* is a fascinating, informed and fact-based view of the future of technology.

GLOSSARY

Access Control List See ACL.

Access Method A low-level hardware protocol used on computer networks. Examples of access methods include Ethernet, Token Ring, and FDDI, although Ethernet has become the de facto standard for home networks.

ACL (Access Control List) When used on a wireless access point, ACLs are tables that maintain lists of MAC addresses that are permitted to transmit and receive data to and from the access point.

Ad Hoc Wireless Network A small wireless network with computers in close proximity to one another that does not use the services of a central access point. Instead computers communicate directly using their wireless PC cards.

Administrative A level of privileges assigned on a Windows XP computer user that grants complete control over the computer and its resources including the ability to make configuration changes, install new software, and manage user accounts.

Advanced Research Projects Agency Network See ARPAnet.

Anti-Virus A software program that protects a computer from being infected by a computer virus by scanning all new files and isolating and removing harmful files.

Application Response A measurement of how long a user must wait for the computer to respond to a command.

ARP A protocol in the TCP/IP protocol suite that locates the MAC address of a network computer using its IP address.

ARPAnet (Advanced Research Projects Agency Network) A project started by the U.S. Department of Defense in the 1960s that eventually led to the development of the Internet. The initial goal of this project was to develop a national computer network that could survive a nuclear attack and continue functioning.

Audit The process of recording event information into log files. Windows XP records event information into different logs based on how it classifies the event. These logs include the System, Security, and Application logs.

BIOS Software stored on a computer's main circuit board or motherboard that is used to start up the computer and initialize its hardware.

Bluetooth A wireless cable replacement technology that supports the creation of personal area networks or PANs.

Broadband Internet Connection A DSL or cable Internet connection generally offering transmission speeds between 300–500KB.

Browsing The process of manually searching a network for its resources instead of specifying the path required to locate the resource.

BUS A type of network design or topology where all computers on the network are connected to a single backbone cable as opposed to the STAR topology where all computers are connected to a central hub.

Cable Internet Access An always-on, high-speed Internet connection that is provided by your local cable company.

Cable Modem A specially designed modem that connects a computer to a cable-based Internet connection. Although speeds up to 1MB are possible, transmission rates of 300–500KB are typical.

Carrier Sense Multiple Access with Collision Detection See CSMA/CD.

Client A computer on a network that accesses resources provided by other computers that are functioning as servers. On a home network computers may double as both clients and servers depending on how they are used.

Client for Microsoft Networks Specialized software that allows a computer to connect to a Microsoft network and act like a client. This allows it to connect to and use resources provided by other computers on the network.

Coaxial Cable A type of network cable used to connect computers together and create a network using the BUS topology. Coaxial cable

is made up of a solid copper wire surrounded by insulation and wire mesh that is then covered by a protective layer of plastic.

Collision Occurs on an Ethernet network when two or more computers attempt to transmit network data at the same time.

CSMA/CD (Carrier Sense Multiple Access with Collision Detection) A network management technique employed on Ethernet networks that governs the transmission of network data and its retransmission in the event of a collision. It allows a computer to send data out over the network anytime that it detects that the network is idle. The network is then monitored for collisions. In the event of a collision all the computers involved wait a random period of time before attempting to retransmit their data.

Demodulation The technique used by dial-up modems to convert analog signals back into their original digital format.

DHCP (Dynamic Host Configuration Protocol) A TCP/IP protocol that provides for the dynamic assignment of IP addresses to network computers. Network devices such as Internet gateways or computers running ICS provide DHCP services. In addition, most ISPs use DHCP to assign a temporary IP address to computers that connect to the Internet.

Dial-Up Networking The process of establishing a network connection over a phone line connection using a dial-up modem. Once connected, the network is accessed in the same manner as it is locally accessed except that the connection speed will be slower for the dial-up connection.

Digital Signal Processing See DSP.

Digital Subscriber Line See DSL.

Disk Quota A capability of the NTFS file system to impose a preset limit on the amount of space a user can consume on a disk drive.

Distributed Denial-of-Service (DDoS) Attack A technique used by Internet hackers to plant a program on your computer that can later be activated and used to instruct your computer to participate in an attack on an Internet Web site in an effort to flood the Web site with more traffic than it can handle, thus effectively shutting down the Web site and perhaps even crashing the site's Web servers.

Domain A collection of computers, users, and network resources that is centrally managed as an organizational unit using a central security database. Domains are used on large corporate networks and are not generally implemented on a home network.

Driver Rollback A Windows XP utility that allows you to restore a software driver to a previous version in the event that the newer driver is not functioning properly.

Drop and Drag A Windows technique that allows you to manipulate one or more files using your mouse. Supported operations include using drag and drop to print files, move and copy them, and load them into applications.

DSL (Digital Subscriber Line) An always on, high-speed Internet connection provided by some local telephone companies using the telephone lines found in your home.

DSP (Digital Signal Processing) An audio technology capable of filtering out non-human generated sounds from the background noise created by EMI.

Dynamic Host Configuration Protocol See DHCP.

Dynamic IP Address An IP address that is dynamically assigned to a network computer. Depending on the network configuration the IP address assignment may come from an Internet gateway appliance, a computer running Microsoft's ICS, or from the computer itself using APIPA. Dynamic IP addresses are also assigned by ISPs to most Internet connections.

Electromagnetic Interference See EMI.

E-mail An electronic form of communication that sends messages over a network using e-mail client software such as Outlook Express.

EMI (Electromagnetic Interference) Electrical signals that emanate from certain electrical devices and that can interfere with network communications.

Ethernet A low-level access method protocol that supports the transport of data packets over local area networks. Ethernet supports a transmission speed of 10Mbps and uses CSMA/CD to determine when data packets can be sent over the network.

External Print Server A small standalone network-connected appliance that provides print server management over printers directly attached to the device.

Fast Ethernet A low-level access method protocol supports the transport of data packets over local area networks. Fast Ethernet supports a transmission speed of 100Mbps and uses CSMA/CD to determine when data packets can be sent over the network.

Fast User Switching A technique introduced by Windows XP that allows two or more people to share a computer without requiring each other to log off. Instead they can switch between each other's sessions while leaving their applications and files open.

FAT (File Allocation Table) The original Microsoft file system used to support the MS-DOS operating system. FAT provides for the insecure storage of files using an 8.3-character name format.

FAT32 A 32-bit upgrade of the FAT that supports long filenames and larger hard drives.

FDDI A low-level access method protocol that supports the transport of data packets over fiber-optic networks. This access method protocol is extremely expensive and is not used on home networks.

FDM (Frequency Division Multiplexing) A form of communication that allows two different types of communication to occur over a single communication medium by assigning different frequency ranges.

File Allocation Table See FAT.

File and Printer Sharing A Microsoft operating system service that enables the sharing of local printers, folders, and drives over a network.

File Sharing The act of making all contents of a folder or entire drive visible and accessible over a network.

Filtering The process a firewall goes through to inspect every network packet that passes through its network connection giving it the ability to determine whether or not the packet should be allowed or blocked.

Firewall A hardware appliance or application that protects a computer or network against external threat by controlling access to and from the computer or network.

Frequency Modulation Distribution See FDM.

FTP A protocol in the TCP/IP suite of protocols that supports the transfer of files over a network.

Gateway A hardware appliance or application that provides shared access to a network such as the Internet.

Guest A default Windows XP account with very limited access to a computer's resources that prevents making configuration changes and installing new software.

Hacker A term used to reference an individual who possesses strong computer skills and who uses them to break into computers and networks.

Hardware Firewall A hardware appliance that connects your computer to an Internet connection and which provides firewall services.

Hidden Share A special type of share resource that is not visible to most network applications and utilities. Hidden shares are created by placing a $ as the last character in their share name.

HomeRF A wireless local area networking technology targeted at the home user that provides equivalent functionality as that provided by 802.11x networks.

Hub A network component that allows you to connect two or more computers and create a local area network.

Hybrid Network A network that is composed of two or more network media that may include powerline, phoneline, wireless, Ethernet, or Fast Ethernet.

ICF (Internet Connection Firewall) A personal firewall integrated into Windows XP Home Edition that provides dynamic packet filtering allowing it to inspect all incoming data packets from the Internet and block any that are considered threatening.

ICMP   A TCP/IP protocol that provides error reporting of data packet delivery.

ICS (Internet Connection Sharing)   A built-in Windows XP service that allows a computer to share its Internet connection with other computers on a local area network.

IEEE 1284 Printer Cable   A cable used to connect a printer to a computer, which supports two-way communications between the two devices.

Internet   A public wide area network sometimes referred to as the World Wide Web.

Internet Connection Firewall   See ICF.

Internet Connection Sharing   See ICS.

Internet Explorer   An Internet browser provided with Windows XP that provides the ability to access the Internet or a local network.

Internet Protocol   See IP.

Internet Service Providers   See ISP.

Internetwork Packet Exchange/Sequential Packet Exchange   See IPX/SPX.

IP (Internet Protocol)   A TCP/IP protocol responsible for addressing and sending data over a TCP/IP network.

IP Address   A unique 32-bit address used on a TCP/IP network to identify a computer's network address and host address.

IPC$ A hidden share created by Windows XP that supports the remote administration of network computers.

IPX/SPX (Internetwork Packet Exchange/ Sequential Packet Exchange)   A proprietary protocol created by Novell for use on NetWare networks. It supports the establishment of large networks and is a routable protocol.

ISP (Internet Service Providers)   A company that provides individuals with leased access to the Internet.

LAN (Local Area Network)   A network the size of a home or small office that is made up of two or more computers that share information and resources.

Limited   A level of access that can be assigned to Windows XP Home Edition user accounts that provides sufficient privileges to perform most day-to-day work.

Local Area Network   See LAN.

Local Printer   A printer that is connected directly to a computer using a parallel, serial, or USB connection.

MAC address (Medial Access Control)   A unique 48-bit address that is embedded on every network adapter. Other devices such as cable modems can also have a MAC address.

Medial Access Control   See MAC address.

Modem   A device that converts digital signals from your computer (modulation) to analog signals so that they can be transported over a telephone connection to a destination computer whose modem converts (demodulation) the signals back into their original digital format.

Modulation   The process of converting digital signals into analog signals so that they can be transmitted over a telephone connection.

NetBEUI (NetBIOS Extended User Interface)   A local area network protocol that supports the operation of small networks. This protocol requires very few computer resources and is self-configuring. However, it is non-routable and is being phased out as a protocol used by Microsoft operating systems.

NetBIOS Extended User Interface
See NetBEUI.

Network Adapter   A hardware device sometimes referred to as a Network Interface Card or NIC that connects a computer to a network.

Network Bridging   A Windows XP feature that allows a computer running Windows XP to seamlessly combine two different network media into a single network. For example, you can use network bridging to connect Ethernet and PhoneLine segments into one home network.

Network Drive   A folder or drive that has been shared over a network.

Network Interface Card   See NIC.

Network Printer   A printer that has been shared over a network. On a home network a network printer can be established by connecting it to a Windows XP computer and sharing it or by attaching it to a print server appliance.

New Technology File System   See NTFS.

NIC (Network Interface Card)   A peripheral device sometimes referred to as a network adapter that connects a computer to a network or a cable or DSL modem.

NTFS (New Technology File System)   An advanced Windows XP file system that provides features not available in the FAT32 file systems including support for fault tolerance, transaction tracking, and Quotas.

NWLink   The name of Microsoft's implementation of Novell's IPX/SPX protocol.

OFDM (Orthogonal Frequency-Division Multiplexing)   A technique that allows powerline networks to piggyback network data over different frequencies using a home's existing electrical wiring.

Operating System   Software that manages a computer, its hardware and software, and which provides you with an interface for working with these resources.

Orthogonal Frequency-Division Multiplexing
See OFDM.

Owner   The default administrative account set up on a Windows XP Home Edition computer. This account has the ability to modify computer settings, open and change any file or folder, manage other user accounts, and install new software.

Packet   The container used to transport data over a network.

Password   A secret code assigned to a user account that is used to identify its owner and provide access to the computer and its resources.

Peer-to-Peer Network   A small home or office network consisting of 2 to 10 computers where each computer acts as both a network client and server.

PAN (Personal Area Network)   A network that spans an area the size of a room and wirelessly connects a computer to its peripheral devices.

Personal Firewall   A software application or small network appliances designed to protect home computer or network Internet intruders.

Phoneline Network   A home network that uses a home's telephone wiring as a network backbone to which all network computers are connected using special phoneline network adapters.

PING   A TCP/IP command that can be used to test the ability of one computer to communicate with another computer over a TCP/IP network.

Plug and Play   A hardware and software standard that allows Microsoft operating systems to automatically detect and install new hardware.

Plug-and-Play BIOS   A type of computer BIOS that can detect and configure hardware during system startup and then pass this information to the operating system.

Powerline   A home network that uses a home's electrical wiring as a network backbone to which all network computers are connected using special powerline network adapters.

Print Driver   A piece of software that is used by the operating system to communicate with and control a printer.

Print Queue   A location on a computer's hard drive or on a network print server appliance where print jobs are spooled and stored until printed.

Print Server   A computer or network appliance that manages the print queue for a network printer.

PRINT$ A hidden share created by Windows XP whenever a shared printer is configured, which allows Windows XP to perform printer management tasks.

Printer   A device that produces printed output.

Printer Sharing   The process of making a printer available to other computers on a network.

Protocol   A set of standards that defines the rules for communicating and exchanging data over a network. Examples of local area network protocols include TCP/IP, IPX/SPX, and NetBEUI.

QoS (Quality of Service)   A networking technique used to guarantee the bandwidth required by applications such as voice and multimedia.

RARP   A TCP/IP protocol that is used to locate a computer's IP address when supplied with the computer MAC address.

RAS (Remote Access Service)   A Windows XP service that allows a computer or network to be accessed remotely.

Redirector   A piece of software that intercepts requests to access computer and network resources and which then determines where the resources reside and either allows the request to proceed to a local resource or redirects the request to the appropriate network computer. On Microsoft networks the Client for Microsoft Networks provides redirector services.

Regedit   A software utility that allows a user with an administrative account to view and make changes to the Windows registry.

Registry   A special database where Windows operating systems store operating system, hardware, and application information. Windows operating systems rely on the information stored in the registry to perform many computer operations.

Remote Access Service   See RAS.

Router   A network appliance that is used to connect two or more network segments into a single logical network.

Server   A computer on a network that provides a service or makes some of its resources available to other computers on the network.

Share   A folder, drive, or printer that can be accessed by other computers on a network.

Shared Drive   A shared disk drive sometimes referred to as a network drive.

Shared Folder   A shared folder sometimes referred to as a network folder.

SMTP   A TCP/IP protocol that supports the transfer of electronic mail.

Sneaker Net   The sharing and movement of data by copying it onto portable media such as floppy disks and manually transporting it to another computer.

Software Driver   A piece of software that is used by the operating system to communicate with and control a peripheral device such as a network adapter.

Spooling   The process of storing print jobs on a print server until they are printed.

Star   A type of network design or topology where all computers on the network are connected to a central hub as opposed to the BUS topology where all computers are connected to a single backbone cable.

Static IP Address   An IP address that is manually assigned to a computer running TCP/IP and which does not change over time.

Subnet Mask   A TCP/IP setting that is used in conjunction with a computer's IP address to determine the location of a network computer.

System Restore   A Windows XP feature that provides the ability to restore a computer to a previous state in the event that a problem occurs after making a major software or hardware change.

TCP (Transmission Control Protocol)   A TCP/IP protocol that is used to set up a logical connection between network computers.

TCP/IP (Transmission Control Protocol/ Internet Protocol)   A suite of protocols that supports the operation of local area and wide area networks including the Internet. TCP/IP is the default protocol for all Microsoft operating systems starting with Windows 98.

Telnet   A TCP/IP protocol that provides remote terminal access.

Token Ring   A low-level access method protocol that supports the transport of data packets over local area networks using a token passing scheme where an electronic token is passed around the network and only the computer possessing the token can transmit data. Token Ring has fallen out of favor and is seldom used except on older corporate networks.

Topology   A description of the logical and physical design of a network that includes an understanding of how the network is physically connected and how data is transmitted.

Tracert   A TCP/IP command that tests the route taken by a data packet as it travels from the source to the destination computer.

Transmission Control Protocol   See TCP.

Transmission Control Protocol/Internet Protocol   See TCP/IP.

Trojan Horse   A software program that sneaks its way onto your computer and operates in a stealth mode. Once implanted the program may send personal information that it finds on your computer back to its creator or perform some other malicious deed.

Trusted Application   An application that has been identified to your personal firewall as being allowed to communicate freely with the Internet.

Twisted-Pair Cable   A type of network cabling where two or more pairs of copper wire are twisted around each other in order to reduce susceptibility to EMI.

UDP   A TCP/IP protocol that establishes connectionless communication between computers on a network as opposed to the TCP protocol where a logical session is maintained as data is being exchanged.

Universal Plug and Play   A variation of traditional plug and play that allows a Windows XP computer to detect the presence of a new network resource such as a network printer and automatically configure itself to use the device.

Universal Serial Bus   See USB.

USB (Universal Serial Bus)   A technology that greatly expands the number of peripheral devices that can be installed on a computer. USB is a plug-and-play compatible technology that allows a Windows computer to automatically detect and install USB hardware.

USB Hub   A device that plugs into a computer's USB port and provides additional USB connections.

User Account   A collection of information about a computer user that includes the user name, password, desktop preferences, and other custom configuration settings.

User Name   The name assigned to a user account, which may be required in order for a user to log on to a Windows XP computer.

User Profile   A collection of information stored on a per-user basis that defines each user's custom settings and preferences. Windows uses the information stored in a user profile to prepare the user's desktop and environment each time he or she logs on.

Virtual Memory   The allocation of a portion of a computer's hard drive space to emulate physical memory and expand a computer's available supply of memory beyond that which is physically available. Data is paged in and out of physical memory and virtual memory as is necessary in order to ensure that sufficient physical memory is always available to meet system requirements.

Virus   A malicious software program that has been designed to infect a computer and cause an assortment of damage ranging from practical jokes to the deletion of all the files on a hard drive.

WAN (Wide Area Network)   A large network that is made up of multiple smaller geographically dispersed local area networks. The Internet is an example of a WAN.

WIA (Windows Image Acquisition)   An imaging technology employed by Windows XP that allows it to transfer digital images from digital cameras and scanners.

Wide Area Network   See WAN.

Windows Image Acquisition   See WIA.

Windows Update   A Windows feature that allows the operating system to check a Windows Update Site for fixes, updates, and service pack updates that can be downloaded and installed.

Wireless Network   A home network that uses wireless network hardware to communicate by transmitting short-range radio signals between a computer and an access point.

WLANS (Wireless Local Area Networking Standards)   A term that refers to the 802.11x family of wireless networking standards.

WLANS

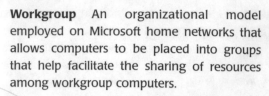

Workgroup An organizational model employed on Microsoft home networks that allows computers to be placed into groups that help facilitate the sharing of resources among workgroup computers.

Worm A software program that attempts to sneak its way onto a computer and hide until a predetermined event or time activates it. Once activated a worm can perform any of an assortment of malicious deeds.

ZoneAlarm A software-based personal firewall that can protect a computer and a home network from attacks launched over the Internet or from worms, Trojan Horse programs, and other malicious programs that attempt to establish secret connections to the Internet from inside your computer.

INDEX

How can we make this index more useful? Email us at indexes@quepublishing.com

313

INSTALLING

INDEX

How can we make this index more useful? Email us at indexes@quepublishing.com

315

INSTALLING

INDEX

How can we make this index more useful? Email us at indexes@quepublishing.com

317

How can we make this index more useful? Email us at indexes@quepublishing.com

319

SERVERS

INDEX

How can we make this index more useful? Email us at indexes@quepublishing.com

321

VIEWING

INDEX

How can we make this index more useful? Email us at indexes@quepublishing.com

Z